T. H. Huxley: Man's Place in Nature

Experience speedily taught them that the shifting scenes of the world's stage have a permanent background; that there is order amidst the seeming confusion, and that many events take place according to unchanging rules. To this region of familiar steadiness and customary regularity they gave the name of Nature. But, at the same time, their infantile and untutored reason, little more, as yet, than the playfellow of the imagination, led them to believe that this tangible, commonplace, orderly world of Nature was surrounded and interpenetrated by another intangible and mysterious world, no more bound by fixed rules than, as they fancied, were the thoughts and passions which coursed through their minds and seemed to exercise an intermittent and capricious rule over their bodies.

T. H. Huxley, "Prologue" to
Controverted Questions

T. H. HUXLEY
Man's Place in Nature

James G. Paradis

UNIVERSITY OF NEBRASKA PRESS
Lincoln and London

Publishers on the Plains

UNP

Copyright © 1978 by the University of Nebraska Press

The publication of this book was assisted by a grant from The Andrew W. Mellon Foundation.

Library of Congress Cataloging in Publication Data

Paradis, James G   1942–
  T. H. Huxley: man's place in nature.

  Bibliography: p. 211
  Includes index.
  1. Huxley, Thomas Henry, 1825–1895. 2. Science–Philosophy. 3.
Biology–Philosophy. 4. Great Britain–Social life and customs–19th century.
5. Biologists–Great Britain–Biography.
QH31.H9P35   574'.092'4 [5B]   78–5492
ISBN 0–8032–0917–7

Manufactured in the United States of America

To the Memory of

Louis Adelard Paradis

Contents

Acknowledgments

I am indebted to Jacob Korg, Edward Alexander, and Richard Dunn for their early interest and encouragement, and their continued support, in the writing of this book on T. H. Huxley. I am grateful, as well, to many additional friends, teachers, and colleagues, but particularly to Malcolm Griffith and Alan Fisher, who, at various phases of my progress, offered me their sundry doubts, criticisms, and suggestions.

For a grant from its Penrose Fund, which made possible my research among the Huxley Papers at the Imperial College of Science and Technology, South Kensington, London, I wish to thank the American Philosophical Society.

I am most grateful to the Governors of the Imperial College of Science and Technology for allowing me to read and to quote from the Huxley Papers. And to Mrs. Jeanne Pingree and her Archive staff, I must express special appreciation for the skill and insight with which they assisted me in my examination of the Huxley manuscripts. I am indebted, as well, to librarians at the British Museum, the Royal Society, the University of London, and the Linnean Society in London.

For their proofreadings and suggestions, I am grateful to Miriam Schmuckler and Jeffrey Alsdorf; and I thank Sherry Laing for her expert typing and retyping of the manuscript.

To Judith Paradis, I am deeply indebted for good-hearted assistance and sympathy.

Note on Textual Citations

Citations of T. H. Huxley's essays in the text are made from his *Collected Essays*, 9 vols. (London: Macmillan, 1893–94):

References to the *Life and Letters* (hereafter cited as *LL*) by Leonard Huxley are from *Life and Letters of Thomas Henry Huxley*, 2 vols. (New York: D. Appleton, 1900).

T. H. Huxley: Man's Place in Nature

Introduction

Nothing great in science has ever been done by men, whatever their powers, in whom the divine afflatus of the truth-seeker was wanting.

T. H. Huxley, "The Progress of Science: 1837–1887"

The Victorian debate over the challenge offered by the new science to traditional concepts of man and man's place in nature found its most prophetic focus in the clear, forceful argument of T. H. Huxley's generalist or popular essays. Huxley, whose professional reputation as a British anatomist and physiologist was well established and growing, undertook a second career, that of an essayist and cultural critic of mid-Victorian England, in the full recognition that technology had proved itself a force to alter society and that theoretical science was proving itself a force to alter assumptions as fundamental as man's conception of himself. This characteristically modern appreciation of the power of theoretical science to define sets Huxley apart from other major essayists of the Victorian period. In such works as *Lay Sermons* (1870), *Critiques and Addresses* (1873), *Science and Culture* (1881), and *Evolution and Ethics* (1893), he made important critical examinations of the new relationship that was being negotiated between man and nature through the intervention of modern science and technology. Few Victorian cultural or social values would remain unaffected by this new relationship. Concepts of human identity, of ethical law, of modern culture as a force for reconciling the progress of the present with the values of the past, would all be profoundly influenced by the new concept of man as a force in nature.

1

I have been drawn to the study of Huxley's thought and vision because he was a Victorian critic of unique accomplishments who brought the perspective of the scientific professional to bear on a society that was itself under the growing influence of science and technology. The nineteenth century was an age, as A. N. Whitehead has observed, which invented the method of invention.[1] But while the new knowledge had brought new power, it also brought a new and perplexing ignorance; while it exerted considerable influence on traditional cultural values and assumptions, it manifested itself intellectually in systems which frequently passed beyond the competence of thinkers and critics of the age. One of the great examples of Victorian interdisciplinary ability, Huxley combined a literary sensitivity and talent with an intimate understanding of the great theoretical and practical developments in nineteenth-century British and continental science. He had made important contributions himself, his research in invertebrate anatomy having earned him entry into the Royal Society at the age of twenty-six and the Royal Medal in physiology a year later, in 1852. From earliest youth he had pursued studies in the history of science and in a variety of literary and philosophical subjects, making his special interest the interrelationship between science and society.

Huxley struggled to comprehend the enigma of the increasing intersections of cultural and natural history, in which ideas of man, nature and deity had come to be defined by conflicting concepts of truth. Natural and supernatural explanations had become attached to identical processes, often creating a debilitating sense of dualism such as is found in much of Victorian literature. In a work like Tennyson's *In Memoriam*, the elemental force of death gave rise to a shattering ambivalence, new and indeed peculiar to Victorian culture, as to the causes and destinies of things. Naturalism and supernaturalism struggled bitterly over the self throughout the dozen years or so that Tennyson devoted to the poem. Critics like Walter Houghton have found that "bourgeois industrial society and widespread doubt about the nature of man, society, and the universe" were main determinants of the Victorian frame of mind.[2] Such doubt revealed that Victorian culture was hard pressed to forge a new

2

synthesis, to discover what Matthew Arnold in the preface to the 1853 edition of the *Poems* had called the "spirit of the whole." Earlier, the Romantic synthesis had taken the form of "natural supernaturalism," Carlyle's term for the fusion of natural and divine. The bridge of self was able to span the great chasm that had begun to loom between a physical nature, ever more clearly defined, and a supernature which had begun to seem somewhat vague and abstract by comparison. For Victorians, the fusion of nature and supernature was more difficult to achieve, for the concreteness with which researchers were documenting physical nature had created a compelling sense of verifiable reality which no evidence in support of divinity could easily match. This growing relativity of truth, as we shall see, was best captured in Huxley's term, "agnosticism," which was more a Victorian than a philosophical word. Victorians discovered, ironically, that the products of scientific precision and certitude could inspire doubt as readily as optimism.

Huxley's maturation as an essayist and critic is particularly instructive in this respect, for, as I shall attempt to show, his philosophical outlook underwent a gradual transition from youthful Romanticism, influenced by writers like Carlyle and Goethe, toward increasing determinism at mid-career, to his final and startling *fin-de-siècle* declaration, almost on his deathbed, that man's hope lay in his revolt against nature. Thus, while in Huxley's essays we witnessthe transition from "supernaturalism" to "natural supernaturalism," as identified by critics like M. H. Abrams, carried its inevitable step further to Victorian "naturalism," we also find, somewhat paradoxically, the great summation of the Victorian disillusionment with and revolt against nature.[3] The last essays, looking boldly out from behind the wall of civilization to an empty, hostile universe, bridge the Victorian and modern sensibilities.

The shaping of a new critical consciousness which would defer to scientific thought and ideals was no casual scientism on Huxley's part, but a carefully considered effort to integrate the forces of Victorian science and culture. It was a Victorian commonplace that the transition occurring in all facets of society had taken a course whose logic few could explain. Like other Victorian critical essayists, Huxley aspired to a theory of transition which would illuminate the great social changes occurring throughout England by revealing the principles of their order. In 1873, he wrote his wife:

> We are in the midst of a gigantic movement greater than that which preceded and produced the Reformation, and really only the continuation of that movement. But there is nothing new in the ideas which lie at the bottom of the movement, nor is any reconcilement possible between free thought and traditional authority. One or other will have to succumb after a struggle of unknown duration, which will have as side issues vast political and social troubles. I have no more doubt that free thought will win in the long run than I have that I sit here writing to you, or that this free thought will organise itself into a coherent system, embracing human life and the world as one harmonious whole. [LL, 1:427–28]

Like Matthew Arnold, Huxley dreamed of the "harmonious whole," doubting, however, the powers of Victorians or their immediate twentieth-century descendants to achieve it. Nevertheless, he invested considerable energy in an attempt to discover the outline of a "coherent system" which would unify "human life and the world," and set out to enlist the scientist as an ally of intellectual freedom in the archetypal struggle between free thought and traditional or ideological authority. Such a unity, he had hoped early in his career, might take the form of a naturalistic system in which ethical order was established as the premise of social order, historical processes of nature and human society were shown to be uniform, and the universal order of nature was accepted by all as the great absolute of existence. Extensive notes Huxley left behind in his manuscripts reveal that his system would have borrowed from Greek Stoical thought and from the philosophy of Spinoza, incorporating the principle of evolutionary progression as the driving force of the whole. But Huxley's system, for reasons which we shall explore, failed to develop beyond the planning stages.

The alternatives which presented themselves to Victorians in their quest for order were those of vision and system, the twin aspects of unity. Each presented possibilities which had a strong attraction for Huxley, the systematic approach appealing to his rationalist appreciation for the formal architectonic, the

4

visionary possibility appealing to his vivid sense of value.[4] The attraction of a system like Herbert Spencer's synthetic philosophy to a scientist like Huxley was considerable, since Spencer offered a systemic unity, formulated along lines of evolutionary development, in which to orient the facts and phenomena of social and historical transition. Karl Marx offered much the same—an ordered theory of historical process which achieved the dimensions of a philosophical system and claimed allegiance to the new science. The systems of Spencer and Marx were great Victorian efforts at synthesis, but Huxley held aloof from Marxist theory and rejected Spencer on the basis of his a priori methodology. A priori thought, divorced as it was from verifiable experience, was of a similar intellectual structure to the "traditional authority" Huxley held to be locked in perpetual conflict with free thought. Its assumptions were frequently vast; its logic was sometimes impervious to fact: "Spencer's idea of a tragedy," Huxley had observed, "is a deduction killed by a fact."[5]

While the scientist might find the alternatives to overt system unattractive, since what was not capable of systematic representation could have little experimental validity, the critic and man of letters operated in a world of value and tradition where the ceremony of consistency was not always stood upon. Experience was important in the critical writings of men like Carlyle, Arnold, and Ruskin, but it rarely assumed the schematized patterns into which the scientist's experience was organized. For the cultural critic, valid experience could also be expressed in moral and emotional modes which originated internally in the personal vision. In his writings, the critic sought to reveal the personal experience of self amid culture, thinking of culture as an organic entity, its complexities not reducible to quantities, whether economic, historical, or biological. Lionel Trilling has observed that "to think in cultural terms is to consider human expressions not only in their overt existence and avowed intention, but in, as it were, their secret life, taking cognizance of the desires and impulses which lie beyond the open formulation."[6] The Victorian cultural critic sought the inward experience that described the sensation of living at a particular moment in history, the frustrations and inspirations of a

5

unique cultural period. In undertaking to consider how the activity of science was influencing Victorian culture, Huxley found himself turning increasingly toward the secret life of Victorian science, seeking to discover the impulses which could be seen as the aspirations of a unique culture. In this critical context, Huxley argued that scientific ideals and accomplishments could furnish material and spiritual means to implement a moral and intellectual revolution such as society had never experienced. In his vision, Huxley dreamed the Baconian dream of a science which, guided by some worthy human aspiration, could shape society anew.

In lieu of realizing his system, Huxley steadily built up a critical edifice from which to view the intersection of science and society, the voices of critic and scientist inevitably becoming one. The result of this union was the creation of a unique cultural agent—the scientist—whom Huxley installed as the primary intelligence of his essays. Essentially a persona, a second self extracted from professional experiences, historical antecedents, and personal ideals, Huxley's idea of the scientist generated a unified vision which lent the essays their consistencies of tone, perspective, and value, or what Oliver Elton has called their "noble unity of mental temper."[7] The scientist figure became Huxley's most significant literary creation, for it allowed him to formulate and sustain what amounted to a scientific world view—a critical consciousness that was able to range freely over diverse materials and to judge them according to ideals and standards it associated with science. The scientist-as-critic, however, added an important dimension to all this, for he was willing to express moral and emotional sensations, to register opinion and to admit error. He was flexible, embracing both the imaginative and the rational, embodying the human element of science, revealing, ideally, the self amid the system.

With origins in the old Baconian vision of the seer, whose methodology filled him with the power of transformation and enabled him to manipulate nature, and with other roots in the Enlightenment, with its cynical regard for authority and its worship of reason, Huxley's man of science was a complicated idea with an interesting intellectual pedigree. He was an ad-

6

venturer, setting out on his quest in nature in order to confront the unknown, with an almost Puritan sense of mission to bring order to the wilderness:

> In fact, the history of physical science teaches (and we cannot too carefully take the lesson to heart) that the practical advantages, attainable through its agency, never have been, and never will be, sufficiently attractive to men inspired by the inborn genius of the interpreter of Nature, to give them courage to undergo the toils and make the sacrifices which that calling requires from its votaries. That which stirs their pulses is the love of knowledge and the joy of the discovery of the causes of things sung by the old poet—the supreme delight of extending the realm of law and order ever farther towards the unattainable goals of the infinitely great and the infinitely small, between which our little race of life is run. In the course of this work, the physical philosopher, sometimes intentionally, much more often unintentionally, lights upon something which proves to be of practical value. Great is the rejoicing of those who are benefited thereby; and, for the moment, science is the Diana of all the craftsmen. But, even while the cries of jubilation resound and this flotsam and jetsam of the tide of investigation is being turned into the wages of workmen and the wealth of capitalists, the crest of the wave of scientific investigation is far away on its course over the illimitable ocean of the unknown. [1:53–54]

The quest theme was essential to Huxley's vision; the man of science sought experience in nature so as to extend the "realm of law and order" even further. One can also detect at such junctures an imperialist element in Victorian science which was consonant with the historical aspirations of the time, the quest for empire, the concern to institute a British order in unknown lands, the romance with the unexplored. Darwin and Huxley, each in his youth, had sailed out from England aboard Her Majesty's ships, the *Beagle* and the *Rattlesnake*, over the "illimitable ocean of the unknown" to return with plans which would bestow order on whole biological realms, Huxley with his rationale for invertebrate classification, Darwin with his theory of natural selection.

We return, then, to the question of man's place in nature, for just as the dynamic between man and nature had always been a subjective one, the definition of the one influencing that of the other, so was the new Victorian extension of law to biological nature to have serious implications for the cultural concept of man and the personal idea of self. Such works as Huxley's *Man's Place in Nature* (1863), Lyell's *The Antiquity of Man* (1863), and Darwin's *The Descent of Man* (1871), brought Victorians face to face with their biological selves, an encounter which proved startling to most, establishing a new concept of self as a physical entity. Because of the Victorian inability to reconcile him with traditional assumptions of self, biological man emerged as yet another version of Victorian dualism. The question of man's place in nature, as Victorians phrased it to themselves, became in this way not only one of the central concerns of several biological sciences—physical anthropology, embryology, physiology, comparative anatomy—but it also found its inevitable way to the center of things, to the human image itself, around which cultures must always be organized.

In the study of Huxley's thought and cultural criticism which follows, I have set out to explore the network of ideas, the vision, in which Huxley labored, concentrating on his special concern with the locus of man amid the powers of nature. In order to examine his vision, I have pursued a series of inquiries which I believe describe the outlines of Huxley's thought, each inquiry cutting across his concern with the human figure in its existential condition. I have also followed a rough chronological pattern in tracing Huxley's intellectual development, beginning with the genesis of his concepts of science and the scientist and concluding with a consideration of his broad critical approach to the problems of Victorian culture and society. Throughout, I have attempted where appropriate to compare Huxley's ideas with those of his leading Victorian antagonists and counterparts so as to weave his thought into the fabric of his era; for Huxley defined and personally symbolized an intellectual and social development which contributed strikingly to Victorian culture.

Victorian culture and science had become deeply, if not consciously, integrated. It was Huxley's critical insight to understand the historical significance of this union and to attempt to raise the relationship to a more conscious level of thought in the minds of his contemporaries. There were those, then as now,

8

whose ideal science was a hidden science, either submerged in an unseen service to society, challenging neither the intellectual discipline nor the cultural tradition, or held aloft from the un-initiated, above the common reach of the masses. Huxley spent a considerable amount of his life's energy arguing the danger, not to mention the intellectual contemptibility, of such positions. If science were merely the slave to the material appetites of humanity, he declared, it were better to do without. And to the Brahmans, scientific and historical, he observed:

> I have not been one of those fortunate persons who are able to regard a popular lecture as a mere *hors d'oeuvre,* unworthy of being ranked among the serious efforts of a philosopher; and who keep their fame as scientific hierophants unsullied by attempts—at least of the successful sort—to be understood of the people. [8:v]

Always Huxley envisioned science as a great social and intellectual venture, a synthesis of knowledge in an endeavor that had been vital to humanity since the beginning of civilization.

I

The Idea of The Scientist

i. the new victorian

If Mary Shelley presented the nineteenth century with the figure of the obsessed man of science, and Charles Dickens and George Eliot created images of the intense young researcher and physician, it was Huxley who formulated for the cultural imagination the ideal scientist as moral figure, prophet of order, and relentless seeker after truth. Selecting almost at random from Huxley's essays, one finds the general outlines and characteristics of the new man of science in the frequent references to what the scientist is, what he is concerned with, and how he carries out his quest for truth, in the voice and assumptions of the essays themselves. Whether the scientist is directly mentioned or not, he is nearly always present by virtue of the fact that a Huxley essay has been written self-consciously by a man of science. This particular perspective, created by a continual scientific presence and voice, characteristically accompanies Huxley's critical essays and constitutes one of their most effective unifying threads.

As a term, "scientist" was a Victorian contribution to the language, coined by William Whewell in his important work *The Philosophy of the Inductive Sciences* (1840), where he set it in contrast to "artist":

> We need very much a name to describe a cultivator of science in general. I should incline to call him a *Scientist*. Thus we might say, that as an Artist is a Musician, Painter, or Poet, a Scientist is a Mathematician, Physicist, or Naturalist.[1]

Apparently taking up Whewell's suggestion, David Scott, a Romantic artist, contributed an essay to the August 1840 issue

11

of *Blackwood's*; looking back to the Renaissance, he compared Leonardo to Correggio by declaring: "Leonardo was mentally a seeker after truth—a scientist: Correggio was an asserter of truth—an artist."[2] And he considered at some length the difference in methodologies between scientist and artist, emphasizing the urge of Leonardo to experiment, his restless drive to perceive anew. For both Whewell and Scott, the scientist or man of science was one who cultivated the pursuit of knowledge with all the determination and intensity of the artist. Whewell's term signaled the scientist's advancing social and cultural status, even though the term "scientist" would not come into common usage until the end of the century. The scientist was becoming a new Victorian professional who lived by means of his intellect, seeking to extend the borders of his discipline, filled with what Whitehead, in referring to the new character of nineteenth-century science, called the "self-conscious realisation of the power of professionalism in knowledge . . . and of the boundless possibilities of technological advance."[3]

The scientist's greatest critic and explicator, his enthusiast, champion, and most visible Victorian representative, in some sense his creator, was Thomas Huxley. For Huxley, the concept of the man of science furnished the foundation for a world view. It had deep personal significance just as it had a vital new cultural implication. A personal and professional concept, it defined Huxley's relationship to his age on both emotional and intellectual planes.

In essays like "On the Advisableness of Improving Natural Knowledge" (1866) and "On the Method of Zadig" (1880), the scientist surfaces as an ancient and honored type; Huxley examines methods, values, and attitudes toward experience which characterize sound scientific thought. Zadig, a mythical figure, becomes the prototypical scientist by virtue of his elegant and superior use of empirical method to extract from mere evidence the attributes of creatures and phenomena he has never seen. In "Joseph Priestley" (1874), "Charles Darwin" (1882), and in essays on Harvey and Descartes, Huxley explored the idea of the scientist through biographical portraits. Priestley emerges as a model of piety and sincerity, who repudiates the myth of amorality which had commonly been evoked to indict the godless scientist. Darwin, "the incorporated ideal of a man of science," is the truth seeker, the great spirit pursuing his vision amid the storm of controversy (2:245). And in yet other essays such as "On a Piece of Chalk" (1868) and in the public Working Men's Lectures, beginning in the 1850s, the featured scientist is none other than Huxley himself, fact and ideal merging on stage at the Huxley theater as he addresses his vast audiences from the halls of Victorian industrial cities.

Letters and journals reveal that even in his earliest years Huxley found a potent personal image in the man of science. Speaking of science as a way of life, a conviction, Huxley generalized on his struggle to become a professional scientist and recorded decisive turns in his scientific career. With reverence for his scientific vocation, he examined the purity of his intentions in a journal entry in 1848: "Have I the capabilities for a scientific way of life or only the desire and wish for it springing from a flattered vanity and self-deceiving blindness?"[4] One is reminded here of a religious novice, preparing for his final vows. The scientist, priest of reason, espoused what Huxley saw as the rationalist commitment and a way of life which promised a unity between belief and deed. Confronting the apparent irrationality and disorder of phenomena, the man of science sought their logic according to his own faith in the ultimate rationality of the natural world.

As a young man, Huxley felt an intense need to find the logic of experience, for his own early life had been a period of disorder and debilitating mental conflict, brought on by what he once referred to as having had his "household gods early overturned & scattered by mis-fortune."[5] Possessed by periodic mental depression and by a terrible sense of his own instability, Huxley appears to have found in the scientist an alternate identity in which he could overcome the anxieties of his youth. We find him at twenty-two, assistant surgeon and unofficial ship's naturalist aboard H.M.S. *Rattlesnake*, writing in his journal as he journeyed on a mapping voyage to Australia and New Guinea in 1846: "In the region of the intellect alone can I find free and innocent play for such faculties as I possess. And it is well for me that my way of life allows me to get rid of the 'malady of thought' in a course of action so suitable to my tastes, as that laid open to me by this voyage."[6] The course of action to which Huxley was referring was not his medical duties, which he found mostly a burden, but his work with South Sea invertebrates, research involving the study of anatomical structure and the search for archetypal anatomical plans. These were suitable objects for his faculties, opening him a path around the "malady of thought," a condition of anxiety which, while vague and diffuse, remained, as we shall see, a lifelong companion. In the same journal entry, written on his twenty-second birthday, he reflected on his birth into the world as a "pulpy mass of capabilities, as yet unknown and save by motherly affection uncared for," and wondered whether it were not better to have been "crushed and trodden out at once." Strident statements like these often punctuate Huxley's early correspondence and suggest that a deep sensitivity and turmoil lay beneath his aggressive rationalism. Some forty years later, Beatrice Webb, fascinated with Huxley while interviewing him about his old associate Herbert Spencer, recorded in her journal: "Huxley, when not working, dreams strange things: carries on lengthy conversations between unknown persons living within his brain. There is a strain of madness in him; melancholy has haunted his whole life."[7] It was a shrewd observation. Huxley's chronic mental depressions and collapses, his sense of isolation and trauma when speaking of his past, suggest that his intense commitment to the rationalist world view, which he identified as the fundamental view of the scientist, was in important ways generated by the impulse to seek and to create external order in the face of impending personal disorder.

From his earliest youth, when he had set out to organize the disciplines of knowledge into objective and subjective categories, to his final years, when he set the human order at odds with the natural order, Huxley was fascinated by philosophical architectonics. "What I cared for," he pointed out in his "Autobiography," "was the architectural and engineering part of the business, the working out the wonderful unity of plan in the thousands and thousands of diverse living constructions, and the modifications of similar apparatuses to serve diverse ends" (1:7). Science opened a bridge between the external world of phenomena and the internal world of intellect and emotion. Writing to Kingsley in 1860, Huxley, emotionally wrought over the death of his son Noel, declared:

> Science seems to me to teach in the highest and strongest manner the great truth which is embodied in the Christian conception of entire surrender to the will of God. Sit down before fact as a little child, be prepared to give up every preconceived notion, follow humbly wherever and to whatever abysses nature leads, or you shall learn nothing. I have only begun to learn content and peace of mind since I have resolved at all risks to do this. [*LL*, 1:235]

Thus it was that death and the apparent irrationalities of the world were brought into rational perspective by the outlook of the man of science. Just as his son Noel had surrendered to the ultimate fact of death, so Huxley resolved to sit down before the same fact and to surrender his will to the reality of the boy's death. It was an act of courage and deep emotion. Like a true Stoic, Huxley sought to live according to the truths of science, believing that they were the truths of life itself, that the work of the scientist was a progressive revelation of the nature of things not only in the laboratory but in the world.

ii. science and self

Huxley's idea of the scientist originated during a period of personal struggle and unrest, when he was uncertain of the direction his life was to take. Born in 1825, the sixth child in an impoverished and factious family, Huxley found his early years full of conflict. For while very early he was keenly interested in acquiring an education as a guide into the world of intellect, he was for the most part left to drift. With little family support and only a year of formal education, he was forced to secure his education through a self-motivated and self-directed process of study, which, while made somewhat easier by his intellectual enthusiasm, was to succeed only through long, grueling lessons in self-discipline. Considering the rigorous educations of his Victorian counterparts, John Stuart Mill and Matthew Arnold, Huxley could only look back on his earlier years with a sense of bitter failure. In 1845, reflecting in a journal on the previous five years of his life, the time of his medical apprenticeship and his study at Charing Cross Hospital in London, he wrote of pain and neglect:

> I hardly care to look back into the seething depths of the working and boiling mass that lay beneath all this froth, and indeed I hardly know whether I could give myself any clear account of it. Remembrances of physical and mental pain . . . absence of sympathy, and thence a choking up of such few ideas as I did form clearly within my own mind. [*LL*, 1:15]

The period remained permanently embroiled in a feeling of despair; it had been a struggle to assemble ideas amid anxieties and circumstances which he would recall in later life with a sense of lonely isolation.

The loss of educational opportunity left Huxley with a sense of intellectual disenfranchisement. While his early journal, "Thoughts and Doings," reveals him at work among studies and experiments in physiology, chemistry, and electricity; readings in English and German Romantic authors like Carlyle, Novalis, and Lessing; and language studies in Greek, Latin, German, and Italian; Huxley was keenly aware that he was without guide and that his studies were often random and incomplete. Left to his own devices in determining his educational program, he found himself ranging over widely diverse materials, and often out of his depth. His future was determined by the fact that his brothers-in-law were medical doctors and that he was expected to follow them; but he demonstrated only slight interest in medicine, devoting much time to the study of his favorite authors, Goethe and Carlyle, and to his readings in philosophy and theoretical science. He managed, in the "boiling mass" of his early years, to obtain a preliminary certificate in medicine at London University in 1845, and a naval position the following year as assistant surgeon aboard H.M.S. *Rattlesnake;* yet he remained anxious, convinced he had wasted his abilities and lost his opportunity. At sea in 1849, writing to his Australian fiancée, Henrietta Heathorn, whom he had met less than a year after he set out on his voyage to Australia and New Guinea, Huxley struck out at his past and expressed his sense of neglect:

> I believe that I possess powers which might by proper training have been made a good deal of. I believe that I have a somewhat acute logical mind and strong appreciation of the Beautiful in whatever shape—I might have made a good critic and an accomplished man. As it is, what am I? A hotch-potch of knowledge and ignorance—facts and fictions picked up from all the highways & byways of knowledge, cheek by jowl with the most absurd ignorance at which a schoolboy might blush. My knowledge is mostly the result of thought and reasoning, whereas all that shows in the world is learning—the result of a good memory and superficial aptness.[8]

Running through the passage is a clash between fact and aspiration, a sense of having fallen far short of capacity. But Huxley's was an exaggerated sense of inferiority—while he had not acquired a classical British university education, he had nevertheless developed his powers of "thought and reasoning" considerably in his struggle to educate himself, and he had read widely, if not systematically, in several disciplines. At the very time he wrote to Henrietta, he was studying ocean invertebrates, research which would prove to be highly innovative and original. It appears, however, that Huxley initially desired a literary rather than a scientific career, and much of his discontent may have arisen from the absence of any choice in his life. His enthusiasm for criticism, the feeling that he might have made a good critic, was undoubtedly inspired by his readings in Carlyle, whose critical essays and *Sartor Resartus* were Huxley's intimate voyage companions. He quoted them and read them for solace; he found Carlyle's essays on Jean Paul deeply appealing, since the conditions of the young Richter's life, the lack of tutors, the neglect by the father of the sons' education, the poverty and struggle, all ran so parallel to his own.[9] Huxley found his own long, introspective flights and depressions considerably amplified and defined by the unrest he encountered in the worlds of Carlyle, Goethe, and the other Romantics whom he read widely. The "malady of thought" he often referred to as his persistent shadow and persecutor was a term used by Carlyle in his essay "Goethe" to describe that Byronic and Goethean sense of despair about the "whole scene of life" which had become barren of belief and hope.[10] It was the "life-weariness" of *Manfred*, the "moody melancholy" of *Werther*. Huxley felt it in his own deep disappointment with the conditions of life, in his sense of alienation, his faltering belief.

The personal struggles of childhood influenced, perhaps even instigated, Huxley's slow synthesis of a professional identity. Few ideals were to be gleaned from the adult models of his early life, and Huxley, precocious, sensitive, and frequently demoralized by a sensation of being entirely alone and adrift, felt a powerful urge to seek out his own. Writing to Kingsley in 1860, he recalled how he had been "kicked into the world a boy without guide or training," and how few men had "drunk deeper of all kinds of sin" than he (*LL*, 1:237). The past was a barrier, complicated with vague yet intense guilt feelings which had their origins at once in childhood incidents and in a diffuse, Romantic sense of sin and alienation, a Byronic *Weltschmerz*.[11] Like Byron's Cain, whose profound discontent with the conditions of human mortality and misery led him to ponder his sleeping child Enoch with the thought that it would have been better to have "snatch'd him in his sleep, and dash'd him 'gainst / The rocks"; Huxley wondered whether it had not been better had he at birth been "crushed and trodden out at once."[12] A similar enmity for experience underlay Huxley's sense of alienation.

Writing to Henrietta Heathorn from 1847, the year they were engaged in Australia, to 1854, the year they were reunited and married in London, Huxley frequently spoke of his past, his painful experiences in the world of men, his private solace in the world of dream and intellect.[13] It was a period of great uncertainty and his letters were often anxious and deeply introspective, at times almost confessional. They revealed a young man, now in his twenties, who had long been alone with his thoughts and who lived intensely in the self. His new love for Henrietta had opened a vista into the external world, much as his scientific research aboard the *Rattlesnake* had been doing. Some letters disclose that as a child he had felt such a burning conflict with the conditions of his life that he had fled inward, constructing a wall between his own mental and the outer

18

physical worlds. In a dream state of consciousness, he had found a personal refuge, away from events which were sources of anxiety and pain. Writing to Henrietta while at sea in December 1848, Huxley spoke of mental and social isolation:

> I fear I have nothing of that fine feeling called "love for one's species." The actions of human beings whether now around me or as they are recorded in history for the most part touch my intellect but not my heart. I like to watch them as I should like to see a play—but I always feel the spectator. It may be Tragedy or Comedy—my feelings may be painfully or pleasantly excited—but I feel more among men than of them. Even among the most real occurrences a dreamy feeling creeps over me—I feel like a man who believes his dream and yet knows he is dreaming.
>
> I fancy that people must occasionally think me very unstable and indeed heartlessly indifferent. I am apt to enter into men's ways and feelings with a certain warmth and enthusiasm which is for the time perfectly real—but in fact only skin deep—and which I fear makes people fancy that I have a feeling of friendship for them when none exists. I go away and forget all about the matter and am as much surprised at their claim of friendship as I should be if, after weeping over the sad fortunes of King Lear, his majesty should doff his robes and beard and request me to back a bill for him on the strength of my sympathy. This may seem hard hearted, but so it is with me. Men's actions often interest me but their motives are either laughable for their folly or contemptible for their selfishness—that is to say, in general, god forbid that I should slander humanity so far as to say that this is universally the case.
>
> I believe that I owe many of these feelings to my early life. My life from eight years age up to manhood was made up of two sets of feelings—joys and anticipations derived from the inward world, those such as a student only knows (and however ill-directed my energies or misspent my time still I *was* a student from my childhood); and sorrows and misfortunes coming from the outward world upon all those whom I had reason to love and value most. Then, too, I was one of the most sensitive, thin-skinned mortals in the world. I had little pleasure in the general pursuits of boys of my own age, cared only for the society of men, and yet was too proud to be treated as one whit of less importance than they—so that I had hardly any friends. There was absolutely nothing to bring me into contact with the world—and I hated and avoided it. Its good was not my good, its ends not my ends, and so I saw it pass before me,

little recking, and dreaming my own dreams.

Since then I have indeed had a few shakes, enough to rouse the dead. But I still fear I am occasionally no better than a somnambulist. [14]

The world was, then, often a stage for the young Huxley, who remained apart, dreaming and yet awake, among men but not of them; he was surprised when their existence was affirmed through the breaking of the frame and he was called upon to respond. As a child, to insulate himself from harm, he drew his energies inward to a place where he might control events as the world passed before him in the distance. He lived with a separate mental convention which systematically disembodied the external world of its materiality and, hence, of its power to inflict pain. Like a dreamer, he saw with the objectivity of one removed, of a keen observer who sees the performances of men fall far short of possibility.

The clash of the real and the ideal in Huxley's youthful mind had its origin in events which were not covered in Leonard Huxley's *Life and Letters*. Very little is known about the Huxley family when Thomas was a child, other than that it was often in desperate financial straits, that it had a history of severe mental disorder, and that factiousness reigned during Huxley's early and later years. It was an atmosphere which bred the permanent rupture between members of the family and the older brother, William, who remained estranged for thirty years because of a family quarrel over the marriage of his brother George. "You will think it strange," Thomas wrote to Henrietta about William, "that you have hardly heard me mention his name before, although he lives in London. But he is completely alienated from the rest of us. You will, I fear, think that we are a very strange set and it is very true. For some inscrutable reason we seem to me to get on with everybody but one another." [15] Exceptions were Thomas and his older sister, Lizzie, who was in many ways his surrogate mother. Of the six children, Thomas Huxley wrote to Lizzie, they were the only two "who seemed to be capable of fraternal love." [16] Beset with financial difficulties, the family was driven inward upon itself, with little guidance from George Huxley, the uncommunicative father who by the time of Thomas's youth was probably slipping into the mental isolation which was well advanced by the time Huxley returned from his *Rattlesnake* voyage in 1850. In an atmosphere of tension and anxiety, and, unable to maintain his equilibrium, the young Huxley withdrew into the private world of dream and intellect.

Huxley's early clash with the world of experience was symbolized by his famous encounter with the corpse in the post mortem scene of his "Autobiography." Written in 1889 when he was nearly sixty-four, Huxley's account of himself follows a pattern beginning with childhood anecdote and ending with a reflection over the most important goals of his scientific life. Midway through the autobiography, he recounts his grim rite of passage from childhood to maturity, the tableside witness, when he was a boy of thirteen or fourteen, of a post mortem dissection. Death was the ultimate reality, the great fact of life which none could escape. There on the table, stiff and grotesque, lay a body before a young man who had had nothing to bring him into contact with the external world, the place of pain and sorrow, and who "hated and avoided" it. Yet, fascinated, Huxley indulged his curiosity for two to three hours in a state of profound but momentarily controlled mental agitation. His recollection that he did not suffer a cut implies that he may even have used the scalpel, perhaps probing and exploring to satisfy his own curiosity after the major dissection had been completed. The scene is full of irony, for while Huxley was actively confronting the fact of death, he was simultaneously submitting to its powerful reality. The corpse belonged to a world he had half disbelieved in, a world of shadows and figures, now suddenly materialized by death. Huxley left to go home in what appears to have been a state of shock and with the feeling of having been "poisoned" (1:8). Sinking into a "strange state of apathy," he languished at home for days.

The family atmosphere was unable to revive him, since it was itself a source of insecurities and the sense of neglect epitomized by the corpse. The corpse, a human figure no longer having an identity, isolated and utterly powerless, was a symbol not only of human materiality, but of human alienation as well. Huxley remained in this strange state of isolated depression until he was removed from home to "the care of some good, kind people . . . who lived in a farmhouse in the heart of Warwickshire''; the following day he arose from the dead, or the very nearly dead: "I remember staggering from my bed to the window on the bright spring morning after my arrival, and throwing open the casement. Life seemed to come back on the wings of the breeze" (1:8). Huxley himself seems to have undergone the experience of death and been reborn with a new knowledge of good and evil.[17]

The experience was important in another sense, for in confronting death Huxley had, if only momentarily, triumphed over his own anxiety. The motivation behind the act of dissection goes to the core of Huxley's thought. The self-destructive impulse to shrink from experience, to exist in dream isolation, was overcome by the scientific necessity to confront the world of fact. There at the dissecting table, the factual curiosity of the aspiring man of science enabled Huxley to control his anxieties and to confront his ultimate fate. As the researcher, he was able to distance himself and to control the object, death, by rendering it the passive subject of his rational intelligence. Science provided a framework in which one might achieve an attitude toward experience which amounted to a negation of the self. In effect, it provided a center of indifference, for its business was with phenomena only insofar as they might be quantified. The flow of consciousness was thus outward and not inward.[18] Confrontation with reality was to become the prime object of Huxley's man of science, and his childhood encounter at the dissecting table would find its ultimate justification in the conclusion of the "Autobiography," which argued that alleviation for the sufferings of mankind could come only through "the resolute facing of the world as it is when the garment of make-believe by which pious hands have hidden its uglier features is stripped off" (1:16).

Death remained for Huxley a vivid symbol of reality, of corporality, a symbol which concentrated all the contingencies which seemed to threaten him as a child. The same vision of mortality which haunted Byron's Manfred and Cain haunted Huxley's private, introspective hours. In a letter to Henrietta written in May 1849, he saw death as a reality against which all ideals seemed impotent:

In my many solitary hours—in this my hermitage—strange thoughts rise in my mind. A weary sense of the vivid emptiness of life—a scorn of my own occupations & the petty aims after which I and others struggle—a miserable feeling of the short coming of all efforts after the noble ideal which now & then for a few bright moments seems so near—so easily attainable. And under all these, as a dark background, showing forth more vividly their lurid colours—the certainty of death. I do not mean in its hackneyed sense. All men tell you they are certain of death as they tell you that they are sinners. But with me this certainty at times assumes a vividness such as I can hardly describe—I see it rather than feel it.[19]

Huxley's vision had likely been intensified by his actual encounters with death in the course of his medical studies, but long before his study at Charing Cross Hospital he had felt the force of death as a threat to his childhood security. Speaking of his mother in a letter to Henrietta, he recalled: "As a child my love for her was a passion—I have lain awake for hours, crying, because I had a morbid fear of her death."[20] His childhood fears must often have bordered on hysteria. Even his love for Henrietta was menaced in his imagination by death: "Will you believe it when I tell you that my foolish fancy carries me to so far as to even imagine you ill, or dying, or even forever . . . parted from me? My imagination has always a pictoral distinctiveness, and I see myself heading over to Holmwood on the day of our return, and hearing that you are no longer mine—no longer of this earth."[21] Reality often seemed to threaten its worst, to dissolve these intangible, emotional attachments in a show of superior force. Given to carrying on long dialogues with the self, Huxley found the private, internal world as threatening as the world without, for there was no insulation from the morbid imagination.

Huxley's early Romantic sense of alienation was thus a distillation of his very real childhood anxieties over death, neglect, and isolation—the "seething depths" and the "boiling mass" he had looked back over in his journal entry of 1845. The Romantic, introspective movement inward, the sullen alienation of Byron's Cain contemplating the injustice of having been called into the world of life only to suffer and die, the sense of dignity in intellectual rebellion, and the enmity toward experience, all conformed to Huxley's youthful sensibilities and conditions. Yet he had also begun to find avenues outward: in his research aboard H.M.S. *Rattlesnake* from 1846 to 1850, in his relationship with Henrietta Heathorn beginning in 1847, and in his increasing grasp of the Carlylean doctrines of antiselfconsciousness and work. Each of these broadened and strengthened his interests in the external world. Research aboard the *Rattlesnake* carried him deeper into the physical world where he found himself increasingly at home in the material world of experience. Living aboard ship for four years brought him into steady contact with a harsh physical world whose laws he disciplined himself to abide by. His work countered his tendency to withdraw, for the labor of the field researcher was among facts which had to be obtained in physical nature. Above all, in the methods of the sciences one found a rational framework in which to approach the phenomena of the external world, even death, since all were a part of the great natural pattern. Science, Huxley declared to Kingsley in 1860, had taught him to "sit down before fact as a little child," and to "follow humbly wherever and to whatever abysses nature leads" (*LL*, 1:235). Only then had he begun to "learn content and peace of mind."

Huxley's conversion from self-centeredness to antiselfconsciousness was a gradual one, and appears to have occurred in the years immediately after his return to London in 1850. He devoted himself intensively to his scientific research for more than four years. Not only did science offer a rational framework in which to view the struggles and pains of life; it also hinted that they were essentially just, since they were universal, without malice, and to varying degrees predictable. "I cannot but think," Huxley reflected in his 1854 essay "On the Educational Value of the Natural History Sciences" "that he who finds a certain proportion of pain and evil inseparably woven up in the life of the very worms, will bear his own share with more courage and submission" (3:62). In spite of pain, one found "the predominance of happiness" among living things, and a "secret and wonderful harmony" in nature. Science offered a Carlylean center of indifference from which to view the whole, for one's obligation was to seek a self-annihilating disinterestedness with which, without fear, one could look upon the worst. "The intellectual perception of truth," Huxley wrote to Henrietta in 1851, "and the acting up to it is so far as I know the only meaning of the phrase 'one-ness with God.' So long as we attain that end, does it matter much whether our small selves are happy or miserable?"[22] It was Carlyle who had cautioned against the morbid introspection, the "malady of thought," that drove one to an inner fury and agony:

> "What is this that, ever since earliest years, thou hast been fretting and fuming, and lamenting and self-tormenting, on account of? Say it in a word: is it not because thou are not HAPPY? Because the THOU (sweet gentleman) is not sufficiently honoured, nourished, soft-bedded, and lovingly cared-for? Foolish soul! What Act of Legislature was there that *thou* shouldst be Happy? A little while ago thou hadst no right to *be* at all . . . Art thou nothing other than a Vulture, then, that fliest through the Universe seeking after somewhat to *eat*; and shrieking dolefully because carrion enough is not given thee? Close thy *Byron*; open the *Goethe*."[23]

The vast scope of the scientific vision served for Huxley as the infinitude in which to dwarf the problems and anxieties of the self. And his Romantic sense of alienation gradually evolved into the "scientific Calvinism" which he identified in a letter to his friend Dyster as the philosophy underlying his 1854 essay. "Pain being everywhere is inevitable," he confided, "and therefore like all other inevitable things to be borne" (*LL*, 1:122). To reach the higher truth, one had to learn the lesson of renunciation, and Huxley found Carlyle's argument compelling enough to list *Sartor Resartus* as one of the "agents" of his redemption (*LL*, 1:237).

The steady confrontation of harsh reality became a high priority of Huxley's intellectual vision, giving rise to his new scientific Calvinism. It was in many ways a fierce vision, a determined commitment to confront, at whatever cost, the abyss that loomed in the world "when the garment of make-believe by which pious hands have hidden its uglier features is stripped off" (1:16). And yet there was a dignity, a courage, in the confrontation that promised a new human possibility and truth. Typically, the confrontation took the form of analysis. Huxley's observation in the 1854 essay "On the Educational

Value of the Natural History Sciences" that the real advantage in the "*trained and organised common sense*" of the scientist was the same as that of the "point and polish of the swordsman's weapon" over the "club" of the savage, demonstrated that he still was at battle with the powers of the earth (3:45). Rebellion was part of his character, and renunciation came much easier to him than submission. His doctrine of confrontation found one of its classic expressions in his 1868 essay "A Liberal Education; and Where to Find it," where death was the outcome of a neglected reality, and science the proper instrument for the confrontation of that reality. He characterized life as a game of chess played against nature by men according to rules which were identical to the laws of nature. While the opponent, nature, was not sinister, but rather a "calm, strong angel," the stakes were high. Those who could not learn to play the game were "plucked," and Huxley carefully pointed out that "Nature's pluck means extermination" (3:85). Death remained the old adversary.

Huxley's 1854 essay was his unofficial inaugural essay. He delivered it at St. Martin's Hall in London on July 22, only a few days after he had been appointed Lecturer in Natural History at the Government School of Mines, replacing his close friend Edward Forbes. For the first time since he had returned to London in 1850, he was able to contemplate a scientific career with some confidence. He had fought for a position in scientific London, but found it difficult to penetrate the inner circle where professional positions were controlled by an intimate polity of researchers and specialists, and very scarce. The pressure was intensified by the absence of Henrietta, whom Huxley could not bring over from Australia until he had a dependable income. The four years from 1850 to 1854 were not unproductive, however, for he earned admission to the Royal Society in 1851, and the society's Royal Medal the following year for his research among ocean invertebrates; he was also earning a reputation as a talented writer and speaker. By midyear 1854, he had published more than twenty papers on technical subjects, including a brilliant study, "On the Morphology of the Cephalous Mollusca," in which he had begun to renovate British theories of anatomy and classification; he had translated and edited, in collaboration with George Busk, Kölliker's *Handbuch der Gewebelehre des Menschen (Manual of Human Histology)*; and he had begun to write scientific columns and reviews for George Eliot in the *Westminster Review*, contributing regularly from 1852 to 1854. He was thus growing familiar with both scientific and literary circles in London, and coming into contact with the main ideas and intellectual trends of his time.

During the four years after his return to London, Huxley's growing commitment to scientific life and work helped him to consolidate his idea of the scientist. But he found a new pattern of adversity dominating his life: the personal alienation of his youth he now saw being recapitulated in the public alienation of the scientist as a type in Victorian society. Huxley's individual struggle formed a basic pattern which was strikingly representative of professional scientists who sought to earn their livings by means of scientific pursuits. In a letter to Henrietta, Huxley wrote in 1851:

> To attempt to live by any scientific pursuit is a farce. Nothing but what is absolutely practical will go down in England. A man of science may earn great distinction, but not bread. . . . A man of science in these times is like an Esau who sells his birthright for a mess of pottage. [LL, 1:72]

In a somewhat different way, Huxley's struggle typified that of Victorian science to become accepted as an intellectual force and a professional body of knowledge. Livings were not often to be made in pure science, although medals and professional plaudits were common enough, for the simple reason that science had yet to be recognized as a social, economic, and cultural force. It remained the amateur's field, that of the gentleman researcher who, like Darwin, might divert himself for years with little concern for income. Huxley wrote, "My opportunities for seeing the scientific world in England force upon me every day a stronger and stronger conviction. It is that there is no chance of living by science. . . . There are not more than four or five offices in London which a Zoologist or Comparative Anatomist can hold and live by. Owen, who has a European reputation, second only to that of Cuvier, gets as Hunterian Professor £300 a year! which is less than the salary of many a bank clerk" (*LL*, 1:74). Professional scientific specialization in England began and developed in a pattern and schedule that roughly paralleled Huxley's professional career.

The search for employment, which for Huxley recalled the childhood anxieties over instability, helped him to formulate a broad notion of the scientist. He was also able to generalize from his own experience to the common experiences of men of science whom he began to characterize as a type in his personal letters. Facing a long period of poverty, continued separation from Henrietta, and uncertainty about his future, Huxley had to consider carefully his motivation for pursuing the way of the scientist, and he began to construct out of his own ideals and those of the men with whom he associated a representative concept of the profession. Looking around him, he found numerous "first-rate men—men who have been at work for years laboriously toiling upward—men whose abilities, had they turned them into many channels of money-making, must have made large fortunes. But the beauty of Nature and the pursuit of Truth allured them into a nobler life" (*LL*, 1:74). In the same letter, written on his twenty-sixth birthday, less than a month after he had been elected a member of the Royal Society, he confided to Henrietta:

> A man who chooses a life of science chooses not a life of poverty, but, so far as I can see, a life of *nothing*, and the art of living upon nothing at all has yet to be discovered. You naturally think, then, "Why persevere in so hopeless a course?" At present I cannot help myself. For my own credit, for the sake of gratifying those who have hitherto helped me on—nay, for the sake of truth and science itself, I must work out fairly and fully complete what I have begun. [*LL*, 1:74–75]

Six months later, Huxley declared that the "real pleasure, the true sphere" of his ambition, lay "in the feeling of self-development—in the sense of power and of growing *oneness* with the great spirit of abstract truth" (*LL*, 1:75). The idealistic dedication to beauty and truth was tempered by an awareness of personal and social conflict. The struggle of the scientist, linked as it was to both truth and adversity, became symbolic for Huxley in a personal as well as a professional sense. It became part of the nobler life, the life which death and childhood misfortunes had often seemed to threaten before they met with the force of his own intellectual enthusiasm. In 1853, he wrote, "I have become almost unable to exist without active intellectual excitement" (*LL*, 1:91). In the scientist, Huxley's personal struggles and values had found their intellectual, public equivalent. In 1860, when he was thirty-five, he confided to Kingsley that he had come to feel as one who had been redeemed from himself. He identified his three "agents . . . of redemption" as *Sartor Resartus*, science, and his love for Henrietta Heathorn (*LL*, 1:237). Carlyle's work had led him from his early alienated scepticism, a Cain-like antipathy for the world that sin had spawned, to the recognition that a "deep sense of religion was compatible with the entire absence of theology." In science he had found an appropriate and constructive resting place for his intellectual rebellion against "authority and tradition." And love had taught him of the "sanctity of human nature" and of the duties and responsibilities of human relationships. Huxley's early Romantic sense of alienation had found its Victorian solution.

iii. the lower world

The idea of a scientist developed into one of the controlling unities of Huxley's nontechnical essays. Exploring the man of science as a type, Huxley investigated his moral, intellectual, and social profile against the Victorian cultural background. As a fusion of personal vision, extracted from Huxley's private experience, and professional generalization, derived from his familiarity with scientists past and present, Huxley's man of science took on the dimensions of a broad ideal. It was an unusual ideal, however, for its preoccupation was with physical reality. Like the poet and the artist, the scientist immersed himself in nature, but in a physical nature where his business was as often as not in the bowels of the earth. As a result, his findings frequently held little aesthetic appeal; they were less likely to reflect the realm of human ideal than to contribute to the book of physical law. The scientist was codifying nature. He was not, as Ruskin had urged, simply the eagle, acting in the conviction that "the glory of the higher creatures is in ignorance of what is known to the lower."[24] While Ruskin argued that great knowledge, "sophia," forbade men to bury themselves in "the mole's earthheap," Huxley held that the pursuit of coarse and inelegant fact was the source of the scientist's power. For Ruskin man had the choice of "stooping in science beneath himself, and striving in science beyond himself," while for Huxley the system of nature was of such unity that the lowliest fact led to the most exalted vista.[25]

In an unpublished, undated fragment, Huxley traced the development from Greek thought to modern thought of the concept of "sophos":

> The early Greeks called a skillful craftsman, one who excelled his fellows, *Sophos*; and hence the term easily extended to cover the shrewd & intelligent in general whence there lay but a step to the men of deep knowledge & wisdom or even of mere worldly wisdom. In fact the fate of the word was pretty much that of our "cunning."[26]

He went on to argue that "sophos" and "sophia" originally meant the craftsman and his skill, but that gradually they came to refer to the wise man and his wisdom, and later to the pedantic art of argumentation. The "philosophos," he noted, was originally the self-designation of one who did not claim to be a "sophos"—a skilled artificer, artist or thinker—but only a lover of such. Only gradually did "philosophos" come to mean the skilled and authoritative wise man. "Sapientia" and "scientia," Huxley observed, were the Latin equivalents of the Greek "sophia," and they had undergone "a most unfortunate narrowing" in modern thought until they were specifically applied to disciplines of chemistry, biology, physics, and mathematics, when in fact they should apply to "organised knowledge whatever its subject matter." For Huxley, the pedigree of human knowledge could be traced back to the precision and skill of the craftsman, whose mastery of detail and preoccupation with materials of the earth, with forging the tools for survival, earned him the admiration of his fellows. Greek technology and science, that is, organized knowledge, laid the foundations for Greek philosophy. Thus while Ruskin's great lectures in *The Eagle's Nest* were delivered at Oxford, Huxley's lectures were given more frequently at working men's clubs; these were the respective symbolic centers of their separate concepts of "sophia."

For Huxley the idea of the scientist had strong proletarian roots. In his address "Technical Education" (1887), he described himself as a teacher of handicrafts, a manual laborer, and emphasized the egalitarian basis of scientific knowledge. Speaking before the Working Men's Club and Institute in London, he referred to anatomy as his "handicraft," and argued that the sciences all required a manual dexterity similar to that of the anatomist, whose skill enabled him to dissect, "say, a blackbeetle's nerves" (3:406). Huxley was careful to emphasize that he meant the comparison in a literal sense, and while his claim seemed somewhat exaggerated, he quite properly drew upon the relationship between the crafts and the laboratory, an association which had endured since the Renaissance. "Doing" was essential to scientific investigation, for the sciences demanded constant verification, and, like the craftsman, the scientist was required to remain in touch with the crude realities of daily experience.

Huxley went on to suggest that the bond between the cobbler and the anatomist lay in their common "contact with tangible facts" (3:407). At the same time, he set in opposition to the scientist and craftsman certain "learned brethren, whose work is untrammelled by anything 'base and mechanical' " (3:408). These were the intellectuals whose histories edified and whose poems charmed; their work illustrated "so remarkably the powers of man's imagination." Yet they were removed from the world of "mother wit" and physical, manual skill. They were the inhabitants of the "empyreal kingdom of speculation," where there were distinct prejudices against mere "grovelling dissectors of monkeys and blackbeetles" (3:408). In his solidarity with his craftsman audience, Huxley gave rein to his sense of antagonism toward the humanities. He emasculated the liberal arts through stereotype: "Mother Nature is serenely obdurate to honeyed words" (3:408). He claimed for the scientist and the craftsman a higher sense of reality and therefore a greater power over nature. The scientist, he argued, is tied to the reality of physical fact by a logic no less compelling than that which demands the attention of the British working classes. For both, it is a matter of survival which, although often prosaic, yields rewards in the increased awareness of physical reality.

Huxley was oversimplifying in identifying the scientist so literally with the working man; in many other essays he had claimed the kingdom of speculation for scientists as well as for intellectuals. Yet he believed that the distinctive character of scientific knowledge and work was their preoccupation with physical nature. The process of accumulating experience had its counterpart in the process of recording factual data. Huxley had formulated reality out of hard, sometimes harsh facts; it was the fundamental lesson of his youth. Imagination and speculation were frequently suspect as pleasant, even lurid, indulgences that for all their edification and charm were not essential to survival. The craftsman's knowledge had its primary value in enabling him to manipulate and thereby change physical reality, to make with his own hands "a veritable chair" (3:407). The man of science had a similar power, only on a larger scale. In his famous lay sermon "On the Advisableness of Improving Natural Knowledge" (1866), Huxley pointed out that natural knowledge had become so fundamental that it had been "incorporated with the household words of men, and . . . supplied the springs of their daily actions" (1:28). He was referring to the largely unconscious behavior of Londoners which averted catastrophes like the great plague and the great fire. The scientist, not the theologian or politician, delivered men from natural catastrophe. Like the working man, he labored in a hidden world, grappling with realities no one else cared to contemplate. Their alliance was a natural one, even to the extent that they suffered in common a certain taint of servility as a consequence of their common residence in lower worlds of fact and utility.

Huxley's belief in the bond between scientists and the working class remained strong throughout his life. His working men's lectures, his energetic pioneering work in technical education and universities for the working classes, suggests a deeply felt identification. British science and labor had secured a close, if stormy, relationship in their shared concern with technology. One remembers the strong ally Dickens finds for the working class in the technology of the Rouncewell iron factory in *Bleak House*, and Carlyle's ambition for British industry.[27] Not only did technology, with its fusion of science and the crafts, supply new possibilities for the British laboring classes, as Huxley noted in his essay on improving natural knowledge, it promised a new independence and dignity. For Marx and Engels, the subjection of nature's forces, resulting from the application of new technology, had revealed that unsuspected "productive forces slumbered in the lap of social labor."[28] Technology promised power for the working classes, even if its exploitation was in the hands of another class. The vast new laboring forces in textiles, commerce, and mining, as Marx had pointed out, promised a new locus of power. The underlying themes of Huxley's working men's lectures and essays treating education, while not Marxist, appreciated similarly the physical power men were exercising over nature. Technical knowledge was that of force and power; it was the new learning which would ultimately revolutionize all human knowledge and human society.

Huxley's thrust in essays like "A Liberal Education; and Where to Find It" and "Technical Education" was the reverse of John Henry Newman's, for Newman's idea of knowledge as its own end rejected the notion that education must have a practical application. Indeed, such knowledge as could be put to distinct use was considered "servile" by Newman to the degree that its worth was to be measured in terms of the efficacy of the particular action it inspired.[29] Newman sought to liberate knowledge from utilitarian standards of value. Liberal knowledge justified itself by fulfilling the basic need of human nature to know. Ruskin, too, found the university the center of "conception" rather than "skill": " The object of University teaching is to form your conceptions;—not to acquaint you with arts, nor sciences. It is to give you a notion of what is meant by smith's work, for instance;—but not to make you blacksmiths."[30] The drive of Newman and Ruskin toward *gnosis*, the contemplative sphere of knowledge, contrasted dramatically with Huxley's advocacy of *praxis*. Scientist and working man were, in their different capacities, oriented toward action. Both were members of "Nature's university," learning to survive and operate in a world that functioned according to natural principle. Physical science was the proletarian of the intellectual world.

Of Huxley's portraits of scientists, fictitious or real, none is more compelling than Zadig in his unique combination of perceptual acumen and that "coarse commonplace assumption, upon which every act of our daily lives is based," the reasoning from effects to causes (4:7). In this 1880 lecture delivered at the Working Men's College, Huxley went to considerable lengths to establish Voltaire's well-known character as a prototype of the modern scientist. Using the "unconscious logic of common sense," Zadig surmises that the king's lost horse has a tail three and a half feet long because the dust of the trees had been disturbed on either side of a narrow, seven-foot alley (4:8). "Nothing can be more hopelessly vulgar," Huxley pointed out, "more unlike the majestic development of a system of grandly unintelligible conclusions from sublimely inconceivable premisses" (4:8). Huxley deliberately set off the portrait in prosaic, even primitivistic, terms, calling Zadig's insight "methodized savagery" (4:8). The point of the portrait was to domesticate the scientist figure, to show that his activities were natural and fundamentally concerned with natural processes, that they were human and "nothing but the method of all mankind" (4:8). Certainly, as Phyllis Rose has suggested, Huxley was oversimplifying the nature of the scientist, but at the same time he was demonstrating the essential human impulse behind the great disciplines that had developed out of empirical investigations.[31] Huxley wished to proclaim the democracy of scientific knowledge by characterizing Zadig as a kind of scientific Everyman. Throughout the essay, the clarity and simplicity of Zadig's method is contrasted with the a priori stances of "magian wisdom, with all its lofty antagonism to everything common" (4:7). Scientific knowledge drew its strength from its vulgar simplicity, its dismissal of intellectual pretension.

Not only was Zadig a plucky antiauthoritarian, like Huxley's scientific Everyman, he served to universalize intellectual procedures commonly associated with scientific method. Precisely because he was not a professional scientist Zadig gave legitimacy to the nineteenth-century scientist, for he illustrated that the scientist had his roots in the distant past, that the unadorned search for fact had moral force, and that the process of scientific method was simple, common, and human. The need to recast the figure of the scientist as a socially responsible being had to be met before science could be taken seriously by society as a means of progress. One suspects that Huxley had something similar to Mary Shelley's *Frankenstein* in mind when he asserted that "Science is not, as many would seem to suppose, a modification of the black art, suited to the tastes of the nineteenth century" (3:45). The gothic obsession of Frankenstein's hideous labor in his isolated laboratory, already by 1823 a popular melodrama in London, presents an interesting contrast to the elegant rationality of Zadig.

Zadig and Dr. Frankenstein belong to different worlds. The science of Frankenstein is a nineteenth-century version of the murky machinery of Cornelius Agrippa, scholar and broker of occult powers over nature. It is a science that still hopes for fabulous "secrets" which promise prodigious power. "I succeeded in discovering the cause of generation and life; nay, more, I became myself capable of bestowing animation upon lifeless matter," records Frankenstein.[32] Mary Shelley attempted to give a solid scientific base to Frankenstein's work, yet for all that, he emerges as the magus, obsessed with his great opus. And it is this isolation while in possession of obscure and demonic power which makes Frankenstein so frightening. By contrast, Zadig's powers appear benign. There is no mystery to them, nor is Zadig outside of society or reason. With his "mere carnal common sense," the common intellectual tool of mankind, he seeks out the obvious in a natural setting. What Zadig discovers is apparent to all; what Frankenstein discovers is shrouded in mystery. In Frankenstein's world, Zadig would seem narrow and dull; in Zadig's world, Frankenstein would seem excessive and mad.

Huxley's essay on Zadig goes on to suggest that Cuvier, the great French naturalist, had used precisely the same method of reasoning from effects to causes to reconstruct the past from the fossil remains of the present. It was, Huxley rightly noted, a demonstrative triumph over the limitations of time; method, it turned out, sought prophecy. The essential characteristic of prophecy, Huxley suggested, is the "apprehension of that which lies out of the sphere of immediate knowledge," in essence, the perception of that which, due to the limitations of time, is no longer physically apparent to the observer (4:6). Cuvier's was a form of "retrospective prophecy" in that his insights, based solidly on evidence gleaned from the present, moved backward into dim epochs of prehistorical time. Interweaving Voltaire's *Zadig* with Cuvier's *Recherches sur les ossemens fossiles*, Huxley eloquently demonstrated not only Cuvier's use of Zadig's method, but the affinities between the French Enlightenment with its philosophical rationalism and nineteenth-century science with its empirical method. Huxley's scientist is very much an offspring of the Enlightenment, bound to an egalitarian ideal by Huxley's continual assertions that his mind and method were essentially the apparatus of all humanity. The great existential constant, "the common foundation of all scientific thought," was the axiom of "the constancy of the order of nature" (4:12). Working on this assumption, the scientist could move not only into the past but into the future. Science offered prophetic powers to laborer and merchant alike. All men were equal before scientific fact; all men stood to gain through scientific knowledge. Prophecy and significant knowledge were democratized.

The simplicity of scientific method was an important issue. In the Zadig essay Huxley was not making claims for the simplicity of actual scientific disciplines, for these involved technical language and a complexity of detail that were the product of extensive intellectual effort. But the basic idea underlying the scientist and his work remained a very simple one: his faith in the constancy of the natural order was justified by daily experience (5:37). The soundness of scientific thought might be demonstrated to all who were prepared to listen to reason. Huxley's scientist had a profound appreciation for order and reason, and he rejected that problematic ingredient, deity. It was an order that was antiauthoritarian, antitraditional, and sometimes even antiintellectual. But even as he was undermining the concept of authority, Huxley was combing tradition for scientific predecessors.

iv. the Huxley theater

If the Zadig essay featured Huxley's scientific Everyman expatiating on the simplicity of scientific method, the lead performer and featured scientist of many essays was none other than Huxley himself. His ability to project to the untutored mind a vision of the new science was nothing short of remarkable. On many a night Huxley's public performances as the new man of science unfolding the great drama of Victorian scientific discovery must have been the best theater in town. As early as 1860 at the famous Oxford clash with Wilberforce over Darwin's *Origin*, Huxley had established his dramatic mettle by challenging and, thought many, defeating Wilberforce at a public forum tailored to the latter's intellectual and oratorical genius. The same projection of self and ideas lifts the Huxley essay to the level of fine dramatic art. Controversy counted for part of the drama, but beyond controversy there was an electrifying motion of ideas, a theatrical clash between tradition and new knowledge, a glimpse into the strange new universe that Victorian science had been quietly assembling. This was Huxley's proletarian theater, frequently offered exclusively to working men with proof of occupational status the condition for entry. "Here he is, this working man, whom I have so often sought and found not," commented Bernard Becker, author of *Scientific London*, as he recounted an evening's performance of Huxley: "His place is not usurped by smug clerks and dandy shopmen."[33]

The drama of Huxley's lectures and essays is frequently achieved through two techniques he relied on consistently. The first involves a process which might be referred to as the dramatization of material entities. It is a theatrical treatment of physical entities and objects whereby Huxley, as scientist-choreographer, presents us with a dance of the material universe. Using such unpromising subjects as chalk, lobsters, coal, yeast, and protoplasm, Huxley describes patterns and rhythms shared between organic and inorganic forms of existence. In such presentations, the boundaries between living and inanimate entities cease to be distinct. Huxley was fascinated by the common organizational principles of the material and the organic universe, and in essays such as "On a Piece of Chalk" and "On the Physical Basis of Life" he probed continually for insights into the shared character of matter and life. The intellectual process becomes dramatic when he begins to call forth and spotlight his entities. "Sit down before fact as a little child, . . . or you shall learn nothing," Huxley had declared in his letter to Kingsley (*LL*, 1:235). And in the Huxley theater one must sit down before the facts and objects which actually seem to perform under the discipline of Huxley's voice. The other dramatic technique Huxley frequently used in his lectures and essays is the projection of the self as scientist-choreographer. The self, as scientist, becomes a stage manager of the material world, demonstrating within the artistic frameworks of stage and essay a variety of existential truths.

Huxley typically designed his performances for a working class audience as in "On a Piece of Chalk," delivered in 1868 to the working men of Norwich. In this famous lecture, subsequently published in *Macmillan's Magazine*, Huxley refers to his presentation as "making the chalk tell us its own history" (8:6). We begin with a descent under the city of Norwich, soon finding ourselves in a great layer of chalk that extends north to Yorkshire, south to Dorset, links London to Paris, runs through Europe and parts of Asia and Africa. "A great chapter of the history of the world is written in the chalk," Huxley declares. It is a history that will give a man "a truer, and therefore a better, conception of this wonderful universe, and of man's relation to it, than the most learned student [will have] who is deep-read in the records of humanity and ignorant of those of Nature" (8:4). A piece of chalk, so common that every carpenter carries it in his pocket, suddenly comes to life as we discover that it is organic, composed of *Globigerinae, Radiolaria* and diatoms, the remains of which have formed vast deposits beneath the surface of the earth and under the ocean floor. Through simple detail and geographical panorama, Huxley slowly assembles his heroic vision: "the earth, from the time of the chalk to the present day, has been the theatre of a series of changes as vast in their amount, as they were slow in their progress" (8:29). The world is the stage of a great drama. One learns not only of buried forests and gradually evolving forms of reptiles sunk in layers of chalk, but that the chalk itself has arisen and descended at least four times relative to sea level. Land and ocean are merely conditions of time. What makes the essay particularly dramatic is Huxley's continual use of active verbs in describing the processes involved in the piece of chalk's history. The essay is alive with motion. Time and its inexorable impress on the material of nature are manifested in vast processes of sedimentation, uplifting, and concretion. The very ground under one's feet must have felt strange after hearing Huxley tell how once it was all the floor of an immense sea.

"A small beginning has led us to a great ending," Huxley notes in his final paragraph (8:36). The piece of chalk is given visionary significance as he observes that if one were to subject it to a flame of burning hydrogen it would glow like the sun, a physical metamorphosis that "is no false image of what has been the result of our subjecting it to a jet of fervent, though nowise brilliant, thought to-night" (8:36). The chalk, then, becomes "luminous," a lantern lit by the intellect of Huxley as scientist, "its clear rays, penetrating the abyss of the remote past" (8:36). It becomes a complex agent which under the influence of the scientist's controlling intellect leads us into the distant past. Its relationship to the scientist is very nearly that of the relationship of Coleridge's aeolian harp to the "intellectual breeze." The piece of chalk, as an image of both common material and the intellectual lantern, carries the significance of being the product of both inorganic and organic forces in nature. At the same time it functions as a dramatic entity within the framework of the essay, performing in a variety of ways to the proddings of Huxley's flames, acids, and pulverizers. It has a story "to tell," and under Huxley's careful direction, the story which began with Norwich well diggers striking a white substance in their downward progress ends with a vision of the eternal process of time.

The organizing voice of the scientist in the chalk essay plays a significant role not only in the stage-management of material entities, but in creating a sense of control, both intellectual and physical, over the entire material world. It is the guiding force of the scientific intellect that irradiates what seems at first so pedestrian a subject. "A small beginning has led us to a great ending," Huxley observes. The scientific mind moves from the common object to reflections that embrace the cosmos, bestowing dignity on rude entities by connecting them with the great network of all things. For Huxley, it was a theatrical process. Who but the scientist could show the way? And yet the way, once seen, was incredibly simple. Huxley's essays reflect that simplicity in their patient reconstruction of fact, always in the simplest and most concrete language he could summon. Observed Professor Howes of the Royal College of Science:

> As a class lecturer Huxley was *facile princeps,* and only those who were privileged to sit under him can form a conception of his delivery. Clear, deliberate, never hesitant nor unduly emphatic, never repetitional, always logical, his every word told. Great, however, as were his class lectures, his workingmen's were greater. Huxley was a firm believer in the "distillatio per ascensum" of scientific knowledge and culture, and spared no pains in approaching the artisan and so-called "working classes." He gave the workmen of his best. [*LL*, 2:438]

Huxley's working men's lectures, models of simplicity and yet full of detail and substance, seemed to proclaim a democracy of knowledge, if only because they were consistently woven around the common objects of experience. The first and final court of intellectual appeal became the great "University of Nature." And this placed a new emphasis on hard physical realities and on an intimate knowledge of the material world.

The Huxleyan "I" looms large in the famous *Six Lectures to Working Men* delivered in 1862 and collected in 1863. It is the "I" of both Huxley the man and Huxley the representative scientist. The first lecture—"The Present Condition of Organic Nature"—makes such extensive use of the first-person pronoun that we cannot read it without sensing an organizing and explicit consciousness at work among diverse materials, the same consciousness that lavished its attention on the piece of chalk. This essay concerns itself with explaining and demonstrating that inorganic and organic forms of existence are composed of the same basic materials, guided by the same physical forces, and engaged in a continual conversion of one into the other. Huxley selects the horse, "an extremely complex

and beautifully-proportioned machine, with all its parts working harmoniously together" (2:313), as a model with which to
demonstrate a number of his most important ideas. The entire
presentation is, again, dramatic in Huxley's mode; it is filled
with physical description and motion as the scientific consciousness works on its object: "if I were to saw a dead horse,
across, I should find that . . ."; "now, suppose we go to work
on these several parts,—flesh and hair, and skin and bone, and
lay open these various organs with our scalpels" (2:308–9).
What makes the essay more than mere demonstration is the
manner in which Huxley has thrust his scientist on stage along
with the various objects of demonstration. We are watching the
scientist perform. There is a dramatic relationship between him
and the materials he examines, a dynamic relationship for
which the image of Victor Frankenstein laboring to bring forth
life from the inanimate is not entirely inappropriate. But for
Huxley the romantic impulse to recreate the external world in
the image of the self is absent; Huxley's mind breathes life into
its material so as to create a lamp, to return to the chalk example, that is capable of illuminating fundamental principles of
natural order. Life itself is a form, but not the apex, of natural
order.

Huxley went on in the other lectures of this working men's
series to present a primer of Victorian life sciences, discussing a
variety of scientific theories and examining the work of such
scientists as Darwin, Pasteur, and Harvey. Darwin is central
and his evolutionary hypothesis becomes the subject of the last
three lectures, with Huxley always pressing, however, toward
his larger themes of the ultimate order and unity of nature and
the rational vision of the scientist. Darwin's model is a
"hypothesis," yet it will remain "the guide of biological and
psychological speculation for the next three or four genera-
tions" (2:475). Abstract concepts are continually made visual for
the audience, traced to their manifestations in the concrete
patterns of daily existence. To illustrate the intricacy of
evolutionary success, Huxley uses as an example a frail historian who, retreating with Napoleon's troops from the advancing Russian army, grabs on to the cloak of a hearty French
cuirassier, who at first curses and cuts at the historian and then,

in order to save himself, struggles across the single narrow bridge amid the general panic, dragging the historian along (2:443). The simplicity of experimental method is enacted in a little drama between shopkeeper and customer in which after twice testing specimens from a batch of apples the customer generalizes that those apples which are hard and green are also sour (2:365–67).

The Huxley theater has, indeed, many qualities in common with the old morality play, in its careful acting out of ideas, its props, its homely, simplifying anecdote.[34] In the second lecture, "The Past Condition of Organic Nature," Huxley evokes the image of the history of nature against which "mere human records sink into utter insignificance," only to turn and tell his audience that the record of nature's history is formed in "mud":

> You may think, perhaps, that this is a vast step—of almost from the sublime to the ridiculous—from the contemplation of the history of the past ages of the world's existence to the consideration of the history of the formation of mud! But, in Nature, there is nothing mean and unworthy of attention; there is nothing ridiculous or contemptible in any of her works." [2:333–34]

We return to the humblest of materials, ordinary mud, for our lesson on the heroic past of earth's slow, elemental change, its ceaseless alteration by unseen forces, the growth of its many life forms. It is a lesson on causality and its subject is life; but no deity lingers in the essay. Sealed in the mud are the imprints and fossil remains of plants and animals, many extinct, many still thriving in the modern world. Examining simple materials, we achieve what few disciplines of knowledge can offer—a physical vision into the past that dwarfs in time and magnitude the mere human present. The vision of the sublime is achieved through the humble contemplation of the ridiculous. The lesson of basic science is a lesson in humility and in the dignity of the material world.

Huxley's lectures were issued in pamphlet form under the title *On Our Knowledge of the Causes of the Phenomena of Organic Nature,* and became an immediate and large-scale success. Ultimately, the Huxley theater was as popular with professional scientists as it was with the working classes. Like Dickens,

Huxley produced material that transcended class boundaries, which made him one of the most widely read essayists of his day. He had reason to seek a wide audience. From his earliest to his final essays, he expressed the conviction that while many were content to assimilate the material achievements of physical science into the basic patterns of their lives, they often lagged dangerously behind in their grasp of scientific method and knowledge. This was true not only of the public, but in the intellectual centers of England as well. The Oxford confrontation with Wilberforce at the British Association meeting in 1860, when Wilberforce asked Huxley whether his ancestry with the ape was to be traced on his grandmother's or his grandfather's side, was an incident which in many ways epitomized the collision of two kinds of knowledge, two habits of thought, two realities which ultimately split the Victorian mind in two. Wilberforce, a subtle and highly intelligent man, had misjudged not only the moral force behind the scientific quest for truth but the substance and magnitude of scientific knowledge. The question he posed about Huxley's ancestry was precisely the question Victorians wanted answered. Given the religious perspective and the perspective of the intellectual tradition of England, who would believe that at ancient Oxford this new science, with its tinge of the ridiculous, its apes, mud and a thousand other materials from the "mole's earthheap," would presume to contemplate itself with such gravity? The clash would echo, again tinged with absurdity, in Huxley's duel with Gladstone in the mid 1880s and the early 1890s, over such things as the legalities of Christ's destruction of the Gadarene swine. Rarely were the details of these controversies of more than incidental interest; more gripping was the conflict of visions, of concepts of human knowledge, conflicts so fundamental that they created an aura of profound absurdity and high intellectual comedy. It was a comic clash which would find expression in the plays of Shaw, and also in the shrewd wit of Shaw's critic William Irvine in *Apes, Angels, and Victorians*.

Huxley declared to Matthew Arnold in 1880 that it was a mistake to attempt a criticism of life without knowing what science had achieved over the past half century. It was not merely a matter of being ignorant of a new fund of knowledge;

43

it was, more seriously, a misapprehension of the very foundations of one's own society. To devalue or underestimate the
fundamental role of physical science in society and culture was
to alienate oneself from vital realities that supported one's own
existence. Culture, in the sense of its being a criticism of life,
was important for assessing such realities in order to influence
the course of human affairs. It was not merely a problem of
misconception, but one of misperception. Modern technology
and theory were elements of reality. The great object of his life,
Huxley declared in his "Autobiography," was "to promote the
increase of natural knowledge and to forward the application of
scientific methods of investigation to all the problems of life"
(1:16). It was, Huxley believed, the only true possibility for the
"alleviation for the sufferings of mankind." Huxley's was a
deeply human and moral ambition, yet it was locked in conflict
with traditions many saw as the mainstays of morality and culture. Huxley found a more receptive, though not more avid,
audience among colleagues and workers than among intellectuals and divines.

The mythos of Huxley's science, the legend of his scientist,
and the vindication of his own personal struggle from childhood to forge a vision worthy of his ideals were all concentrated
in the remarkable Cinderella metaphor which appeared at the
end of his 1886 essay "Science and Morals." Here lay the story
of Victorian science, and of Huxley himself, contemplating intellectual disenfranchisement. The essay had been written in
answer to W. S. Lilly's charges, made in the November issue of
the *Fortnightly*, that modern science had inspired materialism,
fatalism, and was causing the erosion of morality. Huxley responded to Lilly, who was John Henry Newman's advocate and
compiler, with the claim that the only axiom held by the scientist was "the universality of the law of causation," and that this
implied neither materialism, atheism, nor fatalism, but only a
determinism which was not even inconsistent with the
theological notion of an omniscient deity or with predestination
(9:141–44). Huxley summed up his position at the end of the
essay by contrasting the youthful Cinderella of Victorian science with her two elder sisters, philosophy and theology:

44

Cinderella is modestly conscious of her ignorance of these high matters. She lights the fire, sweeps the house, and provides the dinner; and is rewarded by being told that she is a base creature, devoted to low and material interests. But in her garret she has fairy visions out of the ken of the pair of shrews who are quarrelling down stairs. She sees the order which pervades the seeming disorder of the world; the great drama of evolution, with its full share of pity and terror, but also with abundant goodness and beauty, unrolls itself before her eyes; and she learns, in her heart of hearts, the lesson, that the foundation of morality is to have done, once and for all, with lying; to give up pretending to believe that for which there is no evidence, and repeating unintelligible propositions about things beyond the possibilities of knowledge.

She knows that the safety of morality lies neither in the adoption of this or that philosophical speculation, or this or that theological creed, but in a real and living belief in that fixed order of nature which sends social disorganisation upon the track of immorality, as surely as it sends physical disease after physical trespasses. And of that firm and lively faith it is her high mission to be the priestess. [9:146]

Cinderella was science and Huxley at once; a potential queen, she labored at providing for the common needs of others. But as she worked in the prosaic world of physical reality, she had visions of the great cosmic order, of the vast drama of evolutionary terror and beauty. These visions, while they suggested metamorphosis, a future in which scientific knowledge would blossom into something beautiful, as Cinderella had in the fairy tale, asserted with equal strength the existence of an ultimate, macrocosmic order pervading the universe. The vision of "the order which pervades the seeming disorder of the world" was basic to Huxley's thought and faith. Cinderella was the scientist whose solemn quest was to discover, to whatever extent possible, the complexion of the natural order.

II

Huxley and Carlyle: Scientist and Hero

i. penetrating nature

The need to penetrate the secrets of nature struck both Carlyle and Huxley as the most pressing social requirement of the age, since nature stored forces which held ultimate sway over Victorian society and, indeed, over the future of England. Different as their concepts of nature may have been, both men set out, driven by powerful moral imperatives, to discover an approach into the hidden recesses of natural force with the conviction that the results of their efforts could illuminate the path to social harmony and prosperity. Questions which were inevitably raised by such an effort were those of method and leadership. Huxley's writings show that he was considerably influenced by Carlyle in formulating a social response to natural phenomena, and although his youthful enthusiasm for Carlyle's thought was to turn somewhat sour after the Eyre Controversy of 1866, it was not before Carlyle's broad influence had furnished much that was essential to his world view. This influence is best represented in the relationship of the scientist to the hero, which, although problematic, poses a revealing and culturally important series of Victorian moral and intellectual questions.

In the early years of his own largely self-directed education, Huxley had saturated himself in the thought of Carlyle. His journals, letters, and essays were full of quotations from and allusions to Carlyle. Leonard Huxley reveals that his father, in an unpublished autobiographical fragment, referred to *Sartor Resartus* as his "Enchiridion" (*LL*, 1:9). As early as 1842, in his journal "Thoughts and Doings," Huxley had recorded, between

47

observations on physics and descriptions of electrical experiments, fragments from Carlyle's "Characteristics," including Carlyle's declaration: "The ages of heroism are not ages of Moral Philosophy. Virtue, when it is philosophised of, has become aware of itself, is sickly and beginning to decline" (*LL*, 1:14).[1] Carlyle's notion of the heroic interested Huxley, particularly in its contrast with Establishment morality. It combined concepts of leadership and personal force with moods of rebellion shaped by an independent sense of morality. Aboard the *Rattlesnake*, during his four-year voyage as ship's surgeon to Australia and New Guinea, Huxley had kept Carlyle's work close at hand for contemplation during his own fits of frustration and rebellion.[2] And as late as 1860 after the death of his son Noel, he still saw fit to declare to Charles Kingsley that *Sartor Resartus* had exerted a profound influence on his life, even though he was by then well established in and preoccupied with his scientific career. For twenty years, years which saw the slow formation and maturation of his intellect, Huxley looked upon Carlyle as one of the central forces in his life.

While *Sartor Resartus*, as we have seen, taught Huxley the great lessons of self-discipline and disinterestedness and exercised a spiritual influence over his youth, works like *Past and Present* awakened his social sensibilities and inspired him to move beyond the boundaries of the technical essay to a larger criticism of society.[3] The alliance was, of course, unilateral and in many ways highly unlikely, for few Victorians could be more antithetical in their fundamental philosophies of nature and knowledge. Carlyle's cosmos was God-centered, if somewhat vaguely; Huxley's had no center. Carlyle, continually evoking spirit, spontaneity, and unconsciousness as signs of the "healthy body," could not find a more serious opponent than Huxley, who in his 1868 essay "On the Physical Basis of Life" proclaimed that scientific progress meant the "extension of the province of what we call matter and causation, and the concomitant gradual banishment from all regions of human thought of what we call spirit and spontaneity" (1:159).[4] Yet much of Huxley's social theory proceeded from interests which were originally awakened by his readings in Carlyle, and many of the important social ideas and spiritual values that Huxley

48

associated with science and the scientist were of a distinctly Carlylean cast of thought. The language of Carlyle, his sense of the hidden interconnectedness of things and of the forces that moved them, his prophetic stance, all found equivalents in Huxley's thought. As a result, Huxley's ideas often move with a visionary, mystical drive, in dramatic contrast to the staunch commonsensical emphasis of his avowed rationalistic outlook.

In his early journals and letters, Huxley not only borrowed ideas from Carlyle, but often adopted Carlyle's prophetic stance and remarkable language. There is a verbal dauntlessness, a sense of alienated prophecy running through much of his early correspondence whose tone recalls Teufelsdröckh. As an aspiring young scientist, he had reason to see himself as a social and intellectual outsider; even earlier, he had, like the young Teufelsdröckh, experienced the "malady of thought," the intense, spiritual agony of an existence that threatened to become meaningless. In a letter to his sister Lizzie, in 1850, the year he returned from his voyage, Huxley declared,

> There are many nice people in this world for whose praise or blame I care not a whistle. I don't know and I don't care whether I shall ever be what is called a great man. I will leave my mark somewhere, and it shall be clear and distinct ⌐T. H. H., his mark.⌐ and free from the abominable blur of cant, humbug, and self-seeking which surrounds everything in this present world. [*LL*, 1:69]

It was not merely Huxley's use of such select Carlylean words as "abominable," "cant" and "humbug" that suggested he was modeling himself after Carlyle; it was the temperament, what William Irvine once described as Carlyle's real contribution to Huxley.[5] Huxley was adopting the rugged independence of Carlyle's temperament, that combative sense of moral identity and fearless conviction born of alienation. Even the famous and prophetic rectangle around his own initials recalled the odd, rebellious humor of Carlyle.

More importantly, Huxley was contemplating his future as a scientist in terms which were appropriate to and highly suggestive of the Carlylean hero. His indifference about whether he would "ever be what is called a great man," an echo of his observation to Henrietta Heathorn in 1849 that he "might have made a good critic and an accomplished man," was a reference to the concept of the "great man," the *Gelehrter* of Carlyle's critical essays on the German scholar-critics. The attitude of indifference toward greatness was itself a necessary condition for greatness, and Huxley recognized the possibility that he might achieve his early critical ambitions by pursuing the way of the scientist. Fusing his idea of the scientist with the stern moral vision that defined many of Carlyle's great men, he dramatized himself as both scientist and Carlylean truth seeker. It was during this difficult period immediately after his return to London in 1850 that he felt the need to define himself, to "become" something. While he had amassed a large collection of research material, he did not know what he ultimately would do, for there were no paying positions in London for scientific research. Huxley was indeed something of a Teufelsdröckh, a man with ideas and a manuscript whose skills and interests did not conform to the social roles that Victorians were willing to finance. It was his creation of an ideal, a scientist endowed with qualities of the Carlylean hero, that kept him from going the way of his fictional counterpart—George Eliot's Lydgate. "I want something larger, something that should involve sacrifice and danger, and convince me palpably and obviously that I am not utterly absorbed in self," he wrote to Henrietta in 1851.[6] "Like Naaman the Syrian I would be 'bidden to do some great thing.'"

On the deepest level, the influence of Carlyle on Huxley was spiritual. In his famous letter to Charles Kingsley after Noel Huxley's death in 1860, Huxley had attributed to *Sartor Resartus* nothing less than a role in his personal redemption from the nameless depth of sin that he was convinced had blighted his youth. It led him "to know that a deep sense of religion was compatible with the entire absence of theology" (*LL*, 1:237). This insight was vital to Huxley. He had what Gertrude Himmelfarb once referred to as a "basically religious, metaphysical cast of mind," not to be confused with his tendencies to use religious imagery and to conduct his controversies with a religious fervor.[7] In Carlyle's work, he might find a metaphysical feast. Writing to Henrietta in July of 1850, he spoke of Carlyle's thought as a new synthesis of knowledge and religion: "Sometimes in the thoughts his pregnant sayings awake in my mind, I seem to catch an indistinct vision of that union of deep religious feeling with clear knowledge—by which alone the inmost soul of man can live in peace."[8] It was in the vision of Carlyle that Huxley first comprehended the spiritual possibilities of knowledge.

While Huxley would not vulgarize his science by concocting a parochial and formal religious apparatus in which to idealize it, he did find a spiritual object in that sense of surrender he felt in confronting the facts that led to the abyss. Self-renunciation and submission to the great order of the cosmos were elements that Huxley's early scientific Calvinism shared with the transcendental Calvinism of Carlyle. In his letter of 1860 to Kingsley, once again, Huxley had declared his determination to surrender his will to "fact," and to follow humbly "wherever and to whatever abysses nature leads," and this "at all risks" (*LL*, 1:235). Like Carlyle's metaphysics, Huxley's science sought to penetrate into the abyss of nature. And the sense of the unknown, of the void at the edge of inquiry, contributed a visionary, mystical element which transcended the commonsensical basis he had elsewhere attached to scientific thought. Many of Huxley's friends and colleagues, men like Kingsley, John Tyndall, and Herbert Spencer, associated science with the religious impulse. In his essay collection titled *Education: Intellectual, Moral, and Physical*, Spencer spoke of the moral discipline and religious culture which were inspired by science. "Devotion to science, is a tacit worship—a tacit recognition of worth in the things studied," he observed.[9] And he quoted from one of Huxley's 1859 Jermyn Street lectures to working men:

> "True science and true religion," says Professor Huxley at the close of a recent course of lectures, "are twin-sisters, and the separation of either from the other is sure to prove the death of both. Science prospers exactly in proportion as it is religious; and religion flourishes in exact proportion to the scientific depth and firmness of its basis. The great deeds of philosophers have been less the fruit of their intellect than of the direction of that intellect by an eminently religious tone of mind. Truth has yielded herself rather to their patience, their love, their single-heartedness, and their self-denial, than to their logical acumen."[10]

51

Huxley found such a sense of religion in Carlyle's work, which early led him into the study of Goethe and the nature-philosophers who combined their metaphysics with their science.

John Tyndall, with whom Huxley had become intimate in 1851 when both were young scientists adrift in London, was even more markedly the disciple of Carlyle than Huxley. A physicist, sensitive and ebullient and a frequent companion to Carlyle, Tyndall never tired of proclaiming the Carlylean wonders of a scientifically perceived nature. In his "Science and Man" (1877), an address delivered before the Birmingham and Midland Institute, Tyndall compared Robert Boyle's concept of the universe as a machine with Carlyle's symbol of the universe as a tree: "A machine may be regarded as an organism with life and direction outside; a tree may be defined as an organism with life and direction within."[11] Tyndall declared his allegiance to Carlyle's tree and to the internal dynamic of the universe. In his memorial essay on Tyndall which appeared in the *Nineteenth Century* in 1894, Huxley however looked back to their friendship when they were both "zealous students of Carlyle's works" and noted that, unlike Tyndall, he was inclined to approach Carlyle "as a source of intellectual invigoration and moral stimulus and refreshment, rather than of theoretical or practical guidance."[12]

In trying to understand the elements of Carlyle's work which would have appealed to men like Huxley and Tyndall, we may recall that Carlyle's attacks on science were mostly directed against the static, mechanistic notions that were more common in the eighteenth century. He did not feel uncomfortable with the speculations of the Nature-philosophers; Teufelsdröckh himself was suspected of making special contributions to Herr Oken's *Isis*, although this could only be surmised.[13] But Carlyle's general attitude toward science was less than enthusiastic. Darwin observed in his *Autobiography* that Carlyle, who had visited and dined at his house, seemed scornful of British science. He thought Carlyle narrow, somewhat revolting, and "ill adapted for scientific research."[14] Darwin's conclusions were based primarily on his personal encounters with Carlyle, while Huxley, Tyndall, and Kingsley were avid students of Carlyle's works.

Huxley and Carlyle: Scientist and Hero

In *Sartor Resartus*, the clothes philosophy with its solid base in natural phenomena, its persistent stress on experience as an accumulation of evidence for the eternal and infinite, gave a distinctly empirical cast to Carlyle's speculation. "By God's blessing," Carlyle wrote to John Sterling, "one has got two eyes to look with; and also a mind capable of knowing, of believing: that is all the creed I will at this time insist on."[15] *Sartor Resartus* fused hard evidence with belief. Carlyle was often found buttressing his spiritual vision with mathematical and scientific facts. In the famous chapter "The Everlasting Yea," Teufelsdröckh argues renunciation by calling for a lowered denominator: "Nay, unless my Algebra deceive me, *Unity* itself divided by *Zero* will give *Infinity*."[16] In the chapter "Organic Filaments" he observes: "It is a mathematical fact that the casting of this pebble from my hands alters the centre of gravity of the Universe."[17] Reflecting back on Carlyle's relationship with Victorian science, Tyndall observed: "The scientific reader of his works must have noticed the surprising accuracy of the metaphors he derived from Science . . . He laid the whole body of the sciences under contribution."[18] Carlyle's terminology and thought process had a fundamental appeal to the rational mind, for they organized the elements of experience into logical thought patterns. One could follow Carlyle quite rationally to the abyss of the infinite; once there, one either resisted or leapt into belief.

Carlyle had rejected scriptural miracles as well, and he had a fundamentalist's distaste for the didacticism and formal worship of the established Church. While he believed in the basic need of religious forms for society, he declared that the "Church-Clothes" of the age had become "mere hollow Shapes, or Masks, under which no living Figure or Spirit any longer dwells."[19] Such, no doubt, was the basis for Huxley's assessment of Carlyle's book as a deeply religious work without a theology; Carlyle preferred "natural supernaturalism" to the theological supernaturalism of the church. The transcendental vision of the universe was far more compelling than what might be found in a system of theology. Divinity inhered in the vast, sublime ambiguities of the unknowable cosmos. In this sense, God was not part of Teufelsdröckh's argument; what God there was in *Sartor Resartus* existed behind the veil, behind the forces and infinities of the supernatural dynamic. John Sterling found that Teufelsdröckh "does not believe in a God."[20] Huxley's science often contemplated a similar infinity, an abyss which led from the clothes of nature upward to a cosmos in perpetual and measureless flux.

In an important sense, Carlyle changed the directional flow of the miraculous, moving from nature upward toward omega, rather than from heaven downward. The miracle of his chapter "Natural Supernaturalism" was not the Biblical catastrophe, but the fact that the concrete is part, the sleeve, of the infinite to which it is bound. One of the effects of this inversion was that Carlyle was forced to emphasize human works over divine grace as the means to salvation. Human processes, manifested in labor and social institutions, would become modes of worship, lending a new dignity to the interaction between man and the material world. Physical and spiritual salvation were united in labor; without the Biblical supernatural, the messiah had to become the natural messiah—the man hero—finding his salvation in nature. Such was the origin of Carlyle's theory of the heroic. Scientists like Huxley and Tyndall were inspired by the idea of natural salvation as it worked through various Carlylean heroes. In his "On the Advisableness of Improving Natural Knowledge," Huxley identified the preservation of London from various natural catastrophes with the efforts of the scientist. His very power to operate made the man of science a convincing candidate for social leadership and for achieving the general improvement of society's fortune.[21]

Another result of Carlyle's moving from nature up to God was the diffusion of the old anthropomorphic deity; Carlyle's impersonal god had a distinct tendency to become a nameless force: "'Personal,' 'impersonal,' One, Three," he wrote to Sterling, "*what* meaning can any mortal (after all) attach to them in reference to such an object? *Wer darf ihn NENNEN?*"[22] While Carlyle's magificent religious sense is obvious here, a similar reasoning process had led to Spencer's "Unknowable" and even to Huxley's agnosticism.[23] Sterling observed that "what we find everywhere, with an abundant use of the name of God, is the conception of a formless Infinite whether in time or space; of a high inscrutable Necessity."[24] And he pointedly linked the Teufelsdröckhian field of speculation with the "whole spiritual empire of the wisest Pagans."[25]

Carlyle's attack on mechanism, which lay at the center of his philosophy, was based in part on the argument that the nature of infinity was quite beyond the kind of finite limitations that were necessary attributes of the mechanical. But Carlyle did not reject the concept of universal law. Indeed, as Sterling pointed out, Carlyle's sense of necessity was rigid, Calvinistic. Spiritual and natural law, Carlyle asserted in the chapter "Natural Supernaturalism," were essentially the same:

> " 'But is not a real Miracle simply a violation of the Laws of Nature?' ask several. Whom I answer by this new question: What are the Laws of Nature? To me perhaps the rising of one from the dead were no violation of these Laws, but a confirmation; were some far deeper Law . . .
>
> " 'But is it not the deepest Law of Nature that she be constant?' cries an illuminated class: 'Is not the Machine of the Universe fixed to move by unalterable rules?' Probable enough, good friends: nay I, too, must believe that the God, whom ancient inspired men assert to be 'without variableness or shadow of turning,' does indeed never change; that Nature, that the Universe, which no one whom it so pleases can be prevented from calling a Machine, does move by the most unalterable rules."[26]

Carlyle was not arguing against a concept of universal order, but against the reduction of that order to a visible model, a machine, Paley's watch. Even if one were pleased to call the universe a machine, it was of an infinite species and, therefore, beyond human comprehension. Carlyle was also outflanking Hume's argument against the miraculous, with a logic that was nearly identical to that of Huxley's agnostic argument: "To the wisest man, wide as is his vision, Nature remains . . . of quite *infinite* expansion; and all Experience thereof limits itself to some few computed centuries and measured square-miles."[27] The argument is empirical; it is Carlyle's warning to those who habitually appeal to experience that they are excluded by the most obvious facts from considerations of the infinite. The infinity of space and time, relative to men, makes it empirically impossible for them to reduce existence to a mechanism.

Like Carlyle, scientists of the day had begun to think in terms of a universal order which was of infinite extension. The focus of scientific thought in the early nineteenth century was shifting increasingly from the search for some kind of static blueprint for nature to an examination of natural process and flux.[28] Life processes, geological processes, were increasingly seen as part of an open-ended dynamic with no certain beginning or ending. Lyell's *Principles of Geology* was written close to the same time as Carlyle's *Sartor Resartus*, between 1827 and 1833. As different as the two works are, both are obsessed with process. Lyell's uniformitarian principle is expressed in the title of his work: *Principles of Geology, Being an Attempt to Explain the Former Changes of the Earth's Surface, by Reference to Causes Now in Operation.* What Lyell was doing for the features of the earth, Carlyle seemed to be attempting for the spirit. That is, he was evoking a sense of the supernatural "by reference to causes now in operation" rather than by following a priori arguments of Biblical supernaturalism.

The main difference between the *Principles of Geology* and *Sartor Resartus* taking both as studies of phenomena, is that *Sartor Resartus* has at its center a human figure, whose thought processes form a center of consciousness which radiates in numerous directions. In the *Principles*, the authorial center of consciousness is less prominent in the sense that the objects of that consciousness have become the focus and feature of the work. The work seeks to be linear and regular. The "self" or "I" of the *Principles* is of marginal importance to the formal work itself. Metaphysically and emotionally, such a prospect offered little to a layman like Carlyle who, Darwin reported, "thought it a most ridiculous thing that any one should care whether a glacier moved a little quicker or a little slower, or moved at all."[29]

In their similar emphasis on process, Carlyle and Lyell furnish a glimpse into the relationship between the Romantic and scientific mind. M. H. Abrams has maintained that the "cardinal endeavor" of the Romantic generation was precisely defined in Carlyle's term "natural supernaturalism," which described the tendency "to naturalize the supernatural and to humanize the divine."[30] The result of this tendency would be, in part, the reemphasizing of natural processes and objects which, as we have seen, occurs in *Sartor Resartus*. But there the objects are arranged in a profile of the self; in the *Principles,* the self is subdued in the effort to be objective. Like the artist, the scientist immersed himself in nature, and while he disciplined the objects of nature, seeking order and causal links between phenomena, the personal experience of the "I" among its findings was finally of little importance to the validity of his system. The essence of scientific labor was the effort, often collective, to develop a formal system, a paradigm; the object of the Romantic artist was to establish a vision which radiated about the self. Both sought, however, to penetrate the dynamic of nature.

In an earlier day, Huxley might have become one of England's great nature-philosophers. He had all the enthusiasm for seeking unity in diversity, searching for the archetypal, revealing the relationships between man and nature. Indeed, his earliest nontechnical address, "On the Educational Value of the Natural History Sciences," published in 1854, four years after his return from the *Rattlesnake* voyage, treated the phenomena of life as spontaneous and dependent on "vital" rather than physical or chemical forces (3:64). He was still aligned, publicly at least, with the antimechanists, with Carlyle and the German nature-philosophers, Goethe, Schelling, and Oken. Huxley advocated the study of natural history partly in the belief that it led one to seek the beauties of nature and that it enhanced one's sense of beauty with the clarity of distinct knowledge: "To a person uninstructed in natural history, his country or sea-side stroll is a walk through a gallery filled with wonderful works of art, nine-tenths of which have their faces turned to the wall" (3:63). This essay which spoke of the "lavish beauty" and the "secret and wonderful harmony" which pervades all living things reflects the early vision of Huxley's science.

The drift of Victorian science, however, was toward an emphasis on quantification and empirical determinism. In the same essay from 1854, Huxley had furnished a short summary on scientific method, to which he added a footnote pointing out his obligations to Mill's *System of Logic* (3:56). By 1870, when the essay was published as part of his *Lay Sermons*, his point of view had so changed that he took special care to note that he no longer adhered to theories of vitalism. *Lay Sermons* contained his "On the Physical Basis of Life," which rejected all theories of spontaneity and identified life forces with chemical forces. While Huxley had drawn from the Romantics for his early concepts of nature, with the publication of his "On the Advisableness of Improving Natural Knowledge" (1866) he publicly abandoned his earlier Romantic tendencies, rejected spontaneity, and declared scepticism to be "the highest of duties" (1:40). The later essays, while retaining certain ideas and moral insights, and a language and social focus that could be traced to Carlyle, abandoned the vitalism which had linked Huxley philosophically to the Romantics. While Irvine argues that Huxley developed a Carlylean idea of nature as a "moral and spiritual entity," it must be kept in mind that studies in several technical disciplines gave him a professional grounding and orientation that Carlyle did not have, and that Huxley's concept of nature was increasingly determined by his own professional work as a scientific researcher and educator.[31]

Certainly, as both Irvine and Oma Stanley have suggested, Huxley had a tendency to anthropomorphize nature, but this was more a phenomenon of language than of philosophy.[32] Long before the appearance of John Stuart Mill's essay "Nature" in 1874—when, Stanley argues, Huxley abandoned his Romantic concepts of nature—he had set science against spirit and spontaneity. If we look closely at his chess metaphor in "A Liberal Education," which both Irvine and Stanley cite as an instance of his tendency to personify nature, we can see something quite different taking place:

> The chess-board is the world, the pieces are the phenomena of the universe, the rules of the game are what we call the laws of Nature. The player on the other side is hidden from us. We know that his play is always fair, just and patient. But also we know, to our cost, that he never overlooks a mistake, or makes the smallest allowance for ignorance. To the man who plays well, the highest stakes are paid, with that sort of overflowing generosity with which the strong shows delight in strength. And one who plays ill is checkmated—without haste, but without remorse. [3:82]

It is an elaborate extended metaphor, suggestive of a rigorous providential justice paralleling Carlyle's sense of cosmic justice, particularly in the Sphinx symbol in the latter's *Past and Present* that represents one of the great social unknowns of contemporary England.[33] But Huxley's emphasis on the need to know the "laws" of nature lays stress on scientific law, the only kind of law in the realm of natural phenomena whose validity Huxley recognized.

Both Carlyle and Huxley had a strong tendency to dramatize their ideas in concrete images, but with a basic difference. When Carlyle proclaimed that "Nature, like the Sphinx, is of womanly celestial loveliness and tenderness," he used Bacon's old metaphor as a symbol with philosophical overtones, a truth independently contained in the mystical fusion of goddess and lioness:

> Nature, like the Sphinx, is of womanly celestial loveliness and tenderness; the face and bosom of a goddess, but ending in claws and the body of a lioness . . . Nature, Universe, Destiny, Existence, howsoever we name this grand unnameable Fact in the midst of which we live and struggle, is as a heavenly bride and conquest to the wise and brave, to them who can discern her behests and do them; a destroying fiend to them who cannot.[34]

Introduced early in book 1 of *Past and Present*, Carlyle's symbol belongs to the foundation of his prophetic social vision; it is the supreme mystery containing the riddle of English destiny. Huxley's chessboard, on the other hand, is referential, illustrative, and dramatic; it points up our need to know "something of the rules of a game infinitely more difficult and complicated than chess" (3:82). It stresses the inadequacy of language to comprehend the ultimate fact; the chess metaphor does not do justice to the complicated dynamic it is meant to illustrate. In contrast to the immobile mystery of Carlyle's Sphinx, Huxley's game of chess is more concerned with the activity of playing than the process of penetrating the mystery. Huxley's representation, in short, is dramatic, while Carlyle's is symbolic. And even as a dramatization of the interaction between man and nature, Huxley's representation is not to be taken too seriously, since it merely approximates something "infinitely more complicated."

What is most interesting about these two metaphors of man's relationship with nature is that, despite their essential differences, they are structurally similar. The framing of the question through the use of metaphorical language is much the same; but even more striking is that the question itself is nearly identical from one to the other. In both instances the great unknown which has profound social implications is nature; for both Huxley and Carlyle the representation of nature is twofold, suggesting either great beneficence or ultimate destruction. In both metaphors the emphasis is on penetrating the "facts" of nature to avoid becoming her victim. However, Carlyle's "fact" has eternal, mystical origins which must be intuited by the great, heroic mind. To Huxley, fact is a matter of natural law which is determined rationally by the scientist with his method.

Both in Huxley and in Carlyle the law of fact is found to be inexorable and essentially just. Justice for Carlyle rested in a higher order of laws and facts partly hidden from mortal eyes, save those of the hero who, in his different manifestations as prophet and poet, can "read the world and its laws."[35] For Huxley, justice tended to be identified, especially in the early essays, with natural processes representing physical reality. It is the democratic application of physical law to all, the inescapability of its universal validity, that seems to have impressed him with the notion of its justice. The scientist with his tool of method penetrates into the hidden dynamic of nature, collecting detail and determining laws. Both Carlyle and Huxley demonstrated a Calvinistic sense of justice, cosmic justice, large and inexorable, which is not always appreciated or understood by man. In its presence, the individual diminishes in significance.

In spite of his obvious movement away from Romantic ideas, Huxley retained his powerful sense of the interconnectedness of all existence. Like Carlyle, who viewed nature as the physical manifestation of a higher, infinite force, Huxley continually asserted the existence of an ultimate, ineluctable order and cosmic force in the universe. Both men had an overwhelming sense of hidden force and activity lurking beneath the surface of visible reality. Huxley tended to find hidden bonds between various forms of existence, even a bond between inorganic and organic things:

> In nature, nothing is at rest, nothing is amorphous; the simplest particle of that which men in their blindness are pleased to call "brute matter" is a vast aggregate of molecular mechanisms performing complicated movements of immense rapidity, and sensitively adjusting themselves to every change in the surrounding world. Living matter differs from other matter in degree and not in kind; the microcosm repeats the macrocosm; and one chain of causation connects the nebulous original of suns and planetary systems with the protoplasmic foundation of life and organisation. [3:371]

Written in 1881, years after he had abandoned vitalism, Huxley's observation still demonstrates a profound sense of unity between the finite patterns of nature and their infinite extensions into the macrocosm. He regarded as probable that life was simply an advanced and highly specialized condition of material order, a reflection of the physical order prevailing in the universe. His absolute order rested on a Stoical concept of material unity rather than on the spiritual unity of Carlyle. Yet while this suggests a materialistic outlook, Huxley's sense of universal pattern and interconnectedness also points to a single great organism in continual flux.

Carlyle and Huxley reiterate the need to read the laws of nature, making the interaction of man and society with nature's great unknown forces the focal point of significant human knowledge. Prophecy and science thus become great cultural forces. The hero and the scientist become lawgivers, their authority justified by their special insight into the forces and processes of nature. This notion is implicit in the title of Huxley's *Lay Sermons, Addresses, and Reviews,* a collection of fifteen essays published in 1870, which argue among other things the cultural and philosophical relevance of the scientific world view. In one of the earliest addresses of the collection "On the Study of Zoology," first given in 1860 Huxley declared:

> Modern civilization rests upon physical science . . . it is physical science only that makes intelligence and moral energy stronger than brute force.
> The whole of modern thought is steeped in science; it has made its way into the works of our best poets, and even the mere man of

61

letters, who affects to ignore and despise science, is unconsciously impregnated with her spirit, and indebted for his best products to her methods. I believe that the greatest intellectual revolution mankind has yet seen is now slowly taking place by her agency.[36]

Huxley regarded science as a new and basic social and cultural force and the scientist as being at its heroic center. *Lay Sermons*, like the traditional sermon which links a society with its foundations of belief, examines the basis for social action in the faith born of empirical knowledge. The scientist is the hero because he is the source of the new law. By 1880, in his essay "On the Method of Zadig," Huxley would claim that "the power of prediction, of prospective prophecy, is that which is commonly regarded as the great prerogative of physical science" (4:10). Carlyle could only have winced at Huxley's equating of "prediction" and "prophecy," and he undoubtedly would have been astonished to find Huxley citing the *Nautical Almanac*, with its power to predict the "exact position to be occupied by one of Jupiter's moons six months hence," as evidence of the prophetic potency of science (4:10).

While both Huxley and Carlyle insisted on man's need to comprehend the laws of nature, their concepts of fact were, because of their differing methods of arriving at those facts, irreconcilable. Huxley's method, as he noted in "On the Educational Value of the Natural History Sciences," was a combination of experimental induction and logical deduction, formulated along the lines of John Stuart Mill's *System of Logic* (3:52–56). In *Sartor Resartus*, the "Cause-and-Effect Philosophy of Clothes, as of Laws," is plainly suspect.[37] Teufelsdröckh's method "is not, in any case, that of common school Logic, where the truths all stand in a row, each holding by the skirts of the other; but at best that of practical Reason, proceeding by large Intuition over whole systematic groups and kingdoms."[38] Reason is not excluded from Teufelsdröckh's method, but imagination is the highest faculty: "not our Logical, Mensurative faculty, but our Imaginative one is King over us."[39] For him the symbol is the significant unit of human knowledge, in which "man, consciously or unconsciously, lives, works, and has his being." And at its most exalted the symbol becomes the vehicle of prophecy.

Carlyle proceeded intuitively while Huxley advocated empirical method; Carlyle discovered spirit where Huxley found "the practical eternity of matter and of force" (1:37). While Carlyle documented and actively advocated the heroic principle found in the unity between man and nature which his heroes achieved, Huxley, who was by no means indifferent to the heroic, found what he felt to be a more rational and constructive interpreter of nature in his scientist. The age was an ailing body, Carlyle had maintained in his "Characteristics." The question was whether it needed a physician or a metaphysician.

ii. hero and antihero

In early April of 1866, Huxley traveled to Edinburgh to receive an honorary degree at the university in company with Carlyle and Tyndall. By the fall of the same year, as a member of Mill's Jamaica Committee, he was at fierce odds with his fellow conferees over the Eyre controversy. Predictably, the central issue as Huxley saw it was that of hero worship. The Jamaica Revolt had drawn much attention in England to issues of human liberty; Governor Edward Eyre, a self-styled disciple of Carlyle, brutally suppressed the rioting, indiscriminately killing blacks who were British subjects. Under the authority of martial law and without due process, Eyre hanged the black leader and agitator George William Gordon, who was a member of the Jamaican Assembly. Mill formed the Jamaica Committee which sought to remove Eyre from office and prosecute him for murder, and was supported by Darwin, Huxley, Spencer, Frederick Harrison, and Leslie Stephen, among others. Carlyle's Eyre Defence Committee was supported by Tennyson, Ruskin, Dickens, Tyndall, and Kingsley.

In a letter to Kingsley on 8 November 1866, Huxley clarified his position by delivering an attack on the concept of hero worship:

> If English law will not declare that heroes have no more right to kill people in this fashion than other folk, I shall take an early opportunity of migrating to Texas or some other quiet place where

there is less hero-worship and more respect for justice, which is to my mind of much more importance than hero-worship.
. . . .

The hero-worshippers who believe that the world is to be governed by its great men, who are to lead the little ones, justly if they can; but if not, unjustly drive or kick them the right way, will sympathise with Mr. Eyre.

The other sect (to which I belong) who look upon hero-worship as no better than any other idolatry, and upon the attitude of mind of the hero-worshipper as essentially immoral; who think it is better for a man to go wrong in freedom than to go right in chains . . . will believe that Mr. Eyre has committed one of the greatest crimes. [*LL*, 1:303–4]

This marked an important period of intellectual change for Huxley. He had seen the practical implications of Carlyle's social theory and found that his own sense of morality was rationalist and that, like Mill, he was horrified at the prospects of leadership by the supralegal, intuitive mind of the hero.[40]

Huxley's involvement in the slavery issue had actually begun the previous year with the publication of his essay "Emancipation—Black and White" in a May issue of the *Reader*. Emancipation for blacks and women was a single issue, he argued, and natural and moral law both obliged all to reject the physical domination of more powerful over less powerful groups. The enslaver debased himself, diminished the dignity of his own spirit (3:67–68). Apparently recalling Carlyle's argument, more than a decade earlier, in "Occasional Discourse on the Nigger Question," Huxley noted that "emancipation may convert the slave from a well-fed animal into a pauperised man"; but maintained that "no slavery can be abolished without a double emancipation, and the master will benefit by freedom more than the freed-man" (3:67–68). At the same time, he blandly stated that the "facts" clearly demonstrated the average black to be inferior, while "Nature's old salique law" would prevent a revolution at home (3:66–67, 73).[41] John Stuart Mill, whose "The Negro Question" had challenged Carlyle's doctrine of work and idea of destiny and had established a classical liberal argument for emancipation, took a keen, if cautious, interest in Huxley's essay, notwithstanding what he referred to as Huxley's "heretical physiology."[42] In calling for equality before the law and equality of education, Huxley was much closer to Mill's position than to Carlyle's.

Huxley's objections were not without their own irony, for Carlyle had founded his concept of hero worship on the proposition that the hero's life was "a piece of the everlasting heart of Nature herself."[43] The sword of Mahomet was nothing less than an aspect of the dynamic force of nature, the "beak and claws" of the prophet.[44] Carlyle's concept of the heroic suggested that the forces of nature, working unconsciously through the hero, were manifestations of nature itself. Carlyle seemed dazzled by the Gothic prospect of illimitable complexities of force mysteriously surging through the universe: "Force, Force, everywhere Force; we ourselves a mysterious Force in the centre of that."[45] And while he made a strong distinction between the prophet's response to force and the scientist's inclination to bottle it up in Leyden jars, it was nevertheless the same force, the energy diffused throughout nature. Carlyle's metaphor of the Leyden jar was apt, for the scientific impulse was to control. Carlyle's impulse was to release. Indeed, his heroes seemed to lack the means to control the measureless forces that surged within them. His theory of heroism stressed the principle of antiself-consciousness, the instinctual and intuitive. To release the self from the strictures of the conscious mind was to set free the essential forces of nature which furnished the self-transcending energy of the hero. "Shakespeare's Art is not Artifice," he declared. "It grows-up from the deeps of Nature, through his noble sincere soul, who is a voice of Nature."[46] Carlyle's rejection of human consciousness as a controlling agency in heroic achievement slighted the conscious activities of reason and imagination. Destruction was as common in unconscious nature as creation. The "intellectual breeze" that set Coleridge's organic harp to music was not to be compared to the vast, impersonal forces working through the Carlylean supernature.

Having discovered and released the tremendous force or energy in his heroes, Carlyle was left with no human means for controlling it, much as Frankenstein had lost mastery over his creation. It was one thing to find such force released in the fervent atmosphere of St. Edmundsbury in *Past and Present* but quite another in the senseless violence of contemporary Jamaica.

Carlyle's hero functioned in the same natural realm as Huxley's scientist. And it was partly in recognition of this fact that Huxley began seriously to consider the socially redemptive possibilities of Victorian science. In an autobiographical fragment written late in life, Huxley recalled his early impression of Carlyle's intense desire for social reform: "The last recorded speech of Professor Teufelsdröckh proposes the toast 'Die Sache der Armen in Gottes und Teufelsnamen' (The cause of the Poor in Heaven's name and ____'s.) The cause of the Poor is the burden of *Past and Present, Chartism,* and *Latter-Day Pamphlets*" (LL, 1:16). Huxley's positive response to Carlyle's advocacy for the poor was strengthened by his own experiences as a medical student tramping through London slums with his brother-in-law, Dr. Chandler. But whatever social redemption Carlyle had seemed to promise vanished in the wake of the Eyre controversy; the wording of Huxley's letter to Kingsley in which he attacked the notion of the Carlylean hero suggested that he regarded the events of the Jamaica incident as a practical test of Carlyle's social theory. Carlyle himself regarded it so. The laboratory had always been for Huxley the most reliable testing place for a theory, and with a certain sense of shock he concluded that the Carlylean hero was fundamentally immoral.

The social theme in Huxley's essays continued to gain momentum through the mid-sixties to the end of the decade. His essay "On the Advisableness of Improving Natural Knowledge," written early in 1866, had already begun to advocate the spread of scientific knowledge as a vital social activity. Where Carlyle had attempted to bring the prophetic vision to bear as a social corrective, Huxley endeavored to apply scientific insight for a similar objective. But Carlyle's social ideals, concentrated as they were in great men with superior intuitive powers, moved toward the centralization of social power. Huxley's social thought, which was based on his ideal of science as a democracy of knowledge and a social leveling force, moved toward an egalitarian ideal:

All these gifts of science are aids in the process of levelling up; of removing the ignorant and baneful prejudices of nation against na-

tion, province against province, and class against class; of assuring
that social order which is the foundation of progress, which has
redeemed Europe from barbarism. [1:108]

While Huxley and Carlyle both sought social unity and order,
they had different social champions; Carlyle's hero, who had an
intuitive insight into the forces of nature, was supplanted in
Huxley's thought by the scientist, whose insight into nature
was rational. It was as if Huxley, deeply influenced in his early
readings by the great pattern of unity in Carlyle's universe, had
later found in science an alternative approach to satisfying his
own intense need for a sense of order.

This was apparent in Huxley's attempts to install Descartes in
his hall of heroes. Carlyle had warned against mistaking the
"superficial film" above which science operated for the "deep
sacred infinitude of Nescience."[47] If anything, Carlyle's hero
was the arch-opponent of mechanism and method. Huxley certainly was aware of this by 1870 when he wrote his "On Descartes' 'Discourse Touching the Method of Using One's Reason
Rightly and of Seeking Scientific Truth.'" Nevertheless, his
study of the father of mechanism began with the observation
that the thoughts of men were "comparable to the leaves, flow-
ers, and fruit upon the innumerable branches of a few great
stems" which "bear the names of the half-a-dozen men, endowed with intellects of heroic force and clearness," and went
on to identify Descartes' as such a heroic intellect (1:166–67).
His greatness was of that rare kind found in those who "embody the potentiality of their own day, and magically reflect the
future" (1:167). Huxley's root and tree imagery, combined with
his emphasis on Descartes' determination to "strip off all the
garments which the intellect weaves for itself," suggests that he
was writing with Carlyle's concept of heroism in mind (1:166,
177).[48]

Like Carlyle, Huxley began to write biographies of historical
figures possessing qualities to be celebrated as either ideal or
memorable. His portraits of Descartes, Priestley, and Darwin
make a striking contrast to the vivid heroism of Carlyle's subjects. Huxley's Descartes seems in this context an antihero, the
opposite of nearly everything stood for by the heroes of Carlyle.
He was rational, the first great active sceptic, a practical man
who "sought to resolve all the phaenomena of the universe into

matter and motion, or forces operating according to law" (1:181). He was the father of mechanism and the fountainhead of the modern scientific spirit. Yet in his acceptance of only thought as an absolute certainty, he was to be associated as well with the idealism of Berkeley and Kant (1:178). Physically, Descartes was a "sickly and diminutive child" who, like Huxley, found very little of real value in his early education; and the threat of torture and personal ruin for his views and pursuits drove Descartes, unheroically, "into subterfuges and evasions which were not worthy of him" (1:196). Realism had begun to overtake Huxley's vision of the "great man."

In his Descartes essay, Huxley pondered the introduction of Calvinism into science, which he equated with the declaration that "man is nothing but a machine" (1:192). He had no objection to the idea as long as those who would call man a machine admit his ability to adjust himself within certain limits. Such were the views of Descartes, along with the understanding that the mind was the only ultimate reality. Huxley went on to declare that "if some great Power would agree to make me always think what is true and do what is right, on condition of being turned into a sort of clock and wound up every morning before I got out of bed, I should instantly close with the offer" (1:192–93). It was purely a hypothetical proposition, of course, but in a curious manner it depicted the mechanical mirror-image of the Carlylean hero who, similarly, was a force unconsciously driven to do the bidding of nature itself. Material law for Huxley had come to seem as inexorable as spiritual law had been for Carlyle. Huxley had accepted Cartesian dualism. The practical materialism of the mechanistic view of phenomena existed for him beside the idealism "which declares the ultimate fact of all knowledge to be consciousness, or, in other words, a mental phaenomenon" (1:178). This paradox became Huxley's basic philosophical assumption.

Carlyle had once declared that the "Alpha and Omega" of the hero was "that he looks through the shows of things into *things.*"[49] Descartes was the spiritual father of what Huxley alternately called "Critical Idealism" and "thätige Skepsis," or "active skepticism" (1:178, 170). Critical idealism was an admission by the investigator of the mind's inability to transcend its own consciousness, which is the single existential certainty. This led to Goethe's "thätige Skepsis" which Huxley equated with Descartes' stripping away of all beliefs and with the reduction of the self to a "state of intellectual nakedness" (1:170). Huxley's hero also looked through the show of things into things, but did not experience that "Baphometic Fire-baptism" which for Carlyle was the very beginning of vision.[50] Huxley's scientist emphasized scepticism and analysis; Carlyle's prophet, belief and synthesis. Both, however, operated from a center of indifference, for both had reduced the self to an essential nakedness from which it could view things with a minimum of prejudice.

Charles Darwin became for Huxley Descartes' descendant and "the incorporated ideal of a man of science" (2:245). Huxley had asserted that "the essence of the scientific spirit is criticism"; Darwin was the great and heroic instance of that spirit (2:229). *Darwiniana,* the second volume of Huxley's *Collected Essays,* amounts to a critical examination of Darwin's thought and a personal assessment of Darwin as a man. While not a "mere advocate" for Darwin, Huxley was deeply impressed with the productions of Darwin's genius (2:v). In a eulogy which appeared in *Nature* in April 1882, Huxley declared: "One could not converse with Darwin without being reminded of Socrates. There was the same desire to find some one wiser than himself; the same belief in the sovereignty of reason; the same ready humor" (2:246). As fascinated with Darwin's personality as with his work, Huxley found the humility and simplicity of this reserved, self-secluding investigator almost mysterious. In contrast to the Carlylean hero, Darwin was sedentary, a thinker, not an actor. The calm spirit, the truth seeker amid storms of controversy, Darwin was the master of vast seas of detail, the heroic empiricist probing beyond the borders of established knowledge, struggling with the abstract. In his eulogy of Darwin, Huxley speaks of Darwin as both an intellectual and moral model, a Promethean figure, suffused with an "intense and almost passionate honesty by which all his thoughts and actions were irradiated, as by a central fire" (2:246).

In "Joseph Priestley" (1874), an address delivered at the unveiling of Priestley's statue in Birmingham and one of the more successful of Huxley's biographical sketches, Priestley emerges as an innocent yet "fearless defender of rational thought in freedom and in action" (3:2). He was a transmitter of the "fire kindled, in the childhood of the world, at the Promethean altar of Science" (3:3). Yet he was marked by the British public of his day as a moral outcast. Priestley's heroism resided in his unswerving commitment to truth against overwhelming odds. The material progress made possible by such men also contributes to the moral and intellectual progress of a society, for "it is futile to expect a hungry and squalid population to be anything but violent and gross." Huxley's proofs of the moral progress of Victorian society are less convincing than his vindication of Priestley's private moral stature; his argument that "open immorality and gross intemperance" have vanished from the upper and middle classes as a whole suggests that he had not seen very far beneath the surface of contemporary society (3:34).

Huxley was not a good biographer, but his purpose was more didactic than literary: he was attempting to present new models for public consideration. His familiarity with Carlyle's famous critical biographies probably inspired him to explore the backgrounds and lives of his scientist-ideals. For the most part, however, his biographical sketches of men like Hume, Berkeley, and Harvey, and even his deeply felt memorial essays on Darwin and Tyndall, are flat and over-burdened with technical details and moral object lessons.

The man of science was clearly an ideal figure, although not in the same sense as Carlyle's heroes. The values Huxley upheld in his scientist portraits were rationality, honesty, and intellectual courage, all of which he believed exerted a positive moral force on society. Whether or not society knew their names, scientists like Priestley would achieve immortality in their work: "To all eternity, the sum of truth and right will have been increased by their means; to all eternity, falsehood and injustice will be the weaker because they have lived" (3:37). Scientific activity, thus, became imbued with a moral value which Huxley associated with its rigorous standards for truth and assent. "Men of science," he maintained in 1887, "will always act up to their standard of veracity, when mankind in general leave off sinning; but that standard appears to me to be

70

higher among them than in any other class of the community" (5:141). In this scientific ethic Huxley saw an ideal and model for the social ethic and believed that the influence of Victorian science was not primarily material, but moral.

While both Carlyle and Huxley saw the central concern of society in the great unknown forces of nature, their proposed solutions were fundamentally antagonistic. Both recognized, however, that the forces of nature could not be ignored without profound consequences for society. For Carlyle, Victorian society was dangerously fragmented and could not be effectively unified in a democracy, which he equated with the "despair of finding any Heroes to govern."[51] Thus while Huxley's scientist and Carlyle's hero were the products of nearly identical social and intellectual concerns, they became the embodiments of almost opposite ideals. Together they represented a watershed in the concept of social leadership, Carlyle looking to the past for his great examples, Huxley expecting the future to produce ever greater scientific leaders. Huxley's scientists had qualities of the antihero, being primarily methodical thinkers given over to rationality and rumination rather than instinctual action. Darwin, the great modern model, pondered his theory for more than a decade and nearly lost the credit for it to Wallace. Descartes, fearing the stake, was driven to cowardice. These men did not possess the qualities of heroism and intuition in the manner of Carlyle's heroes, although they were certainly not without them. With figures like Zadig, Huxley very nearly elevated common sense to the highest order of insight. Yet while the link between scientist and nature was a rational one, the great ocean of the unknown provided an element of profound emotional mystery that inspired what Huxley called a "religious tone of mind." Carlyle's heroes, with their intuitive, mystical links to the forces of nature, exist outside society in the sense that they transcend the laws of men. They are great individuals, social redeemers who make history; new societies follow in their apocalyptic wakes. Huxley's scientists represent an opposite, collective ideal; they do not operate on knowledge that is unique to them as individuals, but rather build on a continually expanding edifice. Both ideals proved eminently capable of capturing and deeply influencing the Victorian imagination.

71

III

A New Universe

i. the higher science

Huxley's developing ideas of order were full of the dynamism of his day, in which force and motion had become the essence of phenomena at some cost to the idea of permanence. Having abandoned his early Romanticism and his Carlylean tendencies, including vitalism, he was by the mid-sixties faced with the problem of having to imagine a new universe in which he might operate morally and philosophically. In quest of a modern principle of unity, Huxley wished to extrapolate from his growing expertise in a number of scientific disciplines to a higher science that would furnish a new existential model for his thought and criticism. His moral priorities obliged him to look to the past moral experience of the culture, while, philosophically, he felt a growing allegiance to the naturalistic determinism inherent in scientific methodologies. In his drive toward unity, he set out to find a common basis for the moral order and the increasingly well defined natural order, and resurrected, in consequence, the classical conflict between determinism and free will. This conflict, also manifested in the Victorian dualism of matter and consciousness, led ultimately to Huxley's formulation of the agnostic paradox.

In his Royal Institution lecture series "The Physiology of Sensation and Motion," Huxley began with a declaration which might well have served as a motto for the new Victorian world:

> Rest has vanished out of the universe. The stars which we fondly used to call fixed are found to be rushing through space as swiftly as their attendant planets are whirling around them. . . .
>
> The rest which has disappeared from the heavens has found no refuge on the earth.[1]

73

Delivered in 1857 and 1877, this series of eight lectures examined the mechanisms of sensation and traced the origin of human knowledge to the motion of matter. All existence, Huxley declared, was in flux; all permanence therefore was illusory. The hidden molecular motion of what seemed to be solid objects mirrored the activity of the heavens. Connected through an infinite chain of cause and effect, the infinitely small and the infinitely large danced in a harmony that human intellect could perceive only dimly. Life itself, Huxley observed, was known from its motion, since "evidence that a thing lives is furnished by changes of form and size."[2] This emphasis on motion revealed the new direction Huxley's thought had taken in his first years as lecturer at the Government School of Mines. If man's knowledge was of forces, these were known because they were universally resolvable into "modes of motion."[3] Huxley moved a step beyond Carlyle toward naturalism, for while Carlyle had found force surging through heavens and heroes alike, Huxley found motion to be universally distributed.

Motion identified and defined the great phenomena of the universe for Huxley; it was the principle of existence which permeated microcosm and macrocosm, life and the inanimate, matter and consciousness. Its contrast with force was significant, for while force and motion were theoretically one, force was an abstraction—hidden, plastic, and even spiritual. Motion, whether molecular or cosmic, was a manifestation of physical phenomena, observable, directional, and material. Reason guided by an effective method would suffice to identify it, while to locate and define Carlyle's force intuition was required. In this sense, the natural supernaturalism of Carlyle's transcendental force was replaced in Huxley's thought by the naturalism of physical motion. This shift was seen clearly in Huxley's change in emphasis from "vital force" to "vital action," which were respectively the life principles of his 1854 essay "On the Educational Value of the Natural History Sciences" and his 1868 essay "On the Physical Basis of Life."

While vital force emphasized the uniqueness of life, the mystical, unquantifiable energy common to living things, vital motion stressed the view that life forms were simply unique manifestations of a quantifiable energy common to all existence.

Vital motion, while a specialized form, was not discontinuous with other forms of motion; it was a category of a broad physical phenomenon. Furthermore, like all existence, it was subject to perpetual change, since it was part of the universal process. Nothing remained the same from moment to moment. "Even as you speak," Huxley declared in an early fragment, "that which you touch and see is slipping away from you and becoming different from what it was a moment before."[4] Individuality itself was an illusion: "There is no moment in the life of a man . . . in which we can say this is the whole individual—either in the physical or the psychical sense. . . . Our conception of an individual man, in fact, is an abstraction by which we conceive as a whole the several individual states of humanity as we are conscious of them." Huxley's developing vision of flux and universal motion threatened to dissolve the resolution and concreteness of objects and entities into a blur of elemental activity, much as Turner's *Rain, Steam, and Speed* captured on canvas the strange amorphousness of a world thrown out of focus by the driving motion of a steam engine.

The threat of impermanence and dissolution, however, was countered by the order-seeking activity of science. With rest and permanence driven from the heavens, order itself became the principle which rescued man from a random universe. Laws were expressions of regularity in which the flux was given stability in the language of human order. When Darwin's *Origin* appeared in 1959, Huxley found in its mass of detail one of the great justifications of the scientific vision; while Darwin had identified species as life forms which varied with time, he had also described the pattern that the perpetual flux appeared to follow. Darwin had established a new principle of order and motion, a progression. Science, Huxley pointed out in his 1860 essay on Darwin's *Origin*, had begun to set before humanity a vision of harmony and order amid the perpetual flux of matter and force:

> Harmonious order governing eternally continuous progress—the web and woof of matter and force interweaving by slow degrees, without a broken thread, that veil which lies between us and the Infinite—that universe which alone we know or can know; such is the picture which science draws of the world. [2:59]

Huxley's "harmonious order" and "continuous progress," reminiscent of both Goethe and Shelley, were a mixture of naturalism and idealism that frequently characterized his thought, in which he envisioned the progressive revelation of an ideal order and unity out of the slow accumulation of natural knowledge. Order itself was an abstraction, an assertion of cause and effect relationships which, as Huxley knew well that Hume had shown, were impossible to establish empirically.

Science had become more than a discipline through which to achieve practical knowledge about nature. Huxley sought order. Like the Cinderella figure at the end of "Science and Morals" who entertained great visions of "the order which pervades the seeming disorder of the world," Huxley harbored idealistic visions that were compelling, not because they were logical, but because they were mythological (9:146). Some great unity lay in the distant future, promising to embody a philosophical and emotional ideal.[5]

In his 1866 essay, "On the Advisableness of Improving Natural Knowledge," Huxley made it clear that it was the speculative and visionary ends of scientific research he valued most highly. Delivered first as a lecture at London's St. Martin's Hall, the essay came nearly twelve years after "On the Educational Value of the Natural History Sciences," which, delivered also at St. Martin's, had marked the beginning of Huxley's professional scientific career. The difference in the essays was substantial, for while earlier Huxley's ambition had been an increased public appreciation for the "importance" of scientific disciplines, the later essay was offered more as a warning to society that science stood between social cataclysm and social harmony. While the earlier essay suggests that science might enhance one's sense of the beauty of natural things, the second claims that the creative encounter of the scientist with the unknown had produced "ideas which can alone still spiritual cravings" (1:31). The 1866 essay is perhaps the most audacious of the *Lay Sermons*, for in standard sermon form Huxley offered his audience a vision of "fire, famine, pestilence, and all the evils which result from a want of command over and due anticipation of the course of Nature," and then abruptly turned to contemplate the great new creed of Victorian science and the new morality of scientific scepticism (1:28). The essay is an elaborate parody of a sermon, offering the threat of destruction and the alternative spiritual fulfillment of the scientific vision. It was not much different from what so many Victorian missionaries were accomplishing in the far reaches of the Empire—first demonstrating the power of their God by healing the sick and improving physical conditions, and then raising up their heathen fellows to receive the higher rewards of the spiritual vision.

Disseminating the knowledge of natural things meant much more to Huxley than the gradual accumulation of scientific research and the betterment of social conditions. While the scientist was committed to the practical and material interests of society, he was also in quest of an intellectual and spiritual reward. Halfway through the essay, after arguing the vital utility of modern technical knowledge, Huxley turns to scorn the steam pump and spinning jenny as "toys, possessing an accidental value" (1:29).[6] If the scientific endeavor were merely to achieve material comfort, it would be better for men to return to prehistoric times when technology amounted to the simple matter of chipping one's flint axe, and to avoid being "troubled with the endless malady of thought which now infests us all, for such reward" (1:31). The "malady of thought," a term which, as we have seen, Huxley used privately to express the sense of personal disintegration and aimlessness attending the loss of one's traditional certainties of belief, described the anxieties he saw in many of his contemporaries who seemed possessed by the same doubts. Tracing the cause to the growth and success of natural knowledge, he declared that the price was too high if it purchased only material comfort. Like John Stuart Mill who in his *Autobiography* recalled how he had found the prospect of successful social reform strangely unfulfilling, Huxley found the social prospects of technology and science alone incapable of justifying his own commitment to the scientific way of life.[7] Natural knowledge was more than a discipline for achieving the pleasures of utilitarian comfort; it was an Alpine peasant woman knitting for her children as she strode "ever upward, heavily burdened, and with mind bent only on her home" (1:30). Like the Cinderella figure Huxley used twenty years later, the Swiss woman illustrated the humble, proletarian homeliness of natural knowledge, while she awaited a higher destiny than one might guess from mere outward appearance. The structure in both metaphors was mythical, upward toward some higher state and vision.

A deep vein of religious metaphor and imagery throughout the essay suggests that Huxley entertained a spiritual concept of scientific contemplation rivalling, in its intensity and sanctity, the religious traditions he so adamantly opposed. His descriptions of the order contemplated by science read like litanies of a new faith: ". . . the infinite magnitude of space . . . the practical eternity of the duration of the universe . . . the infinite minuteness of its constituent parts . . . the practical eternity of matter and of force . . . the universality of a definite and predicable order and succession of events . . . man to be no centre of the living world, but one amidst endless modifications of life . . ." (1:37). The grand article of faith was the "fixed order and unchanging causation" of nature. This alone offered men something akin to permanence in the universal flux. These were the new universals, infinity extending outward into space and inward into the minute particles that constituted matter. No longer the center of his world, man was his own great limitation, for his powers of perception went but a short distance along the tracks of such immensities.

Early in the essay, the religious theme takes the form of a rivalry in comparative effectiveness between science and religion in averting physical catastrophe such as sickness and fire. The second half of the essay develops the spiritual theme. Huxley's scorn of the utilitarian approach to natural knowledge is similar in tone and attitude to what a deeply religious individual might feel toward those who treated the spiritual activity of prayer as an avenue toward achieving greater material benefits for the self. Scientific efforts to pierce the universal system of natural order are identified with "worship . . . at the altar of the Unknown" (1:38). Scientific advancement is "a great spiritual stream" (1:25). The same "abyss of the unknown" which was the object of primitive religions is the object of modern science (1:33–34). Religion and science are part of the same human impulse to observe and define, to relate cause to effect. The astronomy which arose when early man wished to navigate and predict the seasons has advanced to the stage where it theorizes the infinite extension of matter and force throughout the universe and tells men "that this so vast and seemingly solid earth is but an atom among atoms, whirling, no man knows whither, through illimitable space" (1:35). And like a new believer, the "man of science has learned to believe in justification, not by faith, but by verification" (1:41). For Huxley science was the logical end of a progression of the same human spirit that once found its most useful and compelling certainties in religion. The world has grown older and as the race "approaches its maturity" it begins to abandon the cherished dreams of youth and to recognize that "there is but one kind of knowledge and but one method of acquiring it" (1:41). The basis of belief is no longer to be determined by authority and tradition; experience must be the final arbiter in matters of truth: "scepticism is the highest of duties; blind faith the one unpardonable sin" (1:40).

The essay elaborately transfers the religious impluse from traditional forms to scientific activity. Huxley was not merely appropriating religious terminology to create an ironic effect. Nor was he propagandizing. He was seriously suggesting that the scientific effort to comprehend and define the processes which regulate the natural order is nothing more nor less than a modern manifestation of the primitive impulse that gave rise to the defining processes of religion. As man's experience in the world grows more extensive and precise, two things occur: his god grows more abstract and his natural knowledge becomes more precise and concrete. It is a remarkable essay, alone among mid-Victorian essays in its brilliant analysis of the undercurrent of Victorian science as it slowly yet irrevocably revolutionized men's "conceptions of the universe and of themselves" (1:31). In its stark physical cosmos lay the germ of the vision that was to become a commonplace of the following century, particularly in the dislocation of man from his position at the center of things, the introduction of motion and the concept of change into all facets of existence, the shattering of the old supernatural unities, and the installation of uniformitarian order as their naturalistic equivalents. Of all Huxley's essays "On the Advisableness of Improving Natural Knowledge" is the most succinctly representative of his vision. It is the chief essay of *Lay Sermons, Addresses, and Reviews* (1870), his first important collection, and it followed his short "Autobiography" at the beginning of *Method and Results* (1893), the first volume of his *Collected Essays*.

Huxley's attitude toward science bears an interesting relationship to that other Victorian group which saw religious possibilities in the new science, the positivists. Indeed, Huxley proclaimed war on the positivists in 1868 with his essay, "On the Physical Basis of Life," in which he made his famous observation that the positive philosophy amounted to "Catholicism *minus* Christianity" (1:156). While the occasion which inspired Huxley's attack—the association by the Archbishop of York of the "New Philosophy" of science with Comte's positive philosophy—seems somewhat trivial to justify such a crushing response by Huxley, there were a number of facets to his quarrel which were not examined in the essay. Huxley's argument with the ideas of Auguste Comte had begun long before 1868. His first public dealings with Comte's work came as early as January 1854, when in the science column of the *Westminster Review* he reviewed Harriet Martineau's two-volume *The Positive Philosophy of Auguste Comte* and George Lewes's *Comte's Positive Philosophy of the Sciences*, both of which had appeared in late 1853. Huxley praised Martineau's work, which was essentially a translation and abridgement of Comte's *Cours de philosophie positive* and he criticized Lewes's treatment of Comte, calling Lewes a "book scientist."[8] This caused some friction between Huxley and George Eliot, who had worked on the book herself, was solicitous for Lewes's success, and who was in the difficult position of being the editor of the *Westminster Review*. Less than half a year later, the charge Huxley had leveled at Lewes was extended to Comte himself. In "On the Educational Value of the Natural History Sciences," Huxley discussed the "strange assertions into which speculation . . . may lead even an able man" such as Comte (3:49). He demonstrated that Comte's classification of sciences into various categories such as "experimental" and "comparative" was inaccurate and misleading. Huxley resented the aloof and authoritarian pronouncements on disciplines which he himself had only begun to master after strenuous study and prolonged research. His argument with Comte and Lewes underscored the divergence of the professional from the amateur scientist in England, Huxley charging both men with unprofessionalism. However, Huxley did accept Comte's concept of a science of society or "sociology" (3:58).

In 1866 Huxley again took issue with Comte, this time with the Comtian doctrine of the three stages of history, theological, metaphysical, and positive. He declared in "On the Advisableness of Improving Natural Knowledge" that "it is hardly questionable that mankind from the first took strictly positive and scientific views" on the basic phenomena of the natural world (1:34). "The foundations of all knowledge—secular or sacred—were laid when intelligence dawned," Huxley argued; primitive man was a realist. Furthermore, man's habit of making himself the "centre and measure of the world" was a mistake, since the reality of man's situation in the world was his dislocation from the center of existence. Worship was to be directed not at humanity but "at the altar of the Unknown" (1:38). Although it criticized positivist ideas, Huxley's 1866 essay was not an attack on Comte and, indeed, might have given followers of Comte reason to list Huxley as one of their sympathizers. For Huxley's epistemology was recognizably similar to Comte's, and like Comte and Whewell, he cited astronomy as one of the great examples of the effects of scientific advancement on man's conceptions of the universe and of himself. The vision of the new knowledge, the progression toward a condition where natural knowledge would "become coextensive with the range of knowledge," were ideas which gave Huxley's essay a noticeably Comtian tone.

Months after he had published his 1866 essay, Huxley, as we have seen, was involved in the Eyre controversy and had taken a new view of the concept of hero worship, now finding it brutal and immoral. The reversal of his earlier sympathies with Carlyle was extended to Comte in the 1868 essay "On the Physical Basis of Life," where, as mentioned earlier, he attacked Comte's philosophy as "Catholicism *minus* Christianity" (1:156). Speaking to a Scottish audience, Huxley reminded it that Hume had preceded Comte in tracing the limits of philosophical inquiry, and that Comte's philosophy tendered an authoritarianism that was as opposed to the spirit of free inquiry as was Catholicism, which for Huxley, and no doubt for his audience, represented the ultimate dogmatism. But he offered little additional explanation for his charge against Comte. Challenged by Richard Congreve, founder of the Positivist Society of London, he published "The Scientific Aspects of Positivism" (1869).[9] In this essay, Huxley used Comte's own words to demonstrate that he had urged the adoption of the Catholic organization without the Catholic doctrine as a fit model for the new society. His basic charge was that the spirit of Comte's philosophy was one of an aggressive authoritarianism; its logical manifestation would be "a minutely-defined social organization, which, if it ever came into practice, would exert a despotic authority such as no sultan has rivalled, and no Puritan presbytery, in its palmiest days, could hope to excel."[10] Having rejected the concept of hero worship as a philosophy of oppression, Huxley found the notion of Comte's "Nouveau Grand-Etre Suprême" a threat to the freedom which assured the progress of science and the spirit of free inquiry.[11] The worship of humanity was little more than a variation of the idea of a deity and a new form of anthropomorphism and hero worship. While the Comtists spoke as though they were sympathetic to the sciences, the authoritarian spirit of their vision was antagonistic in the deadliest way to the principle of intellectual liberty.

This was made worse by the fact that Comte himself had no very clear idea of the scientific knowledge he believed himself to be promoting. "What struck me," Huxley recalled, "was his want of apprehension of the great features of science; his strange mistakes as to the merits of his scientific contemporaries; and his ludicrously erroneous notions about the part which some of the scientific doctrines current in his time were destined to play in the future." Huxley went through a list of Comte's pronouncements on the sciences, his high opinion of phrenology, his low opinion of psychology, his odd classifications of the sciences as abstract, comparative, experimental. Much of this was arbitrary, Huxley argued.

He found Comte's Law of Three Stages too schematic and

artificial. Rather than looking at human intellectual development as having passed through theological, metaphysical, and
positive stages, one should consider it as having had from the
dawn of intelligence two distinct ways of "mirroring nature."
On the one hand, the intellect, whether of a child or of the
human species in its childhood, takes in sensations and builds
up associations "which are more thoroughly 'positive,' or devoid of entanglement with hypotheses of any kind, than they
will ever be in after-life"; yet the same intellect soon "becomes
aware of itself as a source of action and a subject of passion and
of thought."[12] Awareness of self, Huxley argued, gives rise to
anthropomorphism when the child intellect begins to endow
other living things with properties similar to its own. Only at a
later stage does the human intelligence become aware of the
apparent conflict between the anthropomorphic and the physical or positive aspects of nature; then it attempts to extend one
of the two views over the whole. The compromise between the
two views gives rise to Comte's metaphysical state:

> What is true of the individual is, *mutatis mutandis*, true of the
> intellectual development of the species. It is absurd to say of men in
> a state of primitive savagery, that all their conceptions are in a
> theological state. Nine-tenths of them are eminently realistic, and as
> "positive" as ignorance and narrowness can make them. It no more
> occurs to a savage than it does to a child, to ask the why of daily and
> ordinary occurrences which form the greater part of his mental life.
> But in regard to the more striking, or out-of-the-way, events, which
> force him to speculate, he is highly anthropomorphic; and, as com-
> pared with a child, his anthropomorphism is complicated by the
> intense impression which the death of his own kind makes upon
> him, as indeed it well may.[13]

Hence there were two principles of explanation in the systems
of human knowledge, and each had been operative from the
beginning. "In the progress of the species from savagery to
advanced civilization," Huxley continued, "anthropomorphism grows into theology, while physicism (if I may so call it)
develops into science; but the development of the two is con-
temporaneous, not successive." The perpetual clash between
the two, he concluded, was resulting in a continually expanding
realm for physicism, while anthropomorphism had "taken

stand in its last fortress—man himself." But the struggle would very likely "for ever remain a drawn one."[14]

The strength of Huxley's argument rested on its psychological insight. What had been described by Comte as a historical process was interpreted by Huxley to be an internal dynamic of mind, a conflict between the impulse to pattern nature after the self and the tendency to view the external world as an objective entity. Primitive man survived through his hearty realism, and did not weave an elaborate system around common events and phenomena of life. He created a superstructure to explain events like death, which forced him to speculate and for which his common experience could supply no satisfactory explanation. Metaphysics formed the territory between supernaturalism and naturalism, "taking from the anthropomorphic view its tendency to personify, and from the physical view its tendency to exclude volition and affection." Looking to the development of the child for a theoretical model from which to postulate the development of the whole race, Huxley suggested that the pattern of cultural maturation was represented in a general but highly revealing manner by the psychological progress of the individual. Civilization was the metaphor of man's psychic progress. As man grew older, his accumulating experience allowed him to formulate explanations for events which before had been mysteries, a process which was manifest in modern society. Comte's historical approach to the progress of human intellect looked forward to the historical determinism of Marx; Huxley's psychological approach, like the work of his contemporaries John Stuart Mill, Herbert Spencer, and William Carpenter, led toward the psychological determinism of Freud.

Huxley's 1869 essay summarized his disagreements with Comte, all of which had been intensified by the shock of the Eyre controversy. The debate with English positivists such as Congreve and Harrison continued over the next twenty years, but while there was a change in emphasis from technical, philosophical questions to problems of morality and political government, little that was new evolved out of the contest. There was excess on both sides—particularly in Huxley's acerbity—but the disagreements were never superficial.[15] There was a clash in attitude, an antagonism that brings to mind the religious differences between the Catholic and the Protestant Fundamentalist (5:260–61). Huxley had once characterized his early outlook as one of "scientific Calvinism"; one could expect little sympathy from such a mind for a scientific vision which aligned itself with Catholic tradition, complete with dogma and ceremony. Positivism was for Huxley very like the second wave of the Oxford Movement in a sinister disguise. More basic was Huxley's aversion, almost fear, of what seemed to him the threat of totalitarian regimentation behind the new Comtist heroes and "saints" who were offered as model governors for society. Like Carlyle's power-men, they concentrated and wielded too much force. This same fear inspired that strange, Quixotic tilt Huxley ran at General Booth and the Salvation Army in 1890.[16] Huxley feared the regimentation of men and the submission of individual will to the authority of a powerful leader; he feared the destruction of private judgment. And his argument with Comte's followers nearly always was formulated along these lines.

In soundly rejecting the program of the positivists, Huxley opened himself to the charge that his advocacy for scientific independence amounted to an abdication of social responsibility, for, as Basil Willey has argued, one of the important goals of Comte's great plan was to turn the sciences away from barren specialization and to link them more clearly with a social objective.[17] While this was without doubt a desirable goal, and one which has yet to be achieved, Huxley had reason to believe that men like Comte, whatever their intentions, did not possess the capacity to rule wisely. The authoritarian structure of their systems promised not a Renaissance of human liberty, but a dark age of human oppression. The worship of humanity, with its vague, drifting ideals, the queer, Gothic ceremonies, struck Huxley as something close to madness. It amounted to the manipulation of reality, a process George Orwell would describe in the society of his *Nineteen Eighty-four*, with its vague "Big Brother" figure and its destruction of science through the authoritarianism of imposed definition. Empirical habits of thought could not survive the regimentation of society. Sympathetic as he was to the plight of mankind, Huxley adamantly refused to "adore the generalized conception of men." To Harrison's charge that he was ignorant of the great outlines of history, Huxley responded:

> I know no study which is so unutterably saddening as that of the evolution of humanity, as it is set forth in the annals of history. Out of the darkness of prehistoric ages man emerges with the marks of his lowly origin strong upon him. He is a brute, only more intelligent than the other brutes, a blind prey to impulses, which as often as not lead him to destruction; a victim to endless illusions, which make his mental existence a terror and a burden, and fill his physical life with barren toil and battle. He attains a certain degree of physical comfort, and develops a more or less workable theory of life, in such favourable situations as the plains of Mesopotamia or of Egypt, and then, for thousands and thousands of years, struggles, with varying fortunes, attended by infinite wickedness, bloodshed, and misery, to maintain himself at this point against the greed and ambition of his fellow-men. He makes a point of killing and otherwise persecuting all those who first try to get him to move on; and when he has moved on a step, foolishly confers post-mortem deification on his victims. He exactly repeats the process with all who want to move a step yet farther. And the best men of the best epochs are simply those who make the fewest blunders and commit the fewest sins.
>
> That one should rejoice in the good man, forgive the bad man, and pity and help all men to the best of one's ability, is surely indisputable. It is the glory of Judaism and of Christianity to have proclaimed this truth, through all their aberrations. But the worship of a God who needs forgiveness and help, and deserves pity every hour of his existence, is no better than that of any other voluntarily selected fetish. The Emperor Julian's project was hopeful in comparison with the prospects of the Comtist Anthropolatry. [5:256–57]

This was indeed a dark pessimism. Delivered in 1889 in his essay "Agnosticism," Huxley's argument seemed to recall the early declaration he had once made to Henrietta Heathorn that he had "nothing of the fine feeling called 'love for one's species.' " On the other hand, his pessimism was balanced by the optimism of other essays such as "On the Progress of Science: 1837–1887," which looked to the future possibilities of an era of human prosperity. Huxley was a man of two visions, the one filled with hope and wonder, the other dominated by a sense of futility and doom. He saw in the very euphoria of systems such as positivism, communism, and various religious movements, cause for concern. The irony and agony of his pessimism was its own powerlessness to formulate a worthy alternative.

ii. microcosm and macrocosm

In spite of his periodic but enduring pessimism, Huxley found self-transcendence in the scientific voyage into nature, the abstract and the ideal. While, one the one hand, the scientist grappled with the common prosaic objects of life, he found in his very preoccupations a simplicity and unity which carried him to the intuition of universal symmetry. Wordsworth, in his preface to the *Lyrical Ballads*, had been one of the first to define the pleasure of scientific knowledge and even to link it with the pleasure of the poetic:

> We have no knowledge, that is, no general principles drawn from the contemplation of particular facts, but what has been built up by pleasure, and exists in us by pleasure alone. The Man of Science, the Chemist and Mathematician, whatever difficulties and disgusts they may have had to struggle with, know and feel this. However painful may be the objects with which the Anatomist's knowledge is connected, he feels that his knowledge is pleasure; and where he has no pleasure he has no knowledge. [18]

A similar appreciation of the higher knowledge of science informed Huxley's aspirations as a scientist. The microcosm, as contemplated by the scientist, was a world of objects which, while often unattractive in themselves, led deeper into the macrocosm of universal order. In his struggle for simplicity, his analysis and reduction, the man of science achieved a vision of the unity common to all things. This was the source of his pleasure. Through materialist reduction lay the path to idealist unity.

The spiritual quality Huxley found in scientific research was the result of the value he placed in contemplating the order of the natural world. Fascinated by the "architectural and engineering part" of the biological world, he found his interests steadily focused on "the working out the wonderful unity of

plan in thousands and thousands of diverse living constructions" (1:7). The idea of investigating the existence of archetypal invertebrate forms was a motivating force behind his
research aboard H.M.S. *Rattlesnake* from 1846 to 1850. Essentially an abstraction, the notion of the archetype, imported into
England from Goethe and the German nature-philosophers,
was first embraced and then rejected by Huxley, probably after
his studies of Berkeley, Hume and Hamilton. Huxley's early
interest in archetypal forms was intense, however, continuing
even after he formally abandoned the notion of archetype early
in his scientific career, surfacing in the persistent echoes of
archetypal idealism throughout his nontechnical prose. In his
acclaimed study "On the Morphology of the Cephalous Mollusca," published in 1853, he concluded that various species of
mollusks were "modifications of the same archetypal mollus-
cous form," and theorized that the "doctrine that every natural
group is organized after a definite archetype" was as important
for zoology as the theory of definite proportions was for
chemistry.[19]

While Huxley's early concept of the archetype, as Julian
Huxley observed, furnished him a pragmatic system for invertebrate classification, it also propelled him in his quest to discover the rational basis for the natural world.[20] Archetypal
theory was a generalizing theory, the object of which was to
discover the characteristics common to all members of a group,
to conceive of a representative, abstract form which was, in
effect, an ideal. Huxley abandoned his search for biological ar-
chetypes quite early, and his *Man's Place in Nature*, published
in 1863, while stressing structural similarities between man and
other animals, particularly the primates, was actually an attack
on archetypal theories. However, much of his nontechnical
prose continued to grope for ideals of order and organization. It
was as if Huxley believed that there existed some ultimate unity
which would answer to the rationalist imperatives of his own
personality.

In an 1860 lecture, reprinted as "A Lobster; or, the Study of
Zoology" which he delivered at the South Kensington Museum,
Huxley declared that "unity of plan everywhere lies hidden
under the mask of diversity of structure" (8:205). At the same

time, he explained that modern physiology regarded animal bodies as "machines" which performed according to the laws of nature. Given such a mechanistic approach, one expects to find unity in living entities, since they are by definition composed of so many identical parts; Huxley, for example, demonstrated how the ideal lobster was a sequence of rings, organized into a definite pattern. To this physical unity of structure, German embryological studies had contributed a dimension of time, showing that individuals developed identically from minute eggs, and revealing that even organisms as diverse as man and fish appeared to be identical in their earliest stages of development. What Huxley found most intriguing was that these unities of structure and development were neither ways of looking at things nor illusions, but "the expression of deep-seated natural facts" (8:205). In nature, then, one found the ideal, for physical unity was not merely the mind's imposition of order on nature; it was a reality. Such unities of plan, he observed, were "wonderful truths, the more so because the zoologist finds them to be of universal application." To understand Huxley's point, one has to recognize that in describing animals as machines he was using the word "machine" as a metaphor for the ideal unity of the physical world. Normally one thinks of a machine in the reductive sense of its being an imperfect and finite product of human ingenuity; the lobster machine Huxley speaks of is a unit of life that functions as an integral part of an order which transcends human comprehension. It could not have been fabricated by man. The study of its mechanism leads only as far as the limits of human perception, comprehension, and metaphor will permit. Nature, not man, encompasses the ideal; its simplest forms outdistance the most exalted human capacities for understanding.

This was the key to Huxley's idealization of nature. It was not an anthropomorphic idealization which endowed the pattern of natural phenomena with human attributes of emotion or thought; nor did it seek to commune in some mystical sense with "forces" represented in nature. Huxley's was the idealization of what he had called "physicism" in his 1869 essay on positivism. Deeply impressed with Lyell's uniformitarian theory, and with what he saw as Darwin's application of the principle to the realm of life, Huxley generalized that all existence was part of a universal harmony and order. As Lyell had shown, all geological features of earth could be seen, regardless of their magnitude and complexity, as conditions created by orderly and perpetual physical processes. Nature itself, Huxley reasoned, was the ideal; its orderly perfection was not imposed by mind, but existed in spite of mind. Mind was, in fact, unequal to it and perceived only dimly the radiant truth of cosmic harmony. The self was, if anything, outside the cosmic harmony, painfully unable to bring its consciousness and actions into conformity with the other patterns of existence. The visions of Lyell and Darwin, imperfect as they were, rumored a physical perfection and magnitude of process in nature beside which the self and the individual consciousness were of no particular moment. Self was the imperfection, the discontinuity. Anthropomorphic deities were far too arbitrary to rule such a universe; Huxley replaced them with a new form of physical perfection. In this sense Huxley was an idealist, for much as he believed science was demonstrating the rational order of the universe to be a reality, he knew he had posited a perfection in nature of a magnitude that was necessarily an article of faith, a synthesis of the mind.

Eight years after his lecture on the lobster, Huxley delivered "On the Physical Basis of Life" to an Edinburgh audience. One of the traumatic literary events of the Victorian age, this 1868 lay sermon examines the basis for a "physical, as well as an ideal, unity" for life (1:131). What many failed to understand was that Huxley's exploration of the hidden organization of living protoplasm was moving into a highly abstract realm of thought. Huxley was in search of the principle that would connect the animate with the inanimate. It is an essay on motion and unity. There is something almost frightening in the way comfortable distinctions determined more or less by convention merge into one another. Form and amorphousness, life and death, plant and animal, dissolve into the strange atmosphere of fluctuating protoplasmic metamorphosis. Beneath the illusory peace of the "wonderful noonday silence of a tropical forest" exists the surging protoplasmic whirl: "and could our ears catch the murmur of these tiny Maelstroms, as they whirl in the innumerable myriads of living cells which constitute each tree, we should be stunned, as with the roar of a great city" (1:136–37). The principle of organization, of fluctuating but orderly process, is epitomized in the phenomena of life.

While Huxley's essay is frequently listed as a classic of Victorian materialism, it is worth remembering that he considered his use of materialistic terminology a matter of necessity and convention, a means whereby to connect "thought with the other phaenomena of the universe" (1:164). He explicitly rejected materialism as an intellectual position involving "grave philosophical error" (1:155). As William Irvine has observed, his defense of free will in a brief phrase that suggested "volition counts for something as a condition of the course of events" was little more than perfunctory.[21] And as many other essays would show, Huxley was willing to admit he was a determinist as long as determinism was not confused with materialism.[22] Pursuing his point to its controversial extreme, he concluded that "thoughts . . . are the expression of molecular changes in that matter of life which is the source of our other vital phaenomena" (1:154). The progress of science, he declared, had always meant "the extension of the province of what we call matter and causation, and the concomitant gradual banishment from all regions of human thought of what we call spirit and spontaneity" (1:159). The object of this essay, as Huxley had revealed in his title, was to demonstrate that life forces could be quantified and examined from a physical point of view; he sought to demonstrate how life itself was part of the physical unity he believed to be the axiom of existence. Perhaps the ultimate end of such a quest was for that materialist monism which, R. G. Collingwood has argued, tries to eliminate the ambiguities caused by the problematic existence of mind in the universe.[23] If such is the case, we come to an impasse in Huxley's essay: he argues a convincing case for a materialism from which he attempts to extricate himself by citing Hume and Hamilton on the limits of philosophical inquiry.

Yet Huxley repudiated the assertion that he was a materialist, and it is at best an oversimplification to attribute to his writings a meaning that he explicitly denied they had. To examine the physical basis of life was to look at life in its physical or sensory manifestations; it did not imply that these alone defined life. Language and sensation were the symbolic representations of a deeper reality, and materialistic and spiritualistic terminologies alike were mere representations of phenomena in no way encompassed by the language in which they were presented. Charles Blinderman has noted Huxley's continual references to the necessary constrictions imposed on thought by language, and has suggested that semantic barriers and prejudices prevented the kind of explanation which could have made Huxley's point of view clear.[24] "Matter and spirit," Huxley had contended, "are but names for the imaginary substrata of groups of natural phaenomena" (1:160). The fault of materialism was that it mistook the image for the reality, the word for the thing itself. When he discussed the physical basis of mental activity, Huxley emphasized he was speaking in terms of equivalents; consciousness and molecular change were capable of being expressed in terms of one another.[25] If the materialistic terminology was successful in facilitating the investigation of physical nature, it was logical for the investigator to adopt it. This did not imply, however, that the investigator was making an ontological judgment in support of materialism.

Huxley's position was that the scientist might use the terminology of materialism while repudiating its philosophy. Like Sir William Hamilton, by whose philosophical criticism he had early been influenced, Huxley considered thought itself as a conditioning process, a human activity of establishing and identifying a reality, the opposite of which was the concept of the unconditioned or absolute. In his essay on Victor Cousin's *Cours de Philosophie* (1829), an essay Huxley frequently cited as an important influence on his early thought, Hamilton dismissed Cousin's thesis that the "Unconditioned" or "Absolute" could be a positive form of conscious knowledge, arguing that it was, rather, a negative idea formed in opposition to concrete, conditioned, knowledge. Thought processes were necessarily limited to the existential order of their origin:

> To think is to condition; and conditional limitation is the fundamental law of the possibility of thought. For, as the grayhound can not outstrip his shadow, nor (by a more appropriate simile) the eagle outsoar the atmosphere in which he floats, and by which alone he

may be supported; so the mind can not transcend that sphere of limitation, within and through which exclusively the possibility of thought is realized.[26]

For Huxley, scientific thought was part of the conditioning process in which the known and concrete were continually carved out of vague or unknown areas; to be unknown or unconditioned did not entitle a possibility to a separate status in the Absolute, for this was simply the apotheosis of ignorance.[27] At the same time, Huxley did not reject the existence of intuition or of abstract, ideal possibilities. He simply insisted that they were not positive or conditioned knowledge.

Consciousness was the barrier which posed insoluble problems for the uniformitarian ambitions of Huxley. Somehow it must be the product of causes, however infinite and complex; yet how was one to explain its apparent independence from the great chain of cause and effect? By what means did it express what appeared to be a unique will of its own, and how did consciousness come to reflect on experience? Huxley's respect for mental phenomena was immense, and he indicated that, forced to choose between absolute materialism and absolute idealism, he would opt for the latter (6:279). Reductive of the autonomy of mind as "On the Physical Basis" seemed, Huxley, in the duality of matter and mind, gave primacy to consciousness. In notes for his lecture series "The Physiology of Sensation and Motion," he declared that all phenomena of life could be shown to be either modes of motion or modes of consciousness.[28] Modes of motion were expressions of matter while modes of consciousness were expressions of mind, spirit, or soul. Language, he suggested, was made up of "symbols in consciousness of the molecular movements which take place in our brain." Its sources were the substrata of matter and consciousness which, while they generated mental activity, were themselves unknowable realities. Hence, while thought and sensation were inevitably accompanied by molecular mental activity, the sources of the activity remained undisclosed. Of matter and consciousness Huxley observed: "we know absolutely nothing of either of these substances as they are termed in the language of philosophy; . . . they are for us simply the unknown causes of phenomena which we call respectively material and mental." They were "absolutely unlike;" yet "matter acts on mind causing the phenomena of sensation and mind acts on matter causing the phenomena of voluntary motion."[29]

Huxley had created an interesting conundrum, for, if the molecular activity generated by external physical motion found its way via the sense organs to symbolization in the consciousness, what motion initiated the molecular activity which was expressed in human reason and emotion? How was one to determine whether molecular action or intellection occurred first, or whether there was any difference between them? While he acknowledged the materialistic doctrine that consciousness was simply a property of matter, Huxley declared that this was impossible to prove or disprove: modes of consciousness have "laws of their own," and these, he added, would be of a different kind than the laws of motion. He was certain only that consciousness did not operate spontaneously, that thoughts and emotions would prove to have origins in antecedent mental phenomena.

Two essays which followed Huxley's "On the Physical Basis" completed a series on mechanism. "On Descartes' 'Discourse' " (1870) and "On the Hypothesis that Animals are Automata" (1874) carefully examine the mechanical aspects of living organisms and very nearly reduce consciousness to a form of motion. While they are conservative by modern standards of cybernetics, Huxley's essays embrace Cartesian mechanism as a valid context in which to explore the mind as a mechanism of nature. He saw no harm in looking at man as "nothing but a machine," so long as one admitted that he was a machine capable of self-adjustment. While this was somewhat further than he was willing to go himself, he saw it as little more than the introduction of Calvinism into science. On the other hand, it was an "indisputable truth that what we call the material world is known to us only under the forms of the ideal world" (1:193). The association of consciousness and matter he found, as Descartes had, to be "an insoluble mystery" (1:194).

In his essay on animal automatism, an expansion of his Metaphysical Society lecture, "Has a Frog a Soul?" Huxley traced the history of the idea of animal mechanism beginning with Harvey and Descartes, and emphasized that the brain, a physiological mechanism, was also the seat of consciousness, and that the capacity of narcotics to influence thought processes demonstrated that in some way "thought and emotion are . . . the consequents of physical antecedents" (1:206). He went on to consider the case of a French soldier, his brain damaged in war, who had been reduced to a mechanism, concluding:

> We are conscious automata, endowed with free will in the only intelligible sense of that much-abused term—inasmuch as in many respects we are able to do as we like—but none the less parts of the great series of causes and effects which, in unbroken continuity, composes that which is, and has been, and shall be—the sum of existence. [1:244]

All states of consciousness were "immediately caused by molecular changes of the brain-substance" (1:244). The core of Huxley's position was the uniformity of nature, the existential probability that all phenomena fit into "the great series of causes and effects." Consciousness would otherwise be un-caused, and this would imply an exception that would shatter the axiom of universal order upon which Huxley has built his universe. Quoting Bonnet and Leibnitz, and citing Jonathan Edwards and Calvin, Huxley argued that man had often been thought of mechanistically (1:246–50).

Huxley was unable to solve the riddle of consciousness and, as a result, his concept of man was deeply divided. Physically part of the universe, mentally an outsider, Huxley's man re-flected a kind of alienation that foretold the modern existen-tialist dilemma of consciousness and existence. In an undated fragment, Huxley wrote:

> Physical man . . . is mere dust in the cosmic machinery—a bottle on the surface of the ocean of things both in magnitude and duration—a bye product of cosmic chemistry. He fits more or less well into the machinery, or it would crush him—but the machinery has no more special reference to him than to other living things.[30]

One thinks of those great natural escarpments in Hardy's novels by which the figures of humanity are so forlornly dwarfed. Like Descartes, Huxley finally rested on the paradox of duality of mind and matter, unable to conceive of a mode by which the two intersected. The riddle was locked, he believed, in the dynamics of molecular activity which reflected the dynamics of the cosmos. Human mental activity was in some way the mirror of activity of the universe, as in the Renaissance commonplace of man, the microcosm. While he could not affirm the existence of a deity, he did believe in the likelihood of innate ideas, which in his *Hume* he compared to instincts (6:131–33). Ultimately, man with his consciousness remained something of an anomaly in a great system which was in harmony with itself.

Two concepts of order emerge in Huxley's thought: the demonstrable, material order of physical nature, and its idealization, the theoretical transcendental order of cosmic eternity. He believed that the accumulating body of natural knowledge—such as that of Lyell and Darwin—was arrived at through an empirical process of investigation, the results of which appealed to human reason as reality or truth. Scientific law described the rational order of nature. And because all nature was interlocked, the laws of observable phenomena somehow approximated the order of the cosmos. In "The Connection of Biological Sciences with Medicine" (1881), he observed:

> In nature, nothing is at rest, nothing is amorphous; the simplest particle of that which men in their blindness are pleased to call "brute matter" is a vast aggregate of molecular mechanisms performing complicated movements of immense rapidity, and sensitively adjusting themselves to every change in the surrounding world. Living matter differs from other matter in degree and not in kind; the microcosm repeats the macrocosm; and one chain of causation connects the nebulous original of suns and planetary systems with the protoplasmic foundation of life and organisation. [3:371]

We approach here a theory of correspondences. Protoplasm becomes a microscopic reflection of the transcendent order Huxley theorized as the fundamental property of the universe. Unlike anything one might find in Hume or even Berkeley, Huxley's universe exists in a perfection that suggests the divine rational order of Spinoza's nature, but not its humanity. There is no hidden anthropomorphism or consciousness here. It is in a cold, crystalline harmony that nature radiates its dazzling perfection.

The speculative drive of Huxley's thought achieved visions

that could be quite arresting. Order seems always to be the highest state in natural and, indeed, cosmic phenomena. If we were to search for a Huxleyan equivalent to Spinoza's enormous machine of the universe, to Kant's *ding an sich*, Berkeley's Divine Mind, or, even, Spencer's Unknowable, we could come no closer than that vision Huxley offered in the relatively late essay "Scientific and Pseudo-Scientific Realism" (1887):

> If a being endowed with perfect intellectual and aesthetic faculties, but devoid of the capacity for suffering pain, either physical or moral, were to devote his utmost powers to the investigation of nature, the universe would seem to him to be a sort of kaleidoscope, in which, at every successive moment of time, a new arrangement of parts of exquisite beauty and symmetry would present itself; and each of them would show itself to be the logical consequence of the preceding arrangement, under the conditions which we call the laws of nature. Such a speculator might well be filled with that *Amor intellectualis Dei*, the beatific vision of the *vita contemplativa*, which some of the greatest thinkers of all ages, Aristotle, Aquinas, Spinoza, have regarded as the only conceivable eternal felicity; and the vision of illimitable suffering, as if sensitive beings were unregarded animalcules which had got between the bits of glass of the kaleidoscope, which mars the prospect to us poor mortals, in no wise alters the fact that order is lord of all, and disorder only a name for that part of order which gives us pain. [5:73–74]

In one of the remarkable visions of order to be found in Victorian literature, Huxley imagines the infinite, ordered machine of eternity. His ultimate vision is perhaps most nearly contained in this single, concentrated intuition. Here lies the spiritual object of the scientist, the object of Huxley's own religious instincts. Here lies imperfect man as well, unable to partake of the transcendentalist order of absolute beauty and truth. The perfect knowledge and the perfect logic are symmetrical, but, unlike the static eighteenth-century visions of the deists, the whole is in a perpetual flux, an infinite sequence of self-rearrangement. The real absolute in the passage is neither matter nor force, but order: "order is lord of all." Huxley fused the real and the ideal in the profound and beatific logic of existence. We approach strangely near to the divine.

At the same time, the passage, in its very stress on order, also suggests a determinism that is rigid and inhuman in its disregard for pain and suffering, which are associated with the flaws of sensitive beings, their inability to harmonize with the universal order. One sees clearly why Huxley, who strove for years to glean a new principle of ethics from natural truths, was unsuccessful: nothing that drives such a great mechanism could provide a special reference to the sufferings of humanity. Humanity has shrunk to "animalcule" insignificance, cursed with pain, with the original sin of consciousness. Pain, in turn, becomes a reminder to man of his own imperfection, of his inability to attain to the ultimate vision, of his disharmony with the universe. Already we find Huxley advancing to his final position in "Evolution and Ethics," where he urged man to revolution against nature and argued that the man-created order of civilization must be accepted as fundamentally at odds with the great cosmic processes of the universe.

A nasty irony hovers about Huxley's great metaphor, however, for the kaleidoscope itself works by an optical illusion, and what through mirrors and lenses is seen as an intricate and fluctuating and spectacularly colored pattern of geometrical order is in reality but a pitiful assembly of tumbling bits of glass. Huxley had played upon himself a cosmic joke that ultimately supported his lifelong contention that human perception and comprehension were prey to endless illusions. The kaleidoscope was possibly the fitting symbol for scientific instrumentation, an imposition of order on otherwise random phenomena. The order that Huxley so yearned for was conceivably nothing more than the asymmetrical tumbling of cosmic flotsam, arranged, as Hume has suggested, by the deluded intellect. This irony justified the principles of agnosticism. Order had to be an article of faith.

Emotion plays no role in the great vision of the *Amor intellectualis Dei*; perfect intellectual and aesthetic faculties along with the absence of the capacity for suffering moral or physical pain are the sole requisites. Such a state is essentially the annihilation of the self. But it is not really mechanistic or Calvinistic in its emphasis on aesthetic and intellectual perfection; rather it is in this sense much closer to the two traditions that fascinated Huxley in "Evolution and Ethics" (1893)—Buddhism and Stoicism. Asserting that modern thought was making a fresh start from the twin traditions of Indian and Greek philosophy, he suggested that the radical idealism of the Indian philosophical tradition and the stringent materialism of the Stoical view had merged in their ultimate objects. "I find it difficult to discover," Huxley decided, "any very great difference between Apatheia and Nirvana" (9:76). Both states, the highest attainable in the two pre-Christian philosophical traditions, emphasized the transitoriness of existence; there was neither the desire nor the possibility for salvation. Both stressed the illusory nature of human perceptions; both brought order to human existence by deemphasizing, even eliminating, emotion. The Indian tradition, which Huxley saw as "a metaphysical *tour de force*" deeper even than the idealism of Berkeley, cultivated a notion of perfection which was "rather a state of painlessness than of happiness . . . the negation of perturbing emotion" (9:108). Stoicism was a philosophy of men who had cast off all illusions and foregone the childish indulgence of despair.

Huxley considered both philosophical traditions primitive; but he retained important elements from them in developing his own philosophical position on man's relationship with nature. The notion that disorder was "only a name for that part of order which gives us pain," focused on the conflict between the ultimate order of nature and the microcosmic order formulated in the sensibility of man; it revealed Huxley midway between the earlier writings in which he advocated natural law as an ethical ideal and the final position he took in "Evolution and Ethics," advocating human revolution against the cosmic process or the essential force of nature.

Huxley's thought was further complicated by the new teleology which he originally associated with Darwin's theory of natural selection and later contrasted with the Logos of ancient Stoic philosophy. In "The Genealogy of Animals" (1869), he suggested that teleology did not necessarily assume a spiritual source:

> It is necessary to remember that there is a wider Teleology, which is not touched by the doctrine of Evolution, but is actually based upon the fundamental proposition of Evolution. That proposition is, that the whole world, living and not living, is the result of the

99

mutual interaction, according to definite laws, of the forces possessed by the molecules of which the primitive nebulosity of the universe was composed. If this be true, it is no less certain that the
existing world lay, potentially, in the cosmic vapour; and that a
sufficient intelligence could, from a knowledge of the properties of
the molecules of that vapor, have predicted, say the state of the
Fauna of Britain in 1869, with as much certainty as one can say what
will happen to the vapour of the breath on a cold winter's day.
(2:110)

It was possible that a creative, self-organizing potential was
inherent in the primitive cosmos, present in the very structure
of the primordial matter; the evolution of life itself would have
been predestined. Huxley's teleology never developed very far,
but while his uniformitarian convictions led him to reject the
possibility of a supernatural first cause, he was willing to
entertain the possibility that matter was becoming ever more
conscious of itself.[31] In his final, unpublished, essay, "Mr.
Balfour's Attack on Agnosticism: II," written in 1895, shortly
before his death, Huxley still found teleology an important argument. Human reason itself, he asserted, was the microcosm
of the rational order of the universe. The order of the universe,
made conscious through its own evolution in the human mind,
was "reason *in excelsis*—a reason so far superior to that incarnate in man, that the profoundest philosopher stands to it in the
relation of a schoolboy stumbling through his primer of arith-
metic to an adept in higher mathematics."[32] This was Huxley's
final vision, the insight he had struggled to grasp throughout
life, the divine "reason *in excelsis*" of his great kaleidoscope.
The gods themselves, according to the "great ancient thinkers,"
were "products, not factors, in the evolution of the cosmos."

iii. agnosticism

The agnostic principle became the only theory of knowledge
adequate to contain Huxley's concept of order. While it certified
the precision of an exclusively empirical approach to natural
phenomena, with the corresponding use of materialistic terminology, it alternately validated the kind of speculative
rationalism Huxley embraced as one of the great objects or

motivating forces of the scientific researcher. "The reconciliation of physics and metaphysics," he argued, "lies in . . . the confession by physics that all the phaenomena of Nature are, in their ultimate analysis, known to us only as facts of consciousness; in the admission by metaphysics, that the facts of consciousness are, practically, interpretable only by the methods and the formulae of physics" (1:194). The term "reconciliation" is somewhat optimistically applied here, for what Huxley was describing was the existence of two realities manifested in separate continua. His argument did not so much reconcile physics to metaphysics as assert the impossibility of reconciliation. The relationship between ultimate truth and specific fact had become one of paradox, characterized by a mutual inapplicability. The very success of Victorian science, which had made the empirical, inductive approach to phenomena so intense and compelling, had rendered the ultimate nature of matter a profound mystery. The trees of nature were emerging with exciting clarity as the great forest passed into indeterminate vagueness. Huxley had recognized that as physical science moved closer to the material objects of its attention, achieving greater clarity and certainty, the ontological considerations were becoming impossible to deal with definitively. Science and philosophy had parted ways. Who labored after ultimates must relinquish the claim to fact; and, conversely, who labored after fact must resist the temptation to universalize. Agnosticism irrevocably severed the bridge between physics and metaphysics, between the natural and the supernatural. The absence of any intersecting point or area other than consciousness meant that the agnostic was on the verge of a perpetual ambivalence—an alternate argument for each theory, a dual reality for every phenomenon. Much as Huxley wished, his science and philosophy were not one.

As a term, "agnosticism" had its origin not in the dispassionate, intellectual effort of Huxley to develop a theory of knowledge, but in the dramatic, somewhat emotional, atmosphere of the early days of the Metaphysical Society, where British intellectuals met, between 1869 and 1880, to debate and discuss a variety of philosophical and religious issues.[33] Whatever agnosticism was to mean later, its origin lay in Huxley's effort to define his identity as a scientist. It was the culminating point of Huxley's idea of the scientist, with both a personal and a professional significance. In his account of the origin of the term, related in the first of the three 1889 essays on agnosticism, he stressed the biographical logic which led to his antignostic position. We are told of the neglected child whose education was interrupted and "who, intellectually, was left, for some years, altogether to his own devices" (5:235). Out of an atmosphere of neglect which typically haunted his returns to the past, Huxley emerges as a young boy influenced by early readings of Guizot's *History of Civilization* and Sir William Hamilton's review-essay "On the Philosophy of the Unconditioned" (5:235–36). He traces his intellectual passage through natural science to the philosophies of Hume and Kant, characterizing his development as an allegorical progress in the manner of Dante:

> I had, and have, the firmest conviction that I never left the "verace via"—the straight road; and that this road led nowhere else but into the dark depths of a wild and tangled forest. And though I have found leopards and lions in the path; though I have made abundant acquaintance with the hungry wolf, that "with privy paw devours apace and nothing said," as another great poet says of the ravening beast; and though no friendly spectre has even yet offered his guidance, I was, and am, minded to go straight on, until I either come out on the other side of the wood, or find there is no other side to it, at least, none attainable by me. [5:238–39]

The concept that Huxley had developed of agnosticism took on an immense moral significance. The allegory contains nothing to identify it substantively with agnosticism; it might as well have been the utterance of Bunyan himself on his own Christian progress. Huxley is stressing agnosticism here less as an intellectual or philosophical position than as a culmination of his own spiritual and scientific progress. It becomes a justification for his personal and professional life. He strikes the characteristic dramatic pose of the self amid forces of opposition; but we should also note the emotional overtones of the rhetoric, the dark, violent images which suggest alienation and abandonment. Ultimately, the allegory is as applicable to the deep personal sense of isolation Huxley associated with his neglected youth as it is to the intellectual isolation he suffered from his less than popular stand as an "unbeliever." Agnosticism, as a unique and logical fusion of Huxley's personal and professional experience, can be understood to represent him emotionally as well as intellectually.

We find further evidence of the complicated origins of the term in Huxley's account of the coining of "agnostic" in 1869, during his early days as a founder of the Metaphysical society:

> Every variety of philosophical and theological opinion was represented [at the Metaphysical Society], and expressed itself with entire openness; most of my colleag[u]es were *-ists* of one sort or another; and, however kind and friendly they might be, I, the man without a rag of a label to cover himself with, could not fail to have some of the uneasy feelings which must have beset the historical fox when, after leaving the trap in which his tail remained, he presented himself to his normally elongated companions. So I took thought, and invented what I conceived to be the appropriate title of "agnostic." It came into my head as suggestively antithetic to the "gnostic" of Church history, who professed to know so much about the very things of which I was ignorant; and I took the earliest opportunity of parading it at our Society, to show that I, too, had a tail, like the other foxes. To my great satisfaction, the term took. [5:239]

Apart from the Huxleyan dramatic presentation of the self in conflict, the passage is perhaps most noteworthy for its humor. The new term apparently arose as much from Huxley's desire for an intellectual costume to display at the meetings of the Metaphysical Society as from any serious effort to conceptualize his philosophical position. The imagery of clothing and the fox tail suggests that he was interested in acquiring a suitable attire for parading in what must have been one of the most exciting intellectual promenades of the century. And few could have been more chic than Huxley, whose agnostic covering bordered on the risqué. The homely Cinderella at the end of "Science and Morals" had finally been invited to the grand ball, and Huxley fit her out in that scanty gown, agnosticism, that seemed to reveal and conceal just the right parts of her youthful figure, to the delight of her peers and the chagrin of her elders.

It is doubtful whether another Victorian word inspired so many different reactions or was subject to so many different interpretations. Adopted by supporters and opponents alike, agnosticism became associated with widely conflicting ideas and values; frequently heralded as the philosophy of a new honesty, it was as often reviled as the symbol of cultural and moral decay. And while it crystallized attitudes and intellectual positions for a variety of like-minded thinkers, including John Tyndall, Leslie Stephen and W. K. Clifford, it also provided a target—although not a very steady one—for the criticism of clerics like Wace, positivists like Frederick Harrison, and a number of statesmen-essayists such as Gladstone, the Duke of Argyll, and A. J. Balfour.[34] At the same time, Huxley, as D. W. Dockrill has demonstrated, was not entirely the originator of the idea of agnosticism; and Huxley himself frequently disclaimed any philosophical innovations on his part, citing precendents as far back as Socrates.[35] Indeed, its very success as a term seems to have been due to its suggestiveness, its communication of an attitude, its ambiguity. It was not so much a philosophical as a Victorian word; as nearly everyone agreed, its essential philosophical content could be found in the scepticism of Hume. Yet, the word "agnostic" also represented something entirely new in that it formalized and materialized many of the doubts raised by the higher criticism of the Bible and the science of Lyell and Darwin. It was a historical term as well, reflecting back on history the wide successes of the new Victorian knowledge. It captured the ambiguity of those who felt the loss of certainty, felt the impact of modern doubt which invalidated many of the most basic assumptions of the past, and yet sought to salvage possibilities and such socially important Victorian conditions as a morality based on theistic belief.

One of the problems of Huxley's agnosticism lies in the thinness of its intellectual content. There is no matrix of ideas which might allow one to grasp its essential meaning through the analysis of a body of formal principles. When examining its philosophical significance, we are forced to discuss its probable implications or to retreat to a range of related, though by no means identical, positions; to those, for example, of empiricism, uniformitarianism, utilitarianism, or scepticism. For the most part, Huxley's agnosticism may be considered formally only by approaching what it is *not*. This is because Huxley explained what he meant by way of controversy and because the term itself is a negation. None of his 1889 essays on agnosticism were expository in any formal sense; rather they corrected the mistaken attempts of opponents such as Wace and Harrison to formalize and then attack the concept. A good deal of Huxley's discussion on the meaning of agnosticism is spent in clarifying what it does not mean—that it is not a sect, that it is not equivalent to materialism, that it is not amoral. On his very deathbed, Huxley was explaining to A. J. Balfour that the agnostic did not hold the universe to be irrational, nor deny the possibility of a supernatural world.[36]

As Dockrill has shown, Huxley himself was not always clear about the precise meaning of agnosticism, alternately presenting it as a theory on the necessity of metaphysical ignorance and as strictly a method of inquiry.[37] In the essay "Agnosticism" (1889), Huxley recognized both a positive and a negative aspect to the term:

> Agnosticism, in fact, is not a creed, but a method, the essence of which lies in the rigorous application of a single principle. . . . Positively the principle may be expressed: In matters of the intellect, follow your reason as far as it will take you, without regard to any other consideration. And negatively: In matters of the intellect do not pretend that conclusions are certain which are not demonstrated or demonstrable. [5:245–46]

Huxley's agnostic conviction on the mutual inapplicability of physical and metaphysical ideas was consistent with the restrictions placed on reason in the philosophies of both William Hamilton and Henry Mansel. Familiar with *On the Limits of Religious Thought*, Huxley declared Mansel an "eminently agnostic thinker" (5:236n). In his lectures, Mansel had acknowledged the incapacity of reason to satisfy the demands of belief. "Let Religion begin where it will," he observed, "it must begin with that which is above Reason."[38] Reason was not equal to the defense of religion, for the infinite and the finite belonged to different existential orders. Not of the realm of reason, religion could neither be proved nor disproved by rational operations, a distinction which Huxley had seen as the essence of the agnostic's position. Mansel argued that "the coexistence of the

Infinite and the Finite, in any manner whatever, is inconceivable by reason . . . We may seek as we will for a 'Religion within the limits of bare Reason'; and we shall not find it; simply because no such thing exists."[39] Mansel had also seen a dualism in the conflict between two forms of experience—physical and mental "In the one," he held, "we are conscious of a chain of phenomenal effects; in the other of *self*, as an acting and originating cause."[40] This corresponded to the conflict between matter and consciousness which Huxley was unable to resolve. But Mansel gave primacy to the human will in the definition of self and in the interaction between matter and consciousness, where Huxley considered will something of an illusion with little real power to escape a determined chain of psychical events.

As an epistemological method, agnosticism was not so much a theory as an attitude, seeking not truth, which was an absolute, but truthfulness, which was the only possibility in a consciousness severely limited by its own physical embodiment. Hannah Arendt argues that after the Cartesian consecration of doubt "the loss of certainty of truth ended in a new, entirely unprecedented zeal for truthfulness" in the modern world, for the doubt that human reason and senses might achieve truth or ontological certainty inspired an alternative emphasis on "truthfulness" as the remaining human capability.[41] As we have seen, Huxley believed the order of the universe to transcend human reason; it was left to man to attempt to be truthful. Thus one followed one's reason as far as it might take him, but did not hope it would attain the ultimate truth or "gnosis" (5:239). Agnosticism argued that man could rely on empirical method to determine a limited knowledge of reality and that, integrating sense experience with human reason, the careful investigator could achieve a conditional certainty.

As an argument against Christianity, agnosticism is perhaps least interesting, if only because the argument against the case for the miraculous had by Huxley's day become fairly well established. Huxley expanded on the argument throughout *Science and Christian Tradition*, volume 5 of his *Collected Essays*; he focused on the integral part the miraculous had played in the Christian tradition, observing that there seemed to be an inverse relation between supernatural and natural knowledge: "As the latter has widened, gained in precision and in trustworthiness, so has the former shrunk, grown vague and questionable" (5:7). It was "becoming less and less possible for the man who puts his faith in scientific methods of ascertaining truth, and is accustomed to have that faith justified by daily experience, to be consciously false to his principle in any matter" (5:37). The successes of scientific method had rendered the positions of a priori disciplines vague and uncompelling. "In spite of prayers for the success of our arms and *Te Deums* for victory," Huxley observed, "our real faith is in big battalions and keeping our powder dry." (5:38). There was a compelling practicality to the empirical or scientific approach to problems, which argued strongly in favor of the exclusive relevance of natural knowledge in the problems of life. On a very basic level, Huxley justified his agnosticism on the strength of its utility: "The justification of the Agnostic principle lies in the success which follows upon its application, whether in the field of natural, or in that of civil, history" (5:310). This argument of success gave Huxley confidence in the force of the agnostic position.[42]

Another dimension of Huxley's agnosticism was its deep moral implication. While Dr. Wace and the Duke of Argyll were attacking agnostic thought in the guise of defenders of faith and morality, Huxley was declaring his position to be the only moral view possible, given the nature of the scriptures. In the same essay, "Agnosticism," Huxley took a twofold view of Christianity, arguing that it was an appropriate "ideal" and worthy of an individual's faith, but that such an individual should not "delude himself with the notion that his faith is evidence of the objective reality of that in which he trusts" (5:245). In history, he noted, the positive aspect of the Christian ethic was cancelled out by the insistence of Christian authorities "that honest disbelief in their more or less astonishing creeds is a moral offence, indeed a sin of the deepest dye" (5:241). And he pointed to the cruelty and inhumanity which attended the history of the Church in its dealings with non-believers. While agnosticism was "not a creed, but a method," its fundamental principle was "of great antiquity"; it was "as old as Socrates; as old as the writer who said, 'Try all things, hold fast by that which is good' " (5:245). Truthfulness was always for Huxley the cornerstone of morality. In "Possibilities and Impossibilities," written in 1891, two years after "Agnosticism," Huxley maintained that while the miracle of the loaves and fishes could not be rejected as an "*a priori* impossibility"; "we not only have a right to demand, but are morally bound to require, strong evidence in its favor before we even take it into serious consideration" (5:201).

Furthermore, agnosticism was a social ideal, quite apart from its methodological and theoretical aspects: "The apostolic injunction to 'suffer fools gladly' should be the rule of life of a true agnostic. I am deeply conscious how far I myself fall short of this ideal, but it is my personal conception of what agnostics ought to be" (5:247). Huxley is advocating a proper code of conduct as well—a code he found particularly uncongenial to his own personality. The degree of agnosticism varied from individual to individual, "according to individual knowledge and capacity, and according to the general condition of science" (5:246). Because the scientific basis of assent was continually in flux, the agnostic occupied a particularly unstable position; new knowledge inevitably meant new possibilities for his outlook. Theoretically agnosticism, in keeping with its scientific base, was to be in a continual state of development: "That which is unproven to-day may be proven by the help of new discoveries to-morrow. The only negative fixed points will be those negations which flow from the demonstrable limitation of our faculties" (5:246). No single individual in this sense could ever measure up to the agnostic ideal, since, by implication, the only perfect agnostic would be one who had mastered the contents of all the sciences at their most advanced stages. If agnosticism, as Huxley indicated, was to be considered as a moral ideal, if science was to be the basis for a new morality, the prospect for complications seemed infinite. For the central principle of an ethic must lie in its stability and universal accessibility. If morality were to be made somehow dependent on the content of the sciences—a proposition which Huxley often seemed to be advocating but never specified—not only would every individual be forced to entertain an entirely relative morality, but the very concept of morality could hardly escape from being confused with that empirical ideal of the laboratory—expediency. Herbert Spencer had fostered his evolutionary theory of social development on the basis of struggle, or what he believed was the dynamic of evolution. Huxley was not advocating the kind of wholesale competition that dominated the thought of the social Darwinists. In "The Struggle for Existence in Human Society" (1888), he wryly observed, "We are told to take comfort from the reflection that the terrible struggle for existence tends to final good, and that the suffering of the ancestor is paid for by the increased perfection of the progeny. . . . it is not clear what compensation the *Eohippus* gets for his sorrows in the fact that, some millions of years afterwards, one of his descendants wins the Derby" (9:198–99). In his final position on the ethical foundation of civilization, in "Evolution and Ethics," Huxley considered science more as a tool which would enable man to modify the forces of nature, and deemphasized the relationship between science and ethics. Although Huxley rejected Spencer's a priori applications of biology to society, he steadily maintained that scientific insights should somehow influence moral behavior. He never managed to specify precisely how this was to be carried out.

In the second of the three 1889 essays on his principle, "Agnosticism: a Rejoinder," Huxley did not notably expand on its theoretical basis. He continued his controversy with Dr. Wace over the question of the historical accuracy of the gospels, offering such insights as the technical unlikelihood that Christ could have died from crucifixion in the mere six hours that it reportedly took (5:280). The second half of the essay concentrates on the evolution of Christianity from a "sect of the Nazarenes" to the position delineated by Justinian in the second century. The essay is mildly interesting, but unsatisfying to anyone interested in determining the meaning of agnosticism. However, it becomes clear that agnosticism was for Huxley a historical concept as well. In the third of the 1889 essays, "Agnosticism and Christianity," Huxley again stressed the moral basis for agnostic thought, claiming that agnosticism expressed "absolute faith in the validity of a principle, which is as much ethical as intellectual" (5:310). The principle could be stated in the following way: "it is wrong for a man to say that he is certain of the objective truth of any proposition unless he can produce evidence which logically justifies that certainty" (5:310). Huxley was asserting that there was an ethics of historical analysis, a morality of criticism.

The historical argument of agnosticism, ironically, was inspired partly by John Henry Newman. It is doubtful whether a more damaging or virulent attack on Newman has ever been launched than Huxley's "Agnosticism and Christianity," in which Huxley formed that strangely perceptive, insidious, and unilateral alliance with Newman the year before the cardinal's death. Actually, the perceptiveness was Leslie Stephen's; musing over Huxley's controversy with Dr. Wace on the biblical account of the Gadarene Swine, Stephen wrote to Huxley in April 1889 about Newman's tracts, pointing out how Newman had shown the historical Christ to be no more than a "Jewish prophet of the usual kind": "If you have anything more to say about it, it would perhaps be worth your while to show that you have a Cardinal to back you."[43] Already at battle with Newman's disciple, W. S. Lilly, Huxley pursued the matter. Primed with knowledge of the higher criticism of German scholarship, with the work of Strauss, Baur, Reuss, and Volkmar, he descended on Newman's tracts and the *Essay on Development*, flushing out the perfect argument for his own case against "Ecclesiasticism." He demonstrated that Newman's path to Rome had largely been negotiated by retracing the historical process that led to the split between the Church of England and the Church of Rome. Quoting Newman's finding that "the Christianity of history is not Protestantism," and that "to be deep in history is to cease to be a Protestant"; Huxley added that the " 'Christianity of history is not' Romanism; and that to be deeper in history is to cease to be a Romanist" (5:343). He went on to declare: "If, with the one hand, Dr. Newman has destroyed Protestantism, he has annihilated Romanism with the other; and the total result of his ambidextral efforts is to shake Christianity to its foundations" (5:343–44).[44] The logic of Huxley's argument was sound, for who could deny that if the path from Rome to England had been a divergent one, the path from Galilee to Rome had been equally so. Huxley argued that an impartial consideration of the evidence "must refuse the authority of Jesus to anything more than the Nazarenism of James and Peter and John" (5:345). If Newman believed that his arguments led to the alternative either of Romanism or "infidelity"—which Huxley preferred to call agnosticism— Huxley declared he merely took the alternative path. "If I were called upon to compile a Primer of 'Infidelity,' I think I should save myself trouble by making a selection from [*Tracts for the Times*], and from the *Essay on Development* by the same author" (5:333n).

Writing to Joseph Hooker in May of 1889, Huxley commented on "Agnosticism and Christianity" which was to appear in the June issue of the *Nineteenth Century*: "By the way, I want you to enjoy my wind-up with Wace in this month's *Nineteenth* in the reading as much as I have in the writing. It's as full of malice as an egg is full of meat, and my satisfaction in making Newman my accomplice has been unutterable. That man is the slipperiest sophist I have ever met with. Kingsley was entirely right about him" (*LL*, 2:240). The letter revealed that the grand attack on Newman was not without a hefty dose of spite on Huxley's part. The agnostic position was capable of becoming a screen in the sense that, while Huxley would have us believe his essay "Agnosticism and Christianity" was a frank consideration of Christian belief from an agnostic's philosophical position, it justified an attack on Newman's integrity.

Agnosticism for Huxley, then, was both a philosophical position and a loose code. Philosophically, it stood for the strict application of empirical method as a condition for determining truth, and rejected observations or declarations which could not be rationally verified. It denied the possibility of rationally determining absolute truth for the simple reason that human faculties, as both Hamilton and Mansel had argued, were inadequate to measure apparent infinities of space and time. Huxley's agnostic principle clearly was focused on humanity and had little to say about ontological questions other than to consider the absurdity of viewing them through the considerably limited vision of finite man. A half century before Camus, Huxley observed: "Generation after generation, philosophy has been doomed to roll the stone uphill; and, just as all the world swore it was at the top, down it has rolled to the bottom again.

All this is written in innumerable books; and he who will toil through them will discover that the stone is just where it was when the work began" (5:312). The remarkable success of empirical method in describing and defining physical nature with precision, concreteness, and in verifiable terms, had left metaphysics and religion vague and uncertain by comparison.

At the same time, Huxley's agnosticism rested on a paradox, that of consciousness. The ambiguity of consciousness as either a physical or purely mental form of activity left Huxley with the ultimate paradox regarding the nature of reality. As early as 1870, he noted in his address on Descartes that it was an "indisputable truth" that the material world was known to the intellect only under the forms of the ideal world, and that one's knowledge of the soul was more intimate and certain than his knowledge of the body (1:193). Huxley qualified his use of the word "soul" by adding a footnote in his 1893 edition which defined soul as "the sum of states of consciousness of the individual" (1:193). It hardly mattered. While it was impossible to prove things existed other than in the consciousness, the mind could disregard the ultimate question and operate on the symbolic levels of language and sensation offered within the empirical disciplines of science and historical and social criticism.

Agnosticism does not emerge as a philosophical system, particularly in the context of Huxley's own work. It was an idea developed largely under the pressure of conflict and controversy. Within Huxley's thought, it was as much an answer to his opponent as an idea that unified the basic strands of his nontechnical essays. More basic to his vision was the idea of order; everywhere he looked he saw arrangements and constructions that verified his rationalist convictions. He saw Victorian science as a vast new argument for the existence of rationality and order and drew great spiritual consolation from this vision. Civilization, he believed, was undergoing the most important revolution of its history, which he presented as a continual process of the freeing of the intellect. In the "Prologue" to *Controverted Questions* (1892), he maintained that the historical process of civilization revealed a progressively expanding realm for rationality. The goal of the Renaissance humanists, whether they recognized it or not, was, he observed, "the attainment of the complete intellectual freedom of the antique philosopher" (5:14). The Christian tradition was the prison of the intellect, and science was preparing to free the mind from the mires of the past.

It was as an epistemological principle that agnosticism supported Huxley's concept of order. In his important essay "The Progress of Science: 1837–1887," originally written as part of T. H. Ward's *The Reign of Queen Victoria* celebrating the golden jubilee of Victoria's reign, he declared that the ultimate object of the physical inquirer was:

> the discovery of the rational order which pervades the universe; the method consists of observation and experiment . . . for the determination of the facts of Nature; of inductive and deductive reasoning for the discovery of their mutual relations and connection. [1:60]

He celebrated scientists as individuals whose pulses were stirred by

> the love of knowledge and joy of discovery of the causes of things sung by the old poet—the supreme delight of extending the realm of law and order ever farther towards the unattainable goals of the infinitely great and the infinitely small. [1:53]

Huxley traced the great ideas of Victorian science as part of a grand historical progress uncovering order and unity in the universe. The essay was thus an epitome of Victorian optimism and faith in the infinite possibilities of progress. Its final point was that men of general culture might now understand that the order of natural phenomena was an "unbroken sequence" extending throughout the duration of the universe (1:129). Huxley envisioned a grand new social order established by the triumph of the physical sciences; his dream was in many respects a distillation representative of that great Victorian dream of an ordered Empire. The successes that studded the pages of his essay were those of the agnostic principle, filling the universe with physical law, bestowing on society a "new birth of time, [a] new Nature begotten by science upon fact" (1:51).

IV

Man's Place in Nature

i. natural man

Huxley's *Evidence as to Man's Place in Nature* (1863) and "Evolution and Ethics" (1893) were not only important contributions to Victorian thought on the question of man's relationship with nature; they were also reflections of Huxley's own unique intellectual development, which took some dramatic and revealing turns over a period of thirty years. The question of nature was very much on the Victorian mind. As Joseph Warren Beach has shown, the earlier enthusiasm of the Romantics who were able to extract a range of moral, metaphysical, and aesthetic values from the bond between self and nature steadily diminished as the century wore on.[1] Nature seemed increasingly indifferent to human concerns, and, as Beach has demonstrated, varying degrees of hostility and suspicion were expressed by such mid-Victorians as Arnold, Tennyson, and Browning toward the Romantic idealization of nature. The mid-century ambivalence of poems such as Arnold's "In Utrumque Paratus" or the fifty-sixth stanza of Tennyson's *In Memoriam* revealed that the idea of nature was undergoing significant change in the cultural imagination. Since they were intimately bound to the idea of nature, concepts of man and of "self" were changing. If man were simply the product of natural forces, Tennyson declared, then he was a monstrosity, a discord, who with his love, justice, and truth, was in conflict with the realities of existence.[2] Arnold, doubly ambiguous, with two final stanzas to a poem with two alternatives, concluded in the second half of "In Utrumque Paratus" that if earth and man existed as mere parts of "the wild unfather'd mass," man's self-image was dangerously alien to the reality of his origins.[3] Both Tennyson and Arnold, in spite of the very different objects of their two poems, were pointing to the overwhelming problem of human identity implicit in the growing dichotomy between man and nature.

Huxley's essays were very much a part of the literature that undertook a fresh examination of the concept of man in light of the developments of nineteenth-century science. Nearly every essay he wrote took into account some new dimension of the idea of nature or generated insights into the physical and psychological aspects of man. His perspective, while different from those of Arnold and Tennyson, carried his thought in directions that frequently crossed the intellectual paths of the two poets; in fact, his most significant early consideration of the concept of man—*Man's Place in Nature*—was concerned with some of the central issues of *In Memoriam*. The striking distinction was that Huxley was in search of a very different man. While Tennyson was in quest of the spiritual self, the essence within his own identity capable of forming a mystical bond with the dead Hallam, Huxley was in quest of the biological self, the physical unity one shared with the organic world. If we were to look for the two poles of the Victorian self-image, we could probably do no better than to consider these two works.

Contrary to what many thought, Huxley did not write *Man's Place in Nature* to take vengeance on the age or to "degrade" man, as a reviewer in the *Athenaeum* declared.[4] His reasons for undertaking such a work were complex, stemming from an internal struggle in the British scientific hierarchy, from his desire to publish his own ideas and findings in primate anatomy and paleontology and, most important, from his belief that recent scientific research efforts might be integrated to provide a portrait of man that was remarkably new, yet unquestionably valid. The success of his work was immediate and substantial in the scientific world and helped him to consolidate his position as one of the major exponents of British anatomy and physical anthropology, gaining him a wide reputation as a leading theoretician in the philosophy and methodology of the biological sciences. Huxley became the first to construct a clear and logical image of biological man. As Houston Peterson has pointed out, it was an "epoch-making" work, the classical statement on the anthropoid nature of man.[5]

Recognized among colleagues, including Darwin, as a brilliant work, comparable to but bolder than Lyell's *The Antiquity of Man*, which was also published in January 1863, Huxley's *Man's Place in Nature* formulated in its concise and lucid prose the truly astonishing theory that man was in fact an animal, an organism bound so intimately to nature as to occupy a common biological order with organisms generally regarded by Victorians as brutes.

It would be difficult to overestimate the far-reaching implications of such an idea, implications which would be recognized in disciplines far removed from the specialized borders of its origin. Huxley was by no means the originator of the concept of man as animal, however. While his idea would gradually be reflected in a spectrum of religious, political, historical, and philosophical thought, its origins led back to ancient mythologies and ancient science alike. The archetypal battle between Lapiths and Centaurs was the primal struggle between civilization and brutality, and was carved in the marble of the Parthenon beside the religious festival of Athena to remind men of the privileges and responsibilities of civilization. Studies of man as animal, as old as Aristotle's classifications and as Galen's human anatomy—which was based on the anatomy of the Barbary Ape—led in the Renaissance to the new dissection, where men like Leonardo and Vesalius slowly divested studies of man from their theological and spiritual overtones by examining him as an anatomical object. Always in the ancient world human function had been linked to a vital principle which was the derivate of some higher entity or cosmic force. William Harvey, while not abandoning vitalism, established circulation in the seventeenth century as a phenomenon common to varied organisms, possessed by man and animal alike; human physiology was thus wedded to animal physiology. Locating vital activities of life in physical, muscular activity, Harvey dispensed with the need for a spiritual explanation, even though he still held spiritual influence accountable for the motion of life. By the end of the Renaissance, man had emerged in the thought of Descartes as both animal mechanism and spiritual entity, a creature with a heart and a mind, the one material and the other spiritual.

Increasing interest in the eighteenth century, as A. O. Lovejoy has shown, centered on anthropological considerations of man's similarity with the ape; Buffon, Linnaeus, Bonnet, Rousseau, all speculated on the remarkable resemblance between man in his primitive state of nature and the ape, his physical counterpart.[6] Rousseau saw primitive man as an innocent who, like the brutes, did not share the original sin of society with civilized man. Linnaeus regarded the troglodytes with keen interest, and considered apes the nearest relations of the human race. With the development of evolutionary concepts at the end of the century in the work of men like Erasmus Darwin and Lamarck, the possibility of a time link between man and his near relations became inevitable. Charles Darwin provided the key, however, for only a clear evolutionary mechanism could force such a notion upon men in general. Natural selection fulfilled that requirement, furnishing an explanation for the development of species from common ancestors by tying survival to the breeding and foraging talents of various groups, emphasizing therefore the physical character of biological identity. Men were forced to think in physical terms when they considered the characteristics of species, were reminded at every turn, if only by implication, that they too were breeders and foragers. Genesis had not only been given a new time schedule; it had been furnished with a perfectly natural explanation as well. Hence the originality of Huxley's work lay neither in the novelty of looking at man as an animal nor in notions of evolutionary development, but rather in the imaginative fusion of the prominent ideas of several disciplines into a new synthesis that brought the historical and biological reality of man's animal nature into the Victorian cultural consciousness.

While Darwin's *Origin* had much to do with Huxley's publication four years later of *Man's Place in Nature*, the original impetus for Huxley's research into the question was furnished by his important controversy with the anatomist Richard Owen.[7] As early as 1858, Huxley delivered a lecture, "On the Theory of the Vertebrate Skull," at the Royal Society, attacking the notion that the skull was a continuation of modified vertebrae, an important theory of the German nature-philosophers, particularly Lorenz Oken, who believed that the archetypal plan of vertebrate animals was a generalized backbone composed of

118

unit vertebra segments. The archetype, an ideal form which corresponded in many respects to the ideal forms of Platonism, was held in the nature-philosophy tradition to be continually manifesting itself through a succession of biological forms. In essence, the archetype was an ideal force, a Logos by means of which unity was made manifest in variety. In this sense, it was a life force which brought into being the evolving forms of the earth. Owen was an adherent to the theory in general, and specifically to the theory that the bones of the vertebrate skull were a series of modified vertebrae.

Although Huxley was not opposed to archetypal idealism in his youthful days—never abandoning his romance with Unity—he began to criticize archetypal theory where he could examine it in terms of his own research. In a report to the British Association in 1852 on his work on the structure of the Ascidians, he took pains to establish that by "archetype" he was merely referring to a diagram of "general anatomical uniformities" of the Ascidians as a group.[8]

His 1854 review of and attack upon Chamber's 10th edition of *Vestiges of the Natural History of Creation* was made on the basis of his theoretical objection to Chambers's concept of law as a physical force. The author of *Vestiges* believed, Huxley declared, "that law is an entity—a Logos intermediate between the Creator and his works."[9] And, in one of his few constructive citations of Comte, he observed that "the mind of the Vestigarian is in the metaphysic stage, and confounds its own abstraction with objective fact," which was the criticism he applied to Argyll more than thirty years later in his 1887 essay, "Science and Pseudo-Science," where he once again but more temperately criticized Chambers (5:108–11). In rejecting the notion that ideals or abstractions could be material forces, Huxley dismissed the possibility of the archetype as well.

The idea of quantity as applied to force was a parallel development in Huxley's thought which effectively dissipated the older idea of a special life force, a philosophical conviction central both to nature-philosophy and Romanticism. Huxley's view was first expressed in a lengthy review, "The Cell Theory," which appeared in 1853; Huxley argued that life forces or "vital forces" were no different from "molecular forces."[10] He warned that "physiology and ontology are two sciences which cannot be too carefully kept apart." Four years later, the most dramatic and chilling of his early anti-vitalist lectures was delivered at the Royal Insitute under the title "On the Present State of Knowledge as to the Structure and Functions of Nerve," which has only survived in abstract. Huxley opened by demonstrating a special apparatus by means of which a pivoting metal "index" was connected through the pericardium to the open, beating heart of a living frog; driven by the muscular action of the heart, it vibrated to and fro for an audience of onlookers. "Where lies the regulative power which governs its rhythm?" Huxley is reported to have asked of the swaying index; and, citing Helmholtz, whose theories on the interconvertibility of forces had recently become current in England, Huxley observed that the "ganglionic" force that kept the heart beating "must be regarded as of the same order with other physical forces."[11] He concluded, in the words of the abstract, with the observation: "Time was when the attempt to reduce vital phenomena to law and order was regarded as little less than blasphemous: but the mechanician has proved that the living body obeys the mechanical laws of living matter."

By 1858, the following year, the stage was set for Huxley's Croonian lecture, "On the Theory of the Vertebrate Skull," in which he directly confronted the archetypalist theory, favored by Owen, that the skull was a fusion of four modified vertebra segments. Huxley drew from the research of German embryologist Martin Rathke, the colleague of Ernst von Baer, to show basic flaws in Owen's trusting to superficial resemblances of bone shape and position. By observing their embryological development, Huxley maintained, the investigator could determine that spinal column and skull were related but divergent structures.

Huxley was not only dealing the death-blow to the nature-philosophy tradition in England, a tradition which had never been strong, but he was also assaulting Romantic thought. In his 1853 review on "The Cell Theory," he had pointed to a parting of ways between the scientist and the transcendentalist:

> But who seeks for absolute truth? Flattering as they were to our vanity, we fear it must be confessed that the days of the high *a priori* road are over. Men of science have given up the attempt to soar

eagle-like to some point amidst the clouds, whence the absolute relations of things could be securely viewed; and at present, their more useful, if more ignoble course, may be compared to that of flocks of sparrows in autumn, which one sees continually halting, yet always advancing—flying from tree to tree. [12]

In the years leading up to his own *Man's Place in Nature*, Huxley openly revolted against Owen's transcendentalist anatomy. He did not question the value of Owen's empirical research, since Owen's mastery of detail in vertebrate anatomy had justly earned him an international reputation. It was the speculative aspect of Owen's anatomical work that Huxley set out to defeat.

For these reasons Darwin and Huxley were attracted to each other. Darwin's consideration of Huxley as a prime candidate for the defense of his *Origin* would most logically have been on the recommendation of Huxley's theoretical position, for in a movement that had its parallel in Germany in the work of men like von Baer, Helmholtz, and Kölliker, Huxley sought to transform the theoretical basis of British biology from the speculative tradition of the nature-philosophers and from the traditionalism of men like Lyell, to a new, empirical, naturalistic basis. It was an audacious ambition for a man so young, but it made Huxley essential to the defense of Darwin's *Origin of Species*, just as it made Darwin's work a most welcome contribution to Huxley in his struggle against Owen. By 1859, Huxley had become the primary exponent in England of scientific naturalism; and, in spite of its substantial debt to speculation, Darwin's work was to be the greatest instance of scientific naturalism of the century. [13]

By the time Huxley published *Man's Place in Nature*, the controversy with Owen had subsided; Huxley included a lengthy note detailing his past argument with Owen over the latter's attempts to salvage a separate biological classification, Archencephala, for man by distorting anatomical findings relating to primate brain structure. [14] *Man's Place in Nature*, with its embryological, anatomical, and paleontological emphases, was in part the research record of Huxley's theoretical struggle with Owen. In consequence, it was a summation of numerous arguments against favored theories of the nature-philosophers. Their vitalism, which Huxley himself had supported in his 1854 essay "On the Educational Value of the Natural History Sciences," was rejected and replaced by a new emphasis on strict causality and determinism. Many of Huxley's essays and technical studies thereafter became standards for methodological approach and were of sufficient importance to win him a substantial international reputation. In Germany and Austria, his work was widely translated and his *The Crayfish* (1879) earned him the admiration of the young Sigmund Freud, whose studies in the Helmholtz school of physical physiology at Ernst Brücke's Vienna Laboratory grounded him in a deterministic tradition that owed something to Huxley's textbooks and thought. [15]

While there were numerous undercurrents of scientific controversy and discovery at work in *Man's Place in Nature*, Huxley's vision of biological man had a much broader cultural significance. The question raised by such a title necessarily addressed various religious, aesthetic, and philosophical traditions on a fundamental level. The basic concept of self and identity, the traditional idea of human nature, indeed many of the most widely accepted assumptions of Western thought were at issue in Huxley's investigation into the hierarchical relationship between man and the rest of nature. It was, he maintained, the great question of the century:

> The question of questions for mankind—the problem which underlies all others, and is more deeply interesting than any other—is the ascertainment of the place which Man occupies in nature and of his relations to the universe of things. Whence our race has come; what are the limits of our power over nature, and of nature's power over us. [7:77]

The question of man's place in nature had occupied a central place in a number of important Victorian poems, as we have already observed; but transferred to a scientific context it acquired a tone of critical objectivity established by the separation of the observer from the object—the self—of the inquiry. Darwin chose to avoid the problem of human origin in his *Origin*; yet, in many ways, his omission rendered his work strange and ambiguous. Unlike the poet, the scientist did not formally seek to identify himself with the forces and objects of nature—the scientific presence in itself was of no moment. Darwin made extensive use of the first person "I," yet the Darwinian landscape was strange and alien to man. Not least among the many remarkable aspects of *On the Origin of Species* was that, while it was the century's greatest work on life and nature, it had virtually nothing to say of man, who presumably existed at the center of things. As in Lyell's *Principles of Geology*, one viewed incredibly vast epochs during which a human presence could hardly be imagined. In taking up the question where Darwin left off, Huxley set out to find the man who arose out of the Darwinian and Lyellian landscapes; and given such beginnings and the anatomical and paleontological data of the day, it was unlikely that he would return with anything resembling the pastoral ideal of natural man.

While Huxley's study examined man as species, it could hardly fail to suggest a great deal about the idea of the self. Subjective or individual notions of the self, while theoretically outside the focus of *Man's Place in Nature*, could not be dispensed with through the mere claim that they were irrelevant. Who could resist the temptation to identify with such a portrait; who could fail to sense the tension building up between one's own familiar self-concept and the strange double emerging from the pages of Huxley's study? Huxley was careful to document his work thoroughly and to avoid claiming human evolution to be a proven fact. Yet one could hardly accept the evidence he offered without also accepting the likelihood that man was a historical refugee from some strange and primitive past. "I have done my best to sweep away this vanity," Huxley declared of the human inclination to proclaim human biology as unique; "I have endeavoured to show that no absolute structural line of demarcation, wider than that between the animals which immediately succeed us in the scale, can be drawn between the animal world and ourselves" (7:152). And in the final chapter, Huxley presented a survey of recent findings of human fossil remains, evidence which looked back to primate origins in a paleontological past that seemed to be peopled with the most fascinating of all doubles, prehistoric man.

In attempting to unify the concept of man by emphasizing his biological affinities with the rest of the natural world, Huxley actually authored a double, a version of the self that had incontestable affinities with the physical nature, yet remained distinctly foreign to one's own sense of individuality and personality. Speaking of the manlike apes which he had taken special care in chapter 1 to identify for their human attributes, Huxley observed:

> Brought face to face with these blurred copies of himself, the least thoughtful of men is conscious of a certain shock, due perhaps, not so much to disgust at the aspect of what looks like an insulting caricature, as to the awakening of a sudden and profound mistrust of time-honoured theories and strongly-rooted prejudices regarding his own position in nature, and his relations to the under-world of life. [7:80–81]

The shock of recognition as one journeyed into the origins and affinities of man could be due only to a face-to-face confrontation with the self; the "blurred copies," as Huxley observed, while capable of arousing disgust, were as likely to awaken a "sudden and profound mistrust" of one's own human prejudices regarding his uniqueness and remoteness from animal nature. In short, Huxley considered the problem of man's place in nature as a problem of identity.

While much has been written on the Victorian double and the divided self, the psychological origins of self-duplication and self-division have been stressed, and the biological, physiological sources of the notion commonly overlooked. Masao Miyoshi has observed that the creature of Frankenstein was, in part, a product of the new science, Mary Shelley infusing into the old gothic tale an artificial supernaturalism that is appropriate to a story of the new scientific man-as-a-kind-of-god.[16] The monster was, of course, a product of the imagination, a perversion of human nature, of physiology and, to a degree, of mind; it was still possible to console oneself with the imaginary nature of the tale. Yet what if the vision were substantially true, if one's ancestor were something heavy and muscular, with a jutting brow that betokened a primitive brutality? At the very beginning of his *Man's Place in Nature*, Huxley pointedly observed:

> Ancient traditions, when tested by the severe processes of modern investigation, commonly enough fade away into mere dreams: but

it is singular how often the dream turns out to have been a half-waking one, presaging a reality. . . . and though the quaint forms of Centaurs and Satyrs have an existence only in the realms of art, creatures approaching man more nearly than they in essential structure, and yet as thoroughly brutal as the goat's or horse's half of the mythical compound, are now not only known, but notorious. [7:1]

He went on to compose a short history of man's encounter with the "man-like apes," ending the chapter with a digression on cannibalism. While the man to emerge from Huxley's study was by no means a monster, he was equally strange and likely to be regarded as more threatening since his origin was in natural process, as certified by legitimate science. Unlike the monster of Frankenstein, he was not the arcane product of a diseased imagination; nor could he be dismissed as an entertaining, if morbid, fiction. In his opening paragraph, Huxley entered into the theme of division, suggesting that the mythological hybrids of man and brute of old presaged a reality; *Man's Place in Nature* consistently pursues that reality, opening up a vista into the natural world that reveals the human species, the biological self.

One of the ironies of Huxley's approach, as has already been noted, is the tone of objectivity he created in separating or distancing himself from man, the object of his inquiry. As a scientist, he could occupy that supposed citadel of objectivity—the scientific mind. Such a complicated mental operation was necessary, since to imagine man as species it was essential to ignore man as self, to suffer absorption and disappearance of the self into the abstraction of one's race. As Huxley approached the general character of biological man more closely, his vision became increasingly alien to notions of individual identity and personality. Instructing the reader as to the frame of mind he should assume in order to comprehend the vision, Huxley suggested that one disconnect oneself from the "mask" of his humanity:

> Bearing this obvious course of zoological reasoning in mind, let us endeavour for a moment to disconnect our thinking selves from the mask of humanity; let us imagine ourselves scientific Saturnians, if you will, fairly acquainted with such animals as now inhabit the

Earth, and employed in discussing the relations they bear to a new and singular "erect and featherless biped," which some enterprising traveller, overcoming the difficulties of space and gravitation, has brought from that distant planet for our inspection, well preserved, may be, in a cask of rum. [7:95]

The images in this dark little piece of humor are startling; yet the disconnecting of the thinking self from the "mask" of one's humanity was essential if one were to comprehend the biological character of one's species. The scene recalls Huxley's childhood experience at the autopsy. Characteristically rendered in dramatic form, the proposal set the scientific Saturnian, a clear, cold, logic-machine, apart from the specimen which was to be preserved in a cask of rum, not only "featherless" but nameless. The mechanism of self-division was essential in order to see as Huxley and the majority of his biological and palentological colleagues saw.

In its original 1863 version, *Man's Place in Nature* consisted of three essays, each of which examined a physical or biological aspect of man from a different perspective. Huxley made it clear that when he spoke of locating man's place in nature, he meant "brute" nature (7:81). Man's brutality, while raising numerous moral issues, was not in itself a moral issue. It was one of Huxley's objectives to show how far removed from ethical or religious considerations the physical portrait of man could be.

In the first essay, "On the Natural History of the Man-like Apes," he examined a variety of accounts of encounters between early explorers, sailors, and naturalists, and African and Asian primates. It was an important introduction, because it surveyed a broad tradition of semi-mythical, quasi-scientific, as well as genuine naturalistic, accounts of manlike apes, mandrills, orangutans and gorillas. Here were also the Linnean anthropomorpha, *Lucifer Aldrovandi, Satyrus Tulpii, Pygmaeus Edwardi*, with illustrations that showed them to be strange fusions of man and ape, with such features as made the Yahoo of Swift notorious (7:18). As we have seen, Huxley opened the chapter, indeed the book, with the observation that the strangest fantasies of the mind frequently presaged a profound truth. This became the underlying theme of his entire work, dominating the basic patterns of exposition. Thus in the first chapter, we begin with those outrageous encounters in the forests between sixteenth-century sailors and apes with oddly human powers and habits, and gradually move into technically sophisticated descriptions of primate behavior by modern observers such as Sir James Brooke and Alfred Wallace. We move from myth and fantasy into carefully collected description and detail, all exploring the human qualities demonstrated by the various primates considered. There is a fragment from *Purchas his Pilgrimes*, published in 1625, describing how an African lived with an ape for a month (7:4–6). Numerous accounts describe how apes cry like children, express affection, become angry and dangerous when intruded upon. Wurmb's Pongo, Huxley relates, was a monster, "of vast strength and fierceness, and very brutal in expression; its great projecting muzzle, armed with strong teeth, being further disfigured by the outgrowth of cheeks into fleshy lobes" (7:27). Part of the brilliance of the chapter lies in the fact that Huxley does not reject the myths but, rather, confirms them by recasting them in more sophisticated, empirical terms. It was a shrewd act of economy, for all the psychic energy one brings to the imagining of those mythological accounts of beast-man fusions is gradually met with the hard evidence of trained observers. The imagination is primed and the reader given a brief but suggestive account of the history culminating in Huxley's main thesis.

The chapter unfolds less in support of a concrete thesis than as a broad portrait, an encounter with ideas and possibilities that hold a perennial fascination for the human imagination. While apes frequently exhibit behavior similar to that of humans, they are also violent and capricious. Illustrations play a fundamental role which in the two later chapters becomes iconographical, symbolizing as well as depicting. In the first chapter, there are illustrations of the Linnean anthropomorpha, of an odd mandrill with a human face, the skull of an orang, and various accurate portraits of primates, including a particularly brutal-looking gorilla baring his teeth. The final illustration, contained in a brief appendix entitled "African Cannibalism in the Sixteenth Century," was lifted by Huxley from a sixteenth-century account of cannibalism by Phillip Pigafetta. It shows an African chopping up the body of a man, with pieces of the body, the head, an arm, hand, and leg, displayed in a jungle market stall in the background. "I must confess," explains Huxley, "that the subject is not strictly relevant to the matter in hand," and he connects Pigafetta's account with the more recent accounts of a Frenchman, M. Du Chaillu, which identify similar modern instances of cannibalism (7:73–75). In spite of Huxley's disclaimer, the appendix on cannibalism removes borders—in this case a primordial taboo—between man and brute. The inclusion of cannibalism as a subject relevant to man's relationship with nature reveals something of the inner logic of Huxley's thought; we descend from the security of civilization into an alien but somehow relevant abnormality for a glimpse of the human potential for brutality.

There is an apocalyptic element in Huxley's vision, a sense of cataclysmic revision of accepted realities and traditions which emerges from the clinical lucidity and objectivity of his careful prose. This becomes particularly apparent in the opening paragraphs of his second chapter, "On the Relations of Man to the Lower Animals," where he begins to speak in terms of a metamorphosis of human knowledge and understanding. Of all the questions that might be raised, he declares, the most basic, and fearful, is that of the relationship between man and nature. It is the question of questions which few dare ask, for its answer contains the deepest implications for the future and freedom of mankind (7:77–78). As Carlyle had done in *Past and Present*, Huxley characterizes the subject as a great riddle, leading its rare investigators—those who have not taken refuge in mere scepticism or beneath the featherbed of tradition—into the construction of theological or philosophical systems, or even into creating the poetry of an epoch (7:78).[17] Yet time proves each answer to have been "a mere approximation of the truth," and slowly or quickly each gives way to the larger knowledge of a successor. The mental progress of the race, he continues, is a process of metamorphosis: "the human mind, fed by constant accessions of knowledge, periodically grows too large for its theoretical coverings, and bursts them asunder to appear in new habiliments" (7:79). Given the progress of physical science over the past fifty years, he concludes, the time has come for a new "ecdysis," a shedding of the dated integument of traditional views of man, "a process not unusually accompanied by many throes and some sickness and debility, or, it may be, by graver disturbances" (7:79–80). Thus Huxley enters into a consideration of those "wide, if not . . . universal" biological truths, a descent into the "under-world of life," rowed across Styx by Ernst von Baer (7:81–82).

The Huxleyan underworld is profoundly new—microscopic and skeletal. Preoccupied with processes of birth and death, it presents verbal images and physical forms that go beyond the average experience, as alien as the mammal egg or the skull of the lemur. It is no small irony that in order to understand the biology of man we peer either into the womb or the grave, those transitional places that remain alien to the conscious mind. In a section on embryological development, Huxley relates how all mammals begin as eggs, then, once fertilized, progress through successive stages during which it is impossible to distinguish one from another. It is only quite late that the embryo of a human becomes differentiated from that of a dog; and only much later is it distinguishable from the embryo of the ape. Hence the ape embryo "departs as much from the dog in its development, as the man does" (7:92). After demonstrating the basic unities revealed in embryological development, Huxley turns to the core of his second chapter—the anatomical unity of man and ape. The basic thesis is that structurally the ape differs less from man than it does from the rest of the animal kingdom. In this chapter Huxley's illustrations take on a symbolic, iconographic significance, something which would never occur in a strictly technical work but which here, given the framework in which Huxley set his study, was nearly inevitable. In endeavoring to establish it in the context of the great systems of human thought, Huxley gave his little treatise symbolic, representative status. The most striking example of the symbolism of his illustrations, his scientific iconography, occurs on the first page of the second chapter where photographic reductions of side views of skeletons, beginning with the gibbon, progressing through the orang, chimpanzee and gorilla, and ending with man, are lined up (7:76). This single illustration communicates Huxley's essential vision—a skeletal apocalypse. In its own homely way, it contains an idea as profound as some great work of art, for in these skeletal remains, these artifacts from the scientific bone closet, man stands beside his relations, intimate with nature beyond the wildest dreams of the Romantics. One sees metamorphosis in glancing at the progressive shortening of the arms, the gradual crouching of the forms as if a single force were passing through them, adapting their structures as each sought to stand erect, striving for balance which is finally achieved in man with the curvature of the spine. In the scientific underworld, the truths of life are found in the forms of death.

The second chapter is a visual boneyard, with Huxley making use of comparative illustration to show similarities in nearly every major bone cluster of the primate form. The entire primate order emerges as a progression of variations; the similarities are undeniable. "It is as if nature herself," Huxley reflects, "had foreseen the arrogance of man, and with Roman severity had provided that his intellect, by its very triumphs, would call into prominence the slaves, admonishing the conqueror that he is but dust" (7:146).

While Huxley sought to convey the unity of structure between man and the other primates in the second chapter, he concentrated on furnishing the biological portrait of man with a valid historical context in the last, "On Some Fossil Remains of Man." The final chapter is perhaps the most remarkable of all, not for what Huxley was able to prove, but for his convincing demonstration of the likelihood that man had existed on earth in some lower, prehistoric form. It was in this chapter that the new concept of man cut deeply into tradition, sweeping away such pastoral myths as the existence of a golden, heroic age, the idea of the noble savage, or the belief that man was of a special, divine origin. If Huxley's speculation and evidence were valid, man was a mutable form with a brute for an ancestor. The alien landscapes of Lyell and Darwin here found their human counterpart.

Huxley based his chapter on the remarkable evidence discovered by two German paleontologists, Schmerling and Schaaffhausen. In 1833, Schmerling published a work detailing his findings of the fossilized remains of what appeared to be a primitive human skull. The skull, called the Engis skull after the

Belgian cave in which it was found, lay among the remains of a woolly mammoth and a woolly rhinoceros and was declared by Charles Lyell to be their contemporary (7:158). Schmerling noted, "From the first, the elongated and narrow form of the forehead attracted our attention" (7:161). Further on, he observed, "For my own part, I hold it to be demonstrated that this cranium has belonged to a person of limited intellectual faculties, and we conclude thence that it belonged to a man of a low degree of civilization: a deduction which is borne out by contrasting the capacity of the frontal with that of the occipital region" (7:161–62). Huxley included three views—side, front and top—of the Engis skull.

In 1856, the famous Neanderthal skull was discovered by Fuhlrott in a limestone cave near Düsseldorf, and Schaaffhausen, a German paleontologist, wrote a description and interpretative essay on the finding, which was translated in 1861 into English for the *Natural History Review* by George Busk, Huxley's close friend and colleague.[18] Schaaffhausen concluded that "the extraordinary form of the skull was due to a natural conformation hitherto not known to exist, even in the most barbarous races"; that the remains belonged to a period "antecedent to the time of the Celts and Germans, and were in all probability derived from one of the wild races of North-western Europe" (7:169). The Neanderthal skull was "of unusual size, and of a long-elliptical form. A most remarkable peculiarity is at once obvious in the extraordinary development of the frontal sinuses. . . . The forehead is narrow and low" (7:170). The thighbones found with the skull were characterized by their unusual thickness and the "great development of all the elevations and depressions for the attachment of muscles" (7:172). Schaaffhausen concluded that the "expansion of the frontal sinuses, which are appendages of the air-passages, also indicates an unusual force and power of endurance in the movements of the body, as may be concluded from the size of all the ridges and processes for the attachment of the muscles or bones" (7:176–77). Portions of the ribs had also been found which from their unusually rounded shape and abrupt curvature resembled more "the ribs of a carnivorous animal than those of a man" (7:174). The picture of primitive man that was emerging from the Neanderthal remains was less to be cherished than to be feared.

Huxley's conclusions are cautious. Remarkable as the fossil findings were, they were not to be regarded as a missing link between ape and man, for modern variations in human skulls, particularly in cranial capacity, could in some instances be found to approximate those of the Neanderthal skull. Nevertheless, in the massive development of its frontal sinuses, the Neanderthal was unique; and its combined bone structure indicated a creature of great force and power with a cultural repertory of only the most basic tools. What *Man's Place in Nature* contributed was an idea. Huxley made no specific evolutionary claims, yet the evidence as he had collected and arranged it leaves little doubt as to the ultimate implications of his study. Man is not only a biological organism; he is quite likely a fluctuating form with roots in a past that could be gauged not by the history of civilization but rather by the history of nature. The idea of a primitive, powerful protohuman had been thrust upon the Victorian cultural consciousness. While Huxley's work was not enthusiastically embraced, it was widely read and translated, and became part of the groundwork of modern thought.[19]

Accurate, cautious, and objective as Huxley's vision was, it was still a deeply divisive one, for in emphasizing the physical unity of mankind with nature it all but eliminated the human consciousness. The profound driving force of the conscious mind, the pyschological unity of the self, perpetually differentiating between subject and object, remained unaccounted for and alien. The title of Huxley's work was in this sense misleading, for while it addressed a basic philosophical issue, it neglected the fundamental problem of the place of the mind in nature. Thus the being that seemed to be revealed in composite from the three chapters was something fearful, an ironical comment on the illusions of civilized man. Such fears would be answered by Huxley with another question:

> Is it, indeed, true, that the Poet, or the Philosopher, or the Artist whose genius is the glory of his age, is degraded from his high estate by the undoubted historical probability, not to say certainty, that he is the direct descendant of some naked and bestial savage,

whose intelligence was just sufficient to make him a little more cunning than the Fox, and by so much more dangerous than the Tiger? Or is he bound to howl and grovel on all fours because of the wholly unquestionable fact, that he was once an egg, which no ordinary power of discrimination could distinguish from that of a Dog? [7:153–54]

The question rightly pointed to the fact that structure and ancestry could not account for the intellectual and social achievements of modern man. Yet Huxley had not examined the question in any detail himself; he assumed in this sardonic and rhetorical question that the answer would be simply a matter of common sense. Many of the implications of the study went far beyond the rational reaches of the mind, for Huxley had penetrated deeply into the intensely private territory of the human self-image. While *Man's Place in Nature* concentrated on man as a biological species, which reader did not belong, as an individual, to the primate group? Whatever the process was that elevated the human species into consciousness and rationality, what mind could, upon close consideration, consider the process complete or irreversible? As Huxley suggested, one's ancestor was very likely a "naked and bestial savage," with an intelligence a mere step in advance of the brutes, enough to make him more dangerous than they. A quick glance at the thickly-browed skull of the Neanderthal man, in Huxley's illustration peering like some portent out of a dim past, was enough to set the imagination in motion. The self contains its own ancestry as part of its unshakable identity. If Huxley was correct, then in some way the Neanderthal man lived within.

Although man must be removed from the center of nature, anthropocentrism abolished, he remained a temporary figure at the apex of the great organic tree. Huxley declared he was strongly convinced "of the vastness of the gulf between civilized man and the brutes," although "the simplest study of man's nature reveals, at its foundations, all the selfish passions, and fierce appetites of the merest quadruped" (7:153–54). While Huxley could declare his faith in these two aspects of man, he could not reconcile them. The mind in *Man's Place in Nature* is the mind of the scientist, the rational intellect pondering the biological aspects of the organism in which it is contained. It is an extreme form of self-consciousness, with the body, not the mind, as the object of its intense focus. This is the essential difference between the psychological and the physiological double. Yet in Huxley's vision, the physiological double with its roots in a brutal past is accompanied by the brute mentality, the "selfish passions and fierce appetites" which, according to Huxley, exist at the foundations of human nature.

A wide and important range of literary figures owes its origins, at least partially, to the concept of a primitive self. These are the "troglodytic" creatures, Stevenson's Mr. Hyde, Conan Doyle's Nottingham Murderer, Wells's Morlocks and even T. S. Eliot's Sweeney.[20] In each case, the physical appearance of the figure recalls a regressive mentality, very often accompanied by psychic excess or behavior outside the norms of civilization. Thus in Doyle's *The Hound of the Baskervilles*, we find, against the background of Grimpen Mire, which is full of the remains of prehistoric man, the reenactment of that primitive drama— murder.[21] What man had in common with nature was brutality, excess of instinct and emotion. By the time of Eliot's crucial Sweeney figures, *Pithecanthropos erectus* had been discovered in Java; and for Eliot the patrimony of man's prehistoric past remained a powerful reality of the present, at war with civilization. Even Huxley, who in *Man's Place in Nature* seemed bent on eliminating the great wall of civilization as some mere illusion or an unhealthy self-indulgence, would in the final decade of his life be found in his "Evolution and Ethics" busily reconstructing the wall. By then, of course, Darwin's illustrious *The Descent of Man* (1871) had broadened the path to Huxley's underworld into a major thoroughfare.

In the years after his *Man's Place in Nature*, Huxley's concept of human division developed increasingly along deterministic lines. The logic of his movement in the direction of determinism was closely tied to the recognition in his earlier work that if man were actually an intimate part of nature, an organism, he must respond to natural forces as other organisms responded, with consciousness and will not being essential to the performance of many operations.

Human division takes on a fascinating aspect in another of Huxley's studies, "On the Hypothesis that Animals are Au-

134

tomata," which was written a decade after the appearance of *Man's Place in Nature*. Huxley was intrigued with the possibilities of the autonomic nervous systems which function independently of the central brain, for they revealed a spectrum of behavior which operates by reflex. The possibilities led him to examine the scope of behavior in the frog with part of its brain matter damaged or removed. Somewhat earlier the same year, in 1874, he had been impressed with the research of E. Mesnet, which described some remarkable findings that the physician had made in his study of a French army sergeant who suffered a head wound in battle. The sergeant went through periodic disturbances of the brain which resulted in behavior he could not recall having performed upon the return to his normal state. "For four years," Huxley reported, "the life of this man has been divided into alternating phases" (1:227). During periods of normality, the sergeant was healthy, intelligent, and kindly; but periodically he was overtaken by a foreign, abnormal state, beginning with a sense of uneasiness and weight about the forehead. During his occupation of the alien state of mind, the sergeant ate, drank, and performed all the necessary activities of life; at the same time he was insensible to pain. Huxley was intrigued by the question of whether he was without consciousness in his abnormal state, since he also mechanically reenacted a battle and sang songs with perfect execution. In a footnote, Huxley observed:

In the unfortunate subjects of such abnormal conditions of the brain, the disturbance of the sensory and intellectual faculties is not unfrequently accompanied by a perturbation of the moral nature, which may manifest itself in a most astonishing love of lying for its own sake. And, in this respect, also, F.'s case is singularly instructive, for though, in his normal state, he is a perfectly honest man, in his abnormal condition he is an inveterate thief, stealing and hiding away whatever he can lay his hands on, with much dexterity, and with an absurd indifference as to whether the property is his own or not. Hoffman's terrible conception of the "Doppelt-gänger" is realised by men in this state—who live two lives, in the one of which they may be guilty of the most criminal acts, while, in the other, they are eminently virtuous and respectable. Neither life knows anything of the other. [1:234–35n]

Science had discovered the doppelgänger through the study of abnormal psychology. Huxley not only recognized the physiological basis for self-division; he understood the possibility of living two lives—one moral and the other criminal. But the criminal state of the French sergeant, the state in which his sense of morality was absurdly absent, was precisely the state in which he seemed to be least conscious of and most intimate with the rest of nature.[22]

Biological, physical man, as he had emerged from Huxley's *Man's Place in Nature*, raised moral questions that were deeply problematic and frightening, since morality was clearly a facet of consciousness, while many varieties of human behavior seemed to be governed by unconscious psychic mechanisms common to the animal world. The Mesnet study had demonstrated the potential for a psychic dualism in which an alien version of the self operated outside the domain of consciousness. In such a state the moral dimension of the conscious mind did not enter into the chain of causation which Huxley believed was the source of all human activity. The dilemma of subconscious motivation, probably more than any other factor, led to his famous proposition, already mentioned, in his 1870 essay "On Descartes' 'Discourse'" on the desirability of being wound up like a clock:

> I protest that if some great Power would agree to make me always think what is true and do what is right, on condition of being turned into a sort of clock and wound up every morning before I got out of bed, I should instantly close with the offer. The only freedom I care about is the freedom to do right; the freedom to do wrong I am ready to part with on the cheapest terms to any one who will take it of me. [1:192–93]

The problem of self-control, of being aware of the effects and motivations of one's action, led to a frustrated sense of the human ability to control and direct moral action. Huxley had a deep anxiety over the capacity of the individual to discriminate between right and wrong. It amounted to a conscious fear of the self, that the ultimate source of one's motives might be born of impulses that functioned apart from and were uncontrolled by the rational mind. If man were an intimate part of nature, as

Huxley had shown in *Man's Place in Nature*, the fact that he had no ultimate control over nature led to the likelihood that he also had no ultimate control over his individual self.

ii. Mill's "nature"

Huxley's earliest concepts of nature were derived from an admixture of Romantic idealism and scientific naturalism which moved increasingly toward the naturalistic, deterministic outlook. *Man's Place in Nature* was a large step in the direction of scientific naturalism in which Huxley sought to place the human organism in its rightful historical position in the embryological, anatomical, and paleontological record. Yet many later essays such as "On the Advisableness of Improving Natural Knowledge" (1866) and "A Liberal Education" (1868) reveal Huxley taking the Romantic view that natural forces are somehow benevolent. The position he took in his often cited letter to Kingsley in 1860, which Irvine has suggested was Huxley's basic faith for the greater part of his life, found the collective forces of nature eminently just:[23]

> The absolute justice of the system of things is as clear to me as any scientific fact. The gravitation of sin to sorrow is as certain as that of the earth to the sun, and more so—for experimental proof of the fact is within reach of us all—nay, is before us all in our own lives, if we had but the eyes to see it. [*LL*, 1:236]

As we have already seen, his chessboard metaphor suggested that natural forces were somehow "fair, just and patient," rewarding the cautious and masterful player of life's game with "overflowing generosity" (3:82). Huxley's early Romanticism faded rapidly however; in spite of the deep and consistent strain of idealism in his work, he gave rationality precedence over imagination as the central human faculty. While Irvine rightly observes that Huxley's basic faith was in the justice of nature, it was a faith held more in the spirit of his "scientific Calvinism," as he had called it in the 1854 letter to his friend Dyster (*LL*, 1:122). Natural law was just in the sense that it was universal and rigorously applied to all. Yet, whether or not the player-force of the chessboard was fair and patient, he was still the opponent with the undeniable power to inflict death.

Huxley's scientific naturalism was grounded in his studies leading up to *Man's Place in Nature*. The reasoning which led him to annex the human organism to the animal kingdom bears an interesting comparison to another central departure from traditional thought on the same subject—John Stuart Mill's "Nature." Mill's remarkable essay, although not published until 1874 when it appeared posthumously as part of his *Three Essays on Religion*, had been completed by 1854. "Nature" anticipated both Darwin and Huxley in its deceptively simple argument:

> The word Nature has two principal meanings: it either denotes the entire system of things, with the aggregate of all their properties, or it denotes things as they would be, apart from human intervention.
>
> In the first of these senses, the doctrine that man ought to follow nature is unmeaning; since man has no power to do anything else than follow nature; all his actions are done through, and in obedience to, some one or many of nature's physical or mental laws.
>
> In the other sense of the term, the doctrine that man ought to follow nature, or in other words, ought to make the spontaneous course of things the model of his voluntary actions, is equally irrational and immoral.[24]

Basing his inquiry on the "Platonic method," Mill approached the problem of physical nature semantically, suggesting that the long tradition of referring to nature as a moral and artistic standard was the result of inaccurate and ambiguous definition. "All praise of Civilization, or Art, or Contrivance," he declared, "is so much dispraise of Nature; an admission of imperfection, which it is man's business, and merit, to be always endeavouring to correct or mitigate."[25] Furthermore, nature was anything but benign: "Nature impales men, breaks them as if on the wheel."[26] And accordingly, almost all respectable attributes of humanity were due to man's "triumph over instinct."[27]

Mill's essay was an attack on eighteenth-century and Romantic pastoral thought, particularly its ethical naturalism. The targets were Pope and Rousseau, both of whom represented the tradition which attempted to make "Nature a test of right and wrong, good and evil."[28] Pope's declaration, "whatever is, is right," Mill pointed out, is demonstrably false, since human behavior which repeats the violent behavior found everywhere in nature is justly punished by men. "In sober truth," Mill argued, "nearly all the things which men are hanged or imprisoned for doing to one another, are nature's every day performances."[29] The attempt to dignify savage life with nobility and virtue was sheer folly: "Savages are always liars. They have not the faintest notion of truth as a virtue."[30] Above all, the "sentiment of justice is entirely of artificial origin."[31] Thus Mill, with insight similar to that of Tennyson and Arnold, had recognized the violence inherent in natural processes. While Huxley was still reflecting, with vaguely Romantic tendencies, on the justice inherent in natural order, Mill was arguing the fallacy of seeking justice anywhere but in society. Natural justice and natural innocence were myths, Mill argued; yet he admitted that instincts were probably valuable aids to survival in primitive social conditions and of some value in modern society. It was the instinct to destroy, to dominate, that must be eliminated.

Compared to Huxley's *Man's Place in Nature*, Mill's "Nature" is more subtle and philosophically aware; for Mill understood the precise nature of the ethical problems raised by using an abstract concept of nature as an ethical standard. Scientific developments had supplied concrete versions of the old ideal forms. Nature, Mill observed, was the proper domain of the sciences, which were continually involved in the process of determining the conditions of phenomena which when discovered were called the Laws of Nature.

Huxley's study of man stood on the premise, expressed by Mill, that the "first principle of all intelligent action," was the study of nature in order "to know and take heed of the properties of the things we have to deal with."[32] For Huxley, the focus on man, the investigation and revelation of his biological nature, was the starting point of all disciplines, no matter how seemingly distant. While Mill emphasized the need to redefine nature from the human perspective, Huxley emphasized the need to redefine man from the natural perspective. Mill's emphasis was on society in its relation to nature, while Huxley's was on man in his relationship to nature. And while Huxley's study seems incomplete in its failure to account for civilization's place in nature, Mill's essay seems incomplete in its treatment of human nature. Mill dealt briefly with the human instinct; however, his concept of primitive man seems inadequate, particularly in the way he generalized on uncivilized man's cowardice, dirtiness, and dishonesty. If Rousseau had projected cultural or personal ideals into primitive man, Mill invested him with all the negative qualities, including a lack of appreciation for British cleanliness and morality. Furthermore, Mill's emphasis on the semantic origin of modern misconceptions about nature, as well as his suggestion that it was a problem that might have been solved for the better portion of historical time had Plato taken up the question in a dialogue, seems historically naive.[33] Could Plato have precluded, through the force of a dialogue, the adoration of nature that inspired so much Renaissance, eighteenth-century, and Romantic poetry, art, and music? What Mill did not appear to realize was that the idea of nature had always been subjectively bound to the idea of man, and that his own observations revealed nothing less than a revolution in sensibility.

Darwin's *Origin*, Mill's "Nature," and Huxley's *Man's Place in Nature*, all written in the decade from 1854 to 1863, furnish a fairly complete theoretical symposium on the revolution in the concepts of man and nature that occurred in Victorian England. What they all have in common is the dramatic change in perception inherent in the quantification of the collective phenomena of nature; nature was neither presence nor force for these three men, but rather a collection of diverse phenomena, of which the human organism was one. Together, they represent the new determinism, each of them assuming all phenomena to be the consequence of natural causation. They were liberals, their main efforts were unsympathetic to traditional views and dogmas, they were against Eyre. Aesthetically they differed widely. Whereas Darwin, who had discovered nature in the Galápagos Islands, could not discover it in the poems of Wordsworth; Mill found in Wordsworth a deep emotional solace. Huxley was an avid reader of poetry throughout his life, but he found scientific speculation more poetic and exhilarating and often quoted the poets in order to secure a point in argument.

140

iii. revolt against nature

In a series of essays undertaken in his final decade, Huxley turned his attention to considering the impulse and process that led man out of his pristine "state of nature" and into the "state of art" or civilization. Chief among these essays was "Evolution and Ethics," which in its final form consisted of two parts—the "Prolegomena" and the title essay. "Evolution and Ethics" was written and delivered as the Romanes lecture for 1893, the second of an annual Oxford series established by G. J. Romanes in 1892. To this Huxley added a prolegomenon in 1894 which served as an introduction to the problem of human ethics and natural process as he viewed it in the year before his death. Together, the two essays represent the culmination of his lifelong concern with the nature of the relationship between humanity and natural phenomena; "Evolution and Ethics" was his final word on a subject he had first explored thirty years earlier in *Man's Place in Nature*. The two works represented the intellectual extremities of his thought on the subject, and while there is evidence of a number of important changes in his concept of man, the consistency of his thought is no less striking.

William Irvine and Gertrude Himmelfarb have found a deep pessimism in Huxley's final vision of man's relationship with nature, Irvine seeing the two essays as the "culmination of Huxley's pessimism," and Himmelfarb suggesting that the two essays were the end point of Huxley's late "case against nature," which he watched develop "with horrified fascination" almost in spite of himself.[34] Both Irvine and Houston Peterson have noted the strong influence of Mill's essay "Nature," Peterson going so far as to find Huxley's essay "little more than a restatement of Mill's essay on nature in the language of a later generation nourished on *The Origin of Species.*"[35] While the response to "Evolution and Ethics" has varied, nearly all critics have seen Huxley's later vision as a reversal of his earlier tendency to find justice in natural laws and processes, and they regard his essay as a general summary of positions either for or against diverse influences identified in Darwin, Mill, and Spencer. Certainly, Huxley's position in "Evolution and Ethics" was influenced by the important strains of thought of his age; indeed, having reflected major theoretical positions of the century, developing some to their logical ends, his essay on ethics became a culmination of Victorian alienation from nature. His final stand on the amorality of nature indicates a reversal from his consistent earlier attitude expressed in his observation to Kingsley that "Nature is juster than we" (*LL*, 1:236). Even in 1860, however, Huxley's concept of justice was characterized less by an acute sense of the personal justice of things than by a conviction that it was futile and unproductive to oppose the order of nature. His was a Calvinistic sense of justice.

While he often vaguely personified natural forces, his most comprehensive early treatment of man and nature is unquestionably *Man's Place in Nature*. Unlike Mill, who had attacked traditional concepts of nature, Huxley focused his criticism on traditional concepts of man, emphasizing the sway of natural law over human affairs, examining man, the organism. While Huxley continued to acknowledge his debt to Mill and was no doubt deeply influenced by "Nature," his final position in "Evolution and Ethics" revealed a vision quite distinct from that of Mill.

Departing even more from Herbert Spencer, Huxley as early as 1871, in his essay "Administrative Nihilism," had taken note of fundamental differences between natural and civilized man. There was a radical difference, Huxley argued, between an individual who existed in a "state of nature" which he associated with "unlimited freedom" and the man who existed within the restrictions of a polity (1:285). Rejecting Spencer's organic concept of society, Huxley declared that there were "certain profound and essential differences between the physiological and the political bodies"; a better conceptualization of the social synthesis would be the chemical compound in which the properties of the aggregate were substantially different from those of the individual units (1:272, 274). "And the great problem," he maintained, "is to discover what desires of mankind may be gratified, and what must be suppressed. . . . That the gratification of some of men's desires shall be renounced is essential to order; that the satisfaction of others shall be permitted is no less essential to progress" (1:275). Huxley differed sharply from

Spencer in the concept of social progress and struggle; civilized man, he asserted, was basically different from natural man. Spencer's ideas about survival of the fittest would be applicable, at best, to the man of *Man's Place in Nature;* they did not apply to civilized man. In some primary way, the condition of civilization eliminated the violent competition that many, including Spencer, found in the Darwinian model of nature.

In "Evolution and Ethics," Huxley set out to examine the argument for civilization, the ethical process which had its origin in the distant historical past and had somehow domesticated that strange being he had unearthed thirty years earlier in his *Man's Place in Nature.* "Evolution and Ethics," then, pushes biological man back into the prehistorical past and emphasizes the ethical facet of conscious mind in contrast to the instinctual nature of the brute mind. This late vision of Huxley, limited as it was, drew from his own early thought and from the work of Darwin and Mill to explore the psychic architecture of civilization in an approach that would ultimately be borne out in the work of Freud.[36] Unable to reconcile biology and civilization, Huxley began to think of them historically, with the one gradually dominating without effacing the other. The result was a dualism that differed from the Platonic distinction between real and ideal and the Cartesian duality of mind and matter. A psychic dualism between instinct and ethical sense began to dominate his thought, to the amazement of many of his friends and colleagues.

The conflict of man and nature is the central theme of the "Prolegomena" to "Evolution and Ethics," Huxley describing the struggle between the primitive condition in England or the "state of nature," and the "state of art" which he attributed to the intervention of man. Constructing a pattern of imagery reminiscent of the long English literary tradition of the garden as the symbol of civilization—Huxley seems, particularly in his old age, to have been thinking of the deathbed speech of John of Gaunt in *Richard II*—he points out that two thousand years before the land was very likely covered with weeds and gorse. This condition represented the vegetative acme of the natural or cosmic process. Human intervention transformed various outpost patches into gardens, where trees, shrubs, and herbs flourished; man, carefully constructing his wall around the garden, protected this new order established by his labors from the external antagonism of the cosmic process. As a result, he established the "state of Art" (9:9). Thus the state of art, "created in the state of nature by man," was sustained by and dependent on him, and without his support would collapse under the "antagonistic influences of the general cosmic process" (9:9–10).

Extending the concept of the garden to the artificial productions of man, Huxley argues that the structuring impulses of man are all of a type, "from a flint implement to a cathedral or a chronometer," and are to be distinguished from products of the cosmic process, those works of nature resulting from alien phenomena independent of man (9:10–11). There is a dichotomy of force in the world—the collective, evolutionary forces of natural processes, and the opposing, stabilizing forces of man. The idea had been introduced by Mill in his "Nature"; however, Huxley goes on to suggest that the situation is not to be resolved.[37] The existence of the two forces is both truth and paradox; man himself is "as much a part of nature, as purely a product of the cosmic process, as the humblest weed" (9:11). Citing his own *Man's Place in Nature*, he admits that he had spent a good portion of his life trying to locate man's position amid natural phenomena. If it were absurd, as Mill had argued, first to place man among the collective phenomena of nature and then to set him up as an antagonist of the essential processes of nature, nevertheless the paradox is true:

> If the conclusion that the two are antagonistic is logically absurd, I am sorry for logic, because, as we have seen, the fact is so. The garden is in the same position as every other work of man's art; it is a result of the cosmic process working through and by human energy and intelligence; and, as is the case with every other artificial thing set up in the state of nature, the influences of the latter are constantly tending to break it down and destroy it. [9:12]

Art is a paradox, a conversion of the ultimate forces of nature into the production of that which is alien and opposed to the cosmic process. The aesthetic artifact is an expression of the most fundamental of human antagonisms—the revolution of man against nature.

Having established his dichotomy, Huxley carefully considered a wide range of conflicting realities and operative principles which separated or joined the two states. The state of art operated on the principle of the horticultural process, which was in conflict with the cosmic process. The characteristic feature of the state of nature, he declares, "is the intense and unceasing competition of the struggle for existence" (9:13). In the state of art, the primary feature was "the elimination of that struggle, by the removal of the conditions which give rise to it" (9:13). Struggle and flux, the great principles of nature, were replaced in the garden with stability and permanence. In nature, organic entities such as plants were continually adjusting to external conditions; in the garden, conditions were adjusted to suit the plants. The gardener usurped the agency of the cosmic process, eliminating the struggle for existence, becoming a new selecting force, molding the state of art to make it conform more closely to "an ideal of utility or beauty" (9:15). The result was that man used his limited mastery over nature not only to eliminate the threat posed by natural forces indifferent to his needs, but also within the scope of his power to force reality to conform to his ideal.

As Voltaire had done in *Candide*, Huxley slowly and lucidly built up his argument against nature, demonstrating how human institutions were in perpetual threat of extinction from the outside forces of the cosmic process. The result is an equally striking picture of human alienation. Huxley's metaphor for civilization became the colony, and he showed how the members occupy the land, "set up a new Flora and Fauna and a new variety of mankind, within the old state of nature" (9:16). Given a preternatural administrator, as "superior in power and intelligence to men, as men are to their cattle," the goals of the colony would be directed toward ending, as far as possible, the external competition of nature with the colony by systematically eliminating and excluding native forms of competition, whether men, beasts, or plants (9:17–18). All members would then be furnished with the means for existence and relieved of the fear of being deprived of such means by their "stronger or more cunning fellows" (9:18). Laws would be established, "sanctioned by the combined force of the colony," which would "restrain the self-assertion of each man within the limits required for the maintenance of peace" (9:18). Thus the struggle between the colony and nature would not only be eliminated to whatever degree possible, but the competitive struggle between men to take by brute force another's means for existence would also be eliminated. The final activity of the ideal administrator would be the creation of "artificial conditions of existence of a more favourable character" with the ultimate goal of increasing the proportions of persons of superior qualities of "courage, industry, and co-operative intelligence" (9:18–19). Such were the conditions which might establish an "earthly paradise," given a preternatural administrator who could actually bring them about.

The state of art as Huxley conceived it was necessarily an ideal, for who could expect to find such an administrator among men? In addition, given such an earthly Paradise, there remained the old problem of Malthus: "Man shares with the rest of the living world the mighty instinct of reproduction" (9:20). The only solution would be a principle of selection, and Huxley rejected the possibility that men might ever be competent to fulfill such a role: "There is no hope that mere human beings will ever possess enough intelligence to select the fittest" (9:34). While Huxley categorically rejected the possibility of human selection in practice, like Darwin he did not reject it in principle.[38] On the one hand, he underscored the inadequacy of "purely scientific considerations" which would lead to the systematic elimination of individuals deemed undesirable, attacking the application of evolutionary engineering to humans as a monstrosity, a "pigeon-fanciers' polity" (9:21, 23). Yet he argued that if some preternaturally endowed being could accurately judge which individuals were morally and intellectually superior, then systematic selection of human beings would be desirable, amounting to a kind of earthly Doctrine of Election. He severely criticized those who advocated the application of "principles of cosmic evolution . . . to social and political problems," warning of despotic governments which were prepared to carry out the principle of human improvement by selection with "preternatural ruthlessness," but without preternatural intelligence (9:22). Yet he regretted being "obliged to

146

admit that this rigorously scientific method of applying the principles of evolution to human society hardly comes within the region of practical politics" (9:34). Huxley concluded that "in the modern world, the gardening of men by themselves is practically restricted to the performance not of selection but of that other function of the gardener, the creation of conditions more favourable than those of the state of nature" (9:43). For the Malthusian problem of overpopulation, he saw no solutions other than in the increased efficiency of the polity. And because there was no obvious solution to the problem, society remained perpetually threatened from within. For the effect of overpopulation was to reintroduce the cosmic struggle for existence, converting the state of art back to the state of nature:

> Even should the whole human race be absorbed into one vast polity, within which "absolute political justice" reigns, the struggle for existence with the state of nature outside it, and the tendency to the return of the struggle within, in consequence of over-multiplication, will remain. [9:43]

Man was his own unwitting enemy. The effects of human reproduction on a massive scale could bring catastrophe to the social structure, since the condition of order depended on the ability of society to meet the needs of its members, to eliminate the motives for initiating a socially destructive struggle.

What Huxley had done, simply and directly, was to describe the relationship between man and nature as one of warfare. What had been a conflict in definition or conceptualization in Mill's "Nature" became a conflict in reality for Huxley. Nature was at war with man; man, being part of nature, was at war with himself. It was not only Huxley who had seen the conflict. A persistent nineteenth-century theme had been the violent antagonism of nature toward man, from Wordsworth's "Elegiac Stanzas," with its troubled recognition of the forces which had destroyed his brother, through the mid-century wanderings of Tennyson and Arnold amid the violent forms of nature, to works like "The Mother Mourns" of Hardy, where the poet picks through the remaining rubble of the once-colossal idea of nature.[39] In the "Prolegomena" of Huxley's "Evolution and Ethics," the theme found an explicit and final declaration in

147

that apocalyptic spirit that seemed to accompany the *fin-de-siècle* ethos. It would become a basic assumption of twentieth-century works such as Freud's *The Future of an Illusion:* "The principal task of civilization, its actual *raison d'etre,* is to defend us against nature."[40]

The second major conflict Huxley examined in the "Prolegomena," one which was ultimately connected to the war between nature and art, was the internal but equally paradoxical conflict within man. Two years earlier in his 1892 "Prologue" to *Controverted Questions,* Huxley had studied the development of human consciousness and associated the mental evolution of man with an increasing capacity for pain and pleasure: "The amount and the severity of the pain, no less than the variety and acuteness of the pleasure, have increased with every advance in the scale of evolution. As suffering came into the world, not in consequence of a fall, but of a rise, in the scale of being, so every further rise has brought more suffering" (5:48). Primordial man suffered less than civilized man, being much closer in sensibility to his "pithecoid kin." "Like them," Huxley observed, "he stood upon his 'natural rights,' gratified all his desires to the best of his ability, and was as incapable of either right or wrong doing as they" (5:48–49). His innocence was, indeed, a fact, but it was the "innocence of the ape and of the tiger, whose acts, however they may run counter to the principles of morality, it would be absurd to blame" (5:52). Biological man, the figure Huxley had examined in *Man's Place in Nature,* was a creature to whom morality did not apply, his "natural rights" entitling him to the gratification of all his desires to the extent of his capabilities. Theorizing on the rise of civilization, Huxley suggested:

> Morality commenced with society. Society is possible only upon the condition that the members of it shall surrender more or less of their individual freedom of action. In primitive societies, individual selfishness is a centrifugal force of such intensity that it is constantly bringing the social organisation to the verge of destruction. Hence the prominence of the positive rules of obedience to the elders; of standing by the family or the tribe in all emergencies; of fulfilling the religious rites, non-observance of which is conceived to damage it with the supernatural powers, belief in whose existence is one of

the earliest products of human thought; and of the negative rules, which restrain each from meddling with the life or property of another. [5:52–53]

As social organization became more complex, the pressure on the individual to abstain from a greater number of acts increased: "With the advance of civilisation . . . the rules which constitute the common foundation of morality and of law became more numerous and complicated, and the temptations to break or evade many of them stronger" (5:53). Huxley concluded that, in lieu of a clear apprehension of the natural sanctions of social rules, "a supernatural sanction was assumed"; and for the sake of social order, religion was grafted on to morality (5:53–54).

Huxley was attempting to formulate a connection between brute and civilized man. If man had existed contentedly in the primitive state of the natural historical record, what was the justification for civil history and the state of art? This approach examined the problem by considering what advantages social organization would bring to a brute organism. Like Darwin, Huxley reflected on human experience in biological terms; however, he did not accept Darwin's position that the advent of social organization was the result of the existence and strengthening of the "social instincts."[41] Darwin believed that man's moral sense, the conscience, resulted from the sense of unfulfilled social instinct an individual might experience upon giving in to some antisocial passion or impulse.[42] Peer pressure was thus a matter of instinct, a collective expression of moral intuition, enjoining the individual to follow his social instinct. To Huxley, instinct seemed primarily antisocial, and he was inclined to see peer pressure as the threat of superior group force over the instincts of the individual. Society was at war with instinct, preempting primitive man's prerogatives and "desire for unlimited self-gratification" (9:35).

In his essay "The Struggle for Existence: A Programme," published in the *Nineteenth Century* in February 1888, Huxley declared that nature was a violent and brutal process, visiting widespread suffering upon the innocent and universal pain on humanity regardless of desert. This essay, which inspired Petr Kropotkin's opposing essays in the *Nineteenth Century* on

149

mutual aid (1890–96), revealed Huxley's lifelong sense of the conflict between self and nature. The earliest men, Huxley argued, were much like the conditions of their surroundings, violent, unpredictable, struggling by means of instinct in strategies of physical force. "The primitive savage," he maintained "appropriated whatever took his fancy, and killed whomsoever opposed him, if he could" (9:205). Unlike Kropotkin, who formulated his ethical vision on Darwin's concept of "social instinct," arguing that morality and instinct were one, Huxley declared that the two were profoundly at war, that human aggression, rather than human cooperation, was the great factor behind man's early success in nature.[43] Human social behavior was the collective resistance of individuals against the internal and external natural forces which men now sought to subdue. Like Kropotkin, Huxley found survival value in ethics, but the state of art was not simply the construct of an evolving and increasingly triumphant social instinct. Civilization was an attempt to escape from the primitive state where law was undifferentiated from force, an effort by man "to escape from his place in the animal kingdom . . . to establish a kingdom of Man, governed upon the principle of moral evolution" (9:205). But the flight from his primitive origins was only a partial success, for man carried with him the same instincts which governed his pre-societal behavior: "The effort of ethical man to work towards a moral end by no means abolished, perhaps has hardly modified, the deep-seated organic impulses which impel the natural man to follow his non-moral course" (9:205). In effect, man had a dual behavioral orientation—a rational, moral self which he acquired through his civilization, and a conflicting instinctual self, which he had inherited from the distant past.

In the "Prolegomena," Huxley linked instincts to aggression and suggested that these were at war with society from within just as the cosmic process was at war with society from without:

> Moreover, with all their enormous differences in natural endowment, men agree in one thing, and that is their innate desire to enjoy the pleasures and to escape the pains of life; and, in short, to do nothing but that which it pleases them to do, without the least reference to the welfare of the society into which they are born. That

150

is their inheritance (the reality at the bottom of the doctrine of original sin) from the long series of ancestors, human and semi-human and brutal, in whom the strength of this innate tendency to self-assertion was the condition of victory in the struggle for existence. That is the reason of the *aviditas vitae*—the insatiable hunger for enjoyment—of all mankind, which is one of the essential conditions of success in the war with the state of nature outside; and yet the sure agent of the destruction of society if allowed free play within [9:27]

In "Evolution and Ethics," he went on to declare that man in his struggle against natural forces had developed instincts of "self-assertion" necessary to survival and which became the universal inheritance of the human race and a negative force in civilization:

For his successful progress, throughout the savage state, man has been largely indebted to those qualities which he shares with the ape and the tiger; his exceptional physical organization; his cunning, his sociability, his curiosity, and his imitativeness; his ruthless and ferocious destructiveness when his anger is roused by opposition. [9:51–52]

The paradox of civilization was that as man passed from anarchy to society "these deeply ingrained serviceable qualities have become defects" (9:52). Modern man, Huxley contended, "would gladly kick down the ladder by which he has climbed":

He would be only too pleased to see 'the ape and tiger die.' But they decline to suit his convenience; and the unwelcome intrusion of these boon companions of his hot youth into the ranged existence of civil life adds pains and griefs, innumerable and immeasurably great, to those which the cosmic process necessarily brings on the mere animal. In fact, civilized man brands all these ape and tiger promptings with the name of sins; he punishes many of the acts which flow from them as crimes; and, in extreme cases, he does his best to put an end to the survival of the fittest of former days by axe and rope. [9:52]

The concept of an organic dualism had begun to take shape in Huxley's final essays. Going beyond the distinctions between instinct and rationality in the work of Mill and Darwin, Huxley began to think in psychic dimensions, to conceive of man as a divided entity, one foot in a primordial past and the other in his civilized present, unable to possess completely either his primitive or his civilized self. The vision was consistent with the man Huxley had revealed thirty years before in *Man's Place in Nature:* the primitive self remained intact, although it shared the body with a rational entity Huxley associated with the conscious mind. Neither aspect of this divided self could eliminate the other half; rather, both existed in a kind of painful equilibrium, a never-ending war. The divided self which had so fascinated the Victorian mind was given Huxley's biological affirmation in "Evolution and Ethics." In Huxley's vision, it had become part of the universal human condition; the opposing principles, identified as instinct and ethic, provided both historical and biological references which were locked in the conflict which he believed ultimately generated civilization. The internalized struggle of the self found its external parallel in the conflict between the state of nature and the state of art. Instinct was that part of the cosmic process which had become internalized in the mind of man. Thus there was a motivation for human behavior which was amoral and devoted to "unlimited self-gratification" and a more recently developed principle of human behavior which was ethical and devoted to self-restraint: "Every child born into the world," Huxley declared, "will still bring with him the instinct of unlimited self-assertion. He will have to learn the lesson of self-restraint and renunciation" (9:44). This was the starting point of Huxley's attempt to discover the structure and justification of human ethical systems.

While such a vision reflected something of the trauma that attended Victorian society's new awareness of physical nature and natural process—an awareness periodically expressed in the literature of Tennyson, Arnold, and Hardy—Huxley did not reject the likelihood of a link between natural and human societies. In the "Prolegomena," he connected human ethics to still other "organic necessities" which in humanity expressed themselves as sympathy (9:28). "Human society," he theorized, "took its rise in the organic necessities expressed by imitation and the sympathetic emotions" (9:35). These, however, had yet to be adequately cultivated. Given man's selfish instincts, to carry the golden rule—of doing unto others as one would have them do unto himself—to its logical consequences would be to repudiate the very laws upon which the security of society depended. The golden rule, he observed, "can be obeyed, even partially, only under the protection of a society which repudiates it" (9:32).

The new dualism intimated that civilization was a more tentative condition than had previously been suggested in Victorian thought. Every child would develop by retracing the process of transformation from brute to civilized man; even after he had become a member of society, the individual would feel his commitment to the social structure threatened by external forces and internal instincts. Sufficient pressure from overpopulation might so dilute the advantages of a given society that men would begin to preach "anarchy; which is, substantially, a proposal to reduce the social cosmos to chaos, and begin the brute struggle for existence once again" (9:215). The vision of culture through which man attempted to force the realities of nature to conform more closely to his ideal was neither obvious nor assured. "Evolution and Ethics" bears an interesting relationship in this sense to Arnold's *Culture and Anarchy,* which a quarter of a century earlier had examined a similar problem. Huxley's late examination of what seemed to him the bedrock of civilization revealed a conflict similar to that emphasized by Arnold in his study of how individual interests conflict with those of the culture, the whole. Huxley's state of art, founded on the principle of "self-restraint," was a conceptual bridge between the history of nature, which had occupied him for so many years, and the history of civilization, which had long lain at the center of Arnold's thought. The origin of sin, Huxley theorized, was the collective inheritance by society of atavistic modes of behavior, the result being that men had the tendency "to do nothing but that which it pleases them to do, without the least reference to the welfare of the society into which they are born" (9:27).

Huxley's application of the concept of organic dualism to the problems of civilization was a step, however limited, in the direction of what was to become the cultural theory of Freud. While Huxley had no clear concept of the subconscious mind, and while he lacked a specific theory of sexuality and the relationship of instinct to consciousness, he had grasped the idea that instinct was an agent somehow competing with consciousness in the determination of human behavior. Since Bentham, the idea that human behavior was motivated by a pleasure principle or instinct had become an important idea in British social theory. The greatest happiness principle had become the justification in utilitarian thought for the establishment of a polity. For John Stuart Mill, "natural sentiment" was one of the important human motivations for living in society. "The social state," he argued, "is at once so natural, so necessary, and so habitual to man, that, except in some unusual circumstances or by an effort of voluntary abstraction, he never conceives himself otherwise than as a member of the body; and this association is riveted more and more, as mankind are further removed from the state of savage independence."[44] For Mill, society was a condition that was natural and habitual to man to such a degree that thinking of oneself as outside of society was possible only through "voluntary abstraction." For Huxley, thinking of oneself as outside of society was the preoccupation of man's instinctual life.

On a more comprehensive level, Freud would also set instinct against social organization in his theory of civilization.[45] *Civilization and Its Discontents* was a studied argument in the manifest revolt of man against nature, where culture opposed instinct. Civilized society began, Freud argued, with the first attempt to regulate social relationships. In consequence of a natural "inclination to aggression," a "primary mutual hostility," he theorized, "civilized society is perpetually threatened with disintegration. . . . Civilization has to use its utmost efforts in order to set limits to man's aggressive instinct."[46] In effect, Freud recapitulated the deep distrust and uneasiness over nature that had increasingly influenced Victorian thought. He rejected virtually all pastoral ideals, much as Huxley and Mill had, and he opposed traditions that cultivated ideas of man's presocietal innocence, including those which supposed that primitive egalitarian society had been fragmented through the institution of land ownership. The innate reality of humanity, Freud theorized, was its aggressiveness.

Huxley had rejected both idealist and laissez-faire politics and ethics as mistaken attempts to posit a social authority in natural process. He was not prepared to abandon the idea of an instinctual origin to the ethical process, however, perhaps because he was aware of Kropotkin's growing case, in essays which were appearing in the *Nineteenth Century* beside his own, for the advantages of mutual aid to social organisms. Huxley suggested that human social organization was the result of instincts for survival and sympathy rather than instincts for cooperation. "Other things being alike," he declared, "the tribe of savages in which order was best maintained; in which there was most security within the tribe and most loyal support outside it, would be the survivors" (9:35). Early group behavior, he continued, gradually gave rise to the "ethical process":

> I have termed this gradual strengthening of the social bond, which, though it arrests the struggle for existence inside society, up to a certain point improves the chances of society, as a corporate whole, in the cosmic struggle—the ethical process. [9:35]

The dynamic of society, then, was a progression in which the strengthening of the social bond had survival value for mankind in general.

An important preliminary study of religion as a cultural phenomenon prepared the way for Huxley's investigation of the "ethical process" in "Evolution and Ethics." In "The Evolution of Theology: an Anthropological Study," which appeared in 1886 in the March and April issues of the *Nineteenth Century*, he studied the structure of religion through a comparative examination of primitive myths, theologies, and ethical systems, concentrating on the development of Judaism and comparing it to religious systems among Polynesian peoples, as described in such anthropological studies as George Turner's *Nineteen Years in Polynesia*. "From my present point of view," he declared, "theology is regarded as a natural product of the operations of the human mind" (4:288). Departing from his old tendencies simply to attack religions as inaccurate efforts to represent reality, Huxley maintained that religions were universal forms of human activity, in which psychic structures were erected by primitive peoples to conceal and, thus, to modify the harsh realities of physical nature. Religions existed at the center of primitive cultures and, still influencing social behavior, evolved gradually into ethical systems. Hence, the ethical process had its origin in the human protest against nature.

The general pattern of progression was from animistic forms of worship, through image worship, polytheism, and tribalized worship of a single god-ancestor, to the genuine monotheism of the Hebrew prophets. Theological systems were constructed from similar elements, even those as removed in time and place as modern Polynesian polytheism and ancient Judaism. Ethical systems were not integral parts of theological systems, but were grafted on to them in order to lend to social behavior the powerful reinforcement of religious belief. The monotheism of the Hebrew prophets, Huxley argued, was the highest and most refined of theological systems, since its god had become largely a moral ideal.

Religions were natural and universal products of the primitive mind. Huxley regarded them as narcissistic, believing that evidence pointed to their likely origins in some form of ancestor-worship (4:308n). Gods, he suggested, were "deified ancestors"; many past rituals such as sacrifices had gradually become symbolized by practices like circumcision. As civilizations evolved, their ethical systems broke from the spiritualism of their theologies.

"The Evolution of Theology" covered important preliminary ground for "Evolution and Ethics," which Huxley delivered nearly a decade later. He not only suggested that religions were the universal meeting ground between the primitive mind and such grim realities as death; he also held that they were the cultural forces by which the primitive man of *Man's Place in Nature* was transformed into a creature of civilization. The ethical significance of this process led him to argue that religion had played the profound role in the evolution of civilization. Only for prehistorical man could natural law and human law be seen as identical; this was the period of brute innocence, the period of Spencer's survival of the fittest, the period in which ethical behavior could not truly be said to occur.

The premise of "Evolution and Ethics" is that man and nature have been at war throughout human history. That the struggle between man and nature had not always been recognized as such was due to the intervention of human systems which reduced the harshness of the clash. As in his "Prolegomena," Huxley identified the conflict between man and nature as occurring on two fronts—the struggle between the state of art and the state of nature, and the "everlasting battle with self" (9:53). What impressed Huxley most about the reality of existence was the struggle and change: "The more we learn of the nature of things, the more evident is it that what we call rest is only unperceived activity; that seeming peace is silent but strenuous battle" (9:49). Evoking a sense of the great beauty and mystery of cosmic infinity reminiscent of the *Amor intellectualis Dei* he had described in "Scientific and Pseudo-Scientific Realism," he found that in the "infinite diversities of life and thought," the greatest attribute of the cosmos is its "impermanence" (9:50). The strain of visionary idealism was still a presence in Huxley's thought. "In the exploration of the cosmic process," he declares, " . . . the highest intelligence of man finds inexhaustible employment; giants are subdued to our service; and the spiritual affections of the contemplative philosopher are engaged by beauties worthy of eternal constancy" (9:50).

But there is a new element to the vision. It is embedded within a myth, the fairy tale of "Jack and the Beanstalk." The hero climbs the stalk and "discovers that the leafy expanse supports a world composed of the same elements as that below, but yet strangely new" (9:46). And this is the world which is subsequently identified with the great macrocosmic dance, the "wonderland in which the common and the familiar become things new and strange" (9:50). The beanstalk as the path to the upper cosmos not only suggests the path of science through nature; it embodies a mythical aspect of the scientific vision, as well. Immediately after introducing the myth theme, Huxley focuses on the plant itself, and we are suddenly faced with the miraculous cyclical metamorphosis of the bean plant as an entity representative of the organic world. As William Irvine once remarked, there is a suggestion of mysticism in Huxley's acute sense of change and illusion in nature, as expressed in this essay.[47]

But amid the vision, there is a reality principle destroying man's harmony with the cosmos—pain. Pain, the "baleful

157

product of evolution," not only becomes more intense and frequent with advancing grades of animal organization, it reaches its very heights in civilized man as a "necessary consequence of his attempt to live [as a member of an organized polity]" (9:51). The great cosmic kaleidoscope, so vast and beautiful yet so disregardful of human pain, becomes in its inexorable and ubiquitous motion the infernal machine, its very harmony and perfection generating widespread human suffering. The "unfathomable injustice of the nature of things" gives birth to tragedy: "Surely Oedipus was pure of heart," Huxley observes; "it was the natural sequence of events—the cosmic process—which drove him, in all innocence, to slay his father and become the husband of his mother, to the desolation of his people and his own headlong ruin" (9:59). Ultimately, Jack must descend the beanstalk to the common world where all must face the "dread problem of evil" (9:53).

Huxley suggests that the evolution of consciousness in man has increased his capacity for suffering and at the same time given him the capacity to confront the realities of existence. Man's earliest efforts as an animal were directed against his brute competitors in the struggle for existence. His physical and mental attributes, combined with his capacity to organize and concentrate his efforts, secured him a brilliant triumph over his competition. The outcome of this struggle was the formation of the primitive human polity: "Having made the very important advance upon wolf society, . . . they agree to use the force of the whole body against individuals who violate it and in favour of those who observe it" (9:56–57). This advance was the origin of group regulation of individual behavior, and it led both to the success of man in the struggle for existence and to the establishment of human law. Over a period of time law was refined into an ethical system sophisticated enough to consider distinctions between involuntary and willful misdeeds, wrong and guilty actions, and, ultimately, the motive behind a given individual's actions: "The idea of justice thus underwent a gradual sublimation from punishment and reward according to acts, to punishment and reward according to desert" (9:57).

But to a developing human sense of law and justice, the cosmic process became increasingly alien, giving rise to the almost universal sense in civilized man of the division between cosmic law and ethical law; this sense, Huxley observes, is expressed in the great religious works, in Job, the Buddhist Sutras, the tragic poetry of Greece. The clash between harsh, cosmic reality and ethical ideality is mitigated by visionary human systems, either through destruction of desire and denial of the reality of the physical world, as in Buddhism; or by a theodicy such as that developed by the Greek Stoics, which submerges evil in the larger context of necessity or universal good. As Mill had done in his essay "Nature," Huxley cites Pope's famous declaration that "whatever is, is right," and then rejects the idea of living according to nature as a system of "applied Natural History" (9:72, 74). While Huxley rejects the Buddhistic and Stoical systems as being clearly inadequate to the modern experience, his admiration for them is obvious. Both developed highly sophisticated ethical senses, Buddhism arriving at its vision through an absolute idealism, Stoicism coming to a remarkably similar moral vision through its materialism. Much as he admired the "apatheia" of the Stoics and the "nirvana" of the Buddhists, Huxley was unable to reconcile them with his views of modern civilization: there was in this profound renunciation of desire and evil a negation of the individual which seemed more like a retreat from than a recognition of physical reality. He complained: "The hero has become a monk. The man of action is replaced by the quietist, whose highest aspiration is to be the passive instrument of the divine Reason. By the Tiber, as by the Ganges, ethical man admits that the cosmos is too strong for him; and, destroying every bond which ties him to it by ascetic discipline, he seeks salvation in absolute renunciation" (9:77). Yet, the greatest moments of civilization were those of man's confrontation with the realities of his own existence. To use the human reason rather than to trust in the existence of the Divine Reason was the moral object of modern civilization.

Huxley's concepts of good and evil, while partly defined on the basis of their advantages to human survival, were also based on what he referred to as their aesthetic appeal. Holding that cosmic evolution is unable "to furnish better reason why what we call good is preferable to what we call evil than we had before," he suggested that good and evil were not merely social concepts, but that they were consequences in man of the evolution of the "aesthetic faculty" (9:80). Thus, while he argued that moral sentiments arise "in the same way as other natural phenomena," he suggested, as Mill and Arnold had, that they possessed an intuitive, aesthetical basis. Good and evil could not be determined solely in terms of social improvement or biological advancement; they were also to be judged by man's sense of beauty and proportion, by the same ideals which shaped his art.

Human progress meant "a checking of the cosmic process at every step and the substitution for it of another, which may be called the ethical process; the end of which is not the survival of those who may happen to be the fittest, in respect of the whole of the conditions which obtain, but of those who are ethically the best" (9:81). The "ethically best," a vague notion, not unlike Arnold's "best self" in *Culture and Anarchy*, was the abstraction Huxley used to suggest a social ideal. This ideal was embodied in the individual who had learned self-restraint and who placed a high value on social cooperation for the survival and strengthening of the polity (9:82). One thinks not only of Arnold's ideal self but of Carlyle's Abbot Samson in *Past and Present* who brought rigor and ethics to his community. The polity featured the establishment of a human context in nature, the humanization of reality through the force of culture. "The history of civilization," Huxley maintained, "details the steps by which men have succeeded in building up an artificial world within the cosmos" (9:83).

While Huxley found a strong argument in the communal effort, he sought to balance priorities of the group with the freedoms of inquiry and expression which, for him, were necessary to the proper assessment and confrontation of reality. He retained a deep sense of human division, however, and placed growing emphasis on the need of "curbing the instincts of savagery in civilized men" (9:85). He objected to the "fanatical individualism" which he identified with "attempts to apply the analogy of cosmic nature to society," a pointed criticism of both the laissez-faire social thought of Spencer and the anarchism of Kropotkin (9:82). Both trends, Huxley felt, advocated the abdication of individual responsibility through an unjustified submergence of individual morality in a group dynamic which drew its models from Darwin's theories of organic progression.

The finality, bold, uncompromising, and unconditional, of Huxley's declaration that man and nature are at strife makes this assertion one of the great epitomes of the alienation that had been developing during much of the century:

> Let us understand, once for all, that the ethical progress of society depends, not on imitating the cosmic process, still less in running away from it, but in combating it. It may seem an audacious proposal thus to pit the microcosm against the macrocosm and to set man to subdue nature to his higher ends; but I venture to think that the great intellectual difference between the ancient times with which we have been occupied and our day, lies in the solid foundation we have acquired for the hope that such an enterprise may meet with a certain measure of success. [9:83]

The urge of revolution against the macrocosm was the impulse of a thinker whose ambition was to convert nature, much as one might establish the garden in the wilderness; that man might fundamentally alter the forces of nature with the products and processes of his technology did not occur to Huxley. Rather, like Bacon, who had dreamed of a human environment consistent with high human ideals, Huxley believed that the strengthening of the state of art could contain the impulse of man toward aggression. It was above all for an improvement in man's ethical condition, rather than an increase in society's material well-being, that Huxley advocated confrontation of the cosmic process. As Matthew Arnold had said close to half a century before:

> Man must begin, know this, where Nature ends;
> Nature and man can never be fast friends.
> Fool, if thou canst not pass her, rest her slave![48]

Science was the means, as Huxley had intuitively understood in his childhood, by which society might confront the opposing realities of nature. Freud also saw the conflict of man with nature as one waged by means of the intervening sciences, although man would gain little increased pleasure for freedom for his efforts. Speaking of "deflections" which allowed men to live with the inevitable disappointments of their lives, Freud pointed to the garden of Voltaire's *Candide:* "Voltaire has deflections in mind when he ends *Candide* with the advice to cultivate one's garden, and scientific activity is a deflection of this kind, too."[49] Against the "dreaded external world," Freud declared, "one can only defend oneself by some kind of turning away from it, if one intends to solve the task by oneself. There is, indeed, another and better path: that of becoming a member of the human community, and, with the help of a technique guided by science, going over to the attack against nature and subjecting her to the human will."[50] This was the essence of Huxley's garden.

In "Evolution and Ethics," Huxley acknowledged in the human will a power it rarely possessed in his earlier, deterministic days. The emergence of the will, a force independent of and opposed to the collective forces of nature, was the great paradox on which Huxley sought to base his ethical revolution. Human will alienated man from nature, for, recognizing his power to do so, man could hardly refrain from altering the conditions of his existence in his own favor. "In virtue of his intelligence," Huxley declared, "the dwarf bends the Titan to his will" (9:84). One of the moral insights of "Evolution and Ethics" was Huxley's recognition that the power of the human will to confront and alter nature was identical to the faculty which allowed humanity the great ethical choice between ruthless self-assertion and social commitment. The assertion of the will over nature must be accompanied by a corresponding assertion of the will over antisocial instinct, the internalized aspect of the cosmic process. This is the ideal of Huxley's ethics, a vague ideal, but one he believed could harness the prodigious potential of science to a human and civilized end. If man could not control himself, his power over nature would become meaningless, indeed, deadly.

Huxley's thought on the relationship between man and nature developed consistently throughout his life, from his early childhood clash with experience, through his *Man's Place in Nature*, to his final "Evolution and Ethics." From the decidedly monistic emphasis of his early portrait of biological man, he moved steadily toward the dualism of his ethical man; his early belief in the justness of nature was supplanted in his later thought by a sense of the utter amorality of natural process. These developments were interlocked, for as Huxley grew to recognize the alien nature of cosmic process, his appreciation of the importance of civilization deepened. The uniqueness of man seemed more obvious as the capacity of nature to absorb human ideals of benevolence and justice diminished. The development of Huxley's thought was consistent, for the dualism of his "Evolution and Ethics" would have been impossible without that early glimpse into the underworld of human biology and history which left him with a deep impression of the intimacy between man and nature. He did not reject this vision in his later thought; rather, he projected it into its historical perspective, recognizing it as a condition of the prehistorical past which remained at hand in the cultural present: "the cosmic nature born with us and, to a large extent, necessary for our maintenance, is the outcome of millions of years of severe training, and it would be folly to imagine that a few centuries will suffice to subdue its masterfulness to purely ethical ends" (9:85).

While Huxley left his century with a guarded optimism about the prospects for civilization and ethical progress, he also expressed deep anxiety over the fragility of the wall separating the state of art from the state of nature. There were, in fact, two walls—the wall without, protecting the polity from physical nature, and the wall within, separating instinctual from ethical man. Huxley's final emphasis was on the need to strengthen the walls. The human race, he maintained, had emerged from its "heroic childhood." Man had awakened to find himself alone in nature.

V

Science and Culture

i. science and criticism

Huxley's state of art was the concept of a critic and moralist who believed that the principle of society must have a rational and ethical basis. At the same time, he held that society required a clear empirical foundation on which to build. He believed such a foundation could be established on a principle of scientific naturalism which set rigorous empirical standards as the conditions for assent. His problem was that in order to assert the existence and value of human critical reason, after Descartes, while verifying the methodological standards of the empiricists, he was obliged to find a meeting ground for two traditions which were at odds on several philosophical premises. Science, he believed, could furnish the required critical and integrative activity which would effect the fusion of rationalist sources of value with empiricist standards for assent.

Huxley consciously sought to establish his new scientific perspective at the broad Victorian forum on culture, where the concept of social and cultural criticism, initiated, as Mill had pointed out, by Bentham and Coleridge, had begun to flourish. The essays and studies of Carlyle, Mill, Ruskin, and Arnold moved within a common sphere of critical activity, examining the ethics and mechanics of society by exploring the meanings and traditions of culture. To this debate, Huxley brought a broad awareness of developments in scientific thought in an effort to furnish a fresh basis for examining Victorian social and cultural issues, many of which had been raised by the frenetic activity within his own scientific disciplines. Matthew Arnold believed that the nineteenth century was a critical age in which there was a pressing need for the establishment of a new order

165

of ideas. It was the object of the critical power "in all branches of knowledge, theology, philosophy, history, art, science to see the object as in itself it really is."[1] Criticism could establish an "intellectual situation of which the creative power can profitably avail itself."[2] To Huxley, seeing the object as it really is was a particular specialty of the scientific mind, scientific naturalism having as its goals the elimination of preconceptions and the critical isolation of its object. "The essence of the scientific spirit is criticism," he declared in his essay, "The Coming of Age of *The Origin of Species*" (1880). And in his Birmingham address in October of the same year, "Science and Culture," he agreed with Arnold that a criticism of life was the essence of culture, but observed that "an army, without weapons of precision and with no particular base of operations, might more hopefully enter upon a campaign on the Rhine, than a man, devoid of a knowledge of what physical science has done in the last century, upon a criticism of life" (3:144). The scientist, with his tool of method, his distinterestedness, with his solid base in the physical world, was potentially an ideal critic.

Just as Matthew Arnold's "best self" in *Culture and Anarchy* identified the cultural center, the intellectual and moral ideal Arnold wished to associate with sound cultural criticism, Huxley's man of science was the rationalist with a deeply ethical cultural ambition. He was what Arnold would have found an incurably infected Hebraist, with a passion for law, a prejudice toward action, and the strictest of moral consciences. These sprang from values which had a high personal significance for Huxley as well.

More deeply, Huxley associated the scientific frame of mind with an innocence he identified in the process of sitting down before fact as a "little child," in the model of childlike simplicity he found in Darwin's mind, in the innocent Cinderella at the end of "Science and Morals," alone in her garret, contemplating the great natural order of existence. From this haven of innocence, where the self often existed in meditative disembodiment from the world, Huxley drew inner moral resources to prepare for the confrontation with material phenomena and the clash of instinct and consciousness. The scientific haven of innocence was also the state of art of "Evolution and Ethics" where one could operate insulated from the struggle going on in brute nature. While its psychic origins seem clearly to have been established in Huxley's childhood mode of withdrawal from the world of men and experience, of which he spoke to his fiancée, Henrietta Heathorn, its primary cultural metaphor Huxley identified in the "Prolegomena" to "Evolution and Ethics" with the colony set up in a hostile environment to make moral law prevail over instinctual or natural law, civilization prevail over nature. The dark side of this vision was its consuming fear of disorder, its sometimes frantic belief that man can create human community through the establishment of law in all quarters of existence. Its hope lay in the unpretentious rationalism of Huxley's scientist, who doggedly resisted the utopian trend toward absolutism and who sought to establish the free expression of thought as the ethical obligation of society.

Huxley's essays established the critical voice and perspective of the scientist-rationalist, just as Huxley molded the essay itself into a lean and versatile literary instrument with which to dissect chosen features of English culture and society. Always clear, direct, and bold, yet gifted in his use of irony and metaphor, he constructed terse and tightly organized essays which reflected in the simplicity of their literary form a simplicity of values and ideals.[3] He began, like Ruskin, with the materials of his specialty, then expanded his considerations into general subjects and, inevitably, into the still broader scope of cultural and social criticism. His insistent appeal to experiment and observation and his views on the duties of scepticism made him, as Walter Houghton has shown, one of the representative voices of the Victorian critical spirit.[4] Uttered with legendary economy, his criticism was rarely subtle, but nearly always of basic importance. His ultimate appeal was neither to utility nor to empirical standards of verification, but to reason, which as he used the term meant the faculty of judgment that integrated experience with permanent value, whether culturally or intuitively derived. This rationalist appeal was a key to his success as an essayist and controversialist. One after another, great spokesmen for differing traditions, Wilberforce, Gladstone, Argyll, A. J. Balfour, rose up to attack what seemed to be an indiscriminate assault on authority, only to find their own positions opposed from the stronghold of reason and morality. Of Huxley's critics, only Matthew Arnold seemed fully to comprehend the basis of his critical appeal, and he responded by seeking a wider perspective in which to interpret the idea of reason, which was still much valued by Victorians.

Few words were more important or more elusive in the Huxley lexicon than "reason." It was consistently placed strategically in his important essays. It dominated his definitions of science; it was integral to his definition of agnosticism; it typically formed the conceptual bridge in his essays between the activities of science and culture. Huxley identified reason with "private judgment" in his 1892 "Prologue" to *Controverted Questions* (5:9). He assumed that the faculty of reason functioned in a commonsensical manner, that it was self-evident, and that it furnished an innate and sufficient intellectual means for the individual to form a private judgment on the truth of an idea. Its most compelling modern tool was empirical method, which for Huxley was the systematization of common human patterns of experience. Reason was superior to but not independent of sense experience, since sensory data established the bridge between mind and nature. Informed by the data of sensation, it justified assent or doubt and negotiated value through processes which were partially intuitive, since they were not entirely represented in the consciousness. Unlike empirical method, in which the mind consciously and methodically constructed inductive and deductive logical sequences in the formal structuring of experience, reason often made rapid unconscious judgments that could not be fully accounted for by explicit logic and in detail. Conviction and doubt, Huxley observed in a fragment, arose from a complex of intellectual materials which were not fully represented in the consciousness:

> The essence of what we call reason in man is the logical process, not the state of consciousness by which sometimes, and more or less partially, the man becomes aware of the process. The essential operations of induction and deduction, the operations which have the effect of what we call generalization and syllogistic reasoning are performed by quadrupeds and by savages as much as by ourselves. But the quadruped has no or next to no representations in con-

sciousness of these operations; the savage very few; the majority more or less of civilized men not many more; and even the most perfected self analyst constantly drops many, and as we say jumps to a conclusion without the least consciousness [of] most of the work that has been done to get him there.[5]

Human reason, then, shared fundamental characteristics with the intuitive mental processes of lower forms of life, although in the human intellect the processes were more complex and better represented in the consciousness. Aware of his reason, man could externalize it with his experimental method.

Huxley considered science the product of an evolved human consciousness which enabled the intellect to direct and control its own operations more deliberately. Science was a refinement of common sense, where method reconstructed experience in such a way as to reproduce the quasi-conscious and more complex operations of reason. In 1886, late in his career and deep in controversy with Gladstone over Genesis, Huxley gave this definition of science: "To my mind, whatever doctrine professes to be the result of the application of the accepted rules of inductive and deductive logic to its subject-matter; and which accepts, within the limits which it sets to itself, the supremacy of reason, is Science" (4:193). Reason and method were in this way interdependent, but with reason as the ultimate justification for assent. Similarly, in "Science and Culture," his essay addressed to Arnold six years earlier, Huxley had associated reason with method: "We falsely pretend to be the inheritors of [Greek] culture, unless we are penetrated, as the best minds among them were, with an unhesitating faith that the free employment of reason, in accordance with scientific method, is the sole method of reaching truth" (3:152). Huxley's emphasis on method, an explicitly patterned form of consciousness, countered Arnold's stress in *Culture and Anarchy* on spontaneity and the free play of consciousness. While both he and Arnold were strong advocates of reason, Huxley, with his Hebraic love of law, considered reason the faculty for eliminating error in logic and for integrating the results of empirical effort with standards of value, while Arnold frequently used the word in close association with the imagination.

In his essay, "Heinrich Heine," Arnold associated "idea" and "reason" intimately with one another: "The enthusiast for the idea, for reason, values reason, the idea, in and for themselves; he values them irrespectively of the practical conveniences which their triumph may obtain for him."[6] While reason was associated with an antidogmatic principle for Huxley, it was associated with an anti-Philistinic principle for Arnold, the Philistine being one who was willing to tolerate the absence of reason and ideas in exchange for practical convenience. Reason was associated with method for Huxley, and this combination laid a heavy stress on order and on the logical arrangement of parts. Science was, above all, an order-seeking activity in pursuit of law and causation. In Arnold's thought, reason, associated with imagination or ideas, was manifested in balance or harmony, that is, an order that would appeal to the aesthetic sense rather than to standards of inductive or deductive logic. This would account, in part, for the concern with wholeness and harmony characteristic of Arnold's thought.[7]

This contrast extended to the two concepts of criticism Huxley and Arnold supported. Arnold's criticism aspired to inclusiveness, the collection of the best that is known and thought about a given question. Huxley's criticism stressed exclusiveness, the elimination of erroneous and undemonstrable assumptions. The scientific spirit was identical to the critical spirit, its method was empirical, and its ultimate appeal was to the reason:

> The scientific spirit is of more value than its products, and irrationally held truths may be more harmful than reasoned errors. Now the essence of the scientific spirit is criticism. It tells us that whenever a doctrine claims our assent we should reply, Take it if you can compel it. The struggle for existence holds as much in the intellectual as in the physical world. A theory is a species of thinking, and its right to exist is coextensive with its power of resisting extinction by its rivals. [2:229]

While Huxley had rejected social laissez-faire, he embraced its intellectual equivalent in the spirit of Mill's *On Liberty*. Truth was the product of competitive struggle, various theories and ideas vying for supremacy as each stood equal before the reason. The compelling truth was the one that could be traced to its origin via an empirical structure. And since "irrationally held truths may be more harmful than reasoned errors" the means—properly, empirical—of arriving at truth might be more important than the truth itself, truthfulness becoming as important as truth. For Arnold, methodology, whatever its efficacies, was clearly not to be stressed; the important critical object was, through disinterestedness and free play of imagination, to seek and to establish a sense of the whole. Like Huxley, Arnold believed that reason was self-evident and compelling: "But the prescriptions of reason are absolute, unchanging, of universal validity; *to count by tens is the easiest way of counting*—that is a proposition of which every one, from here to the Antipodes, feels the force."[8] While Huxley found specialist knowledge compelling to the reason, knowledge, for example, of Darwin's great argument, Arnold found generalist knowledge compelling to the reason. These attitudes formed the separate foundations of their critical theories.

In "On the Method of Zadig," which also appeared in 1880, Huxley went to considerable lengths to show that "Zadig's method was nothing but the method of all mankind" (4:8). The argument, reminiscent of his early declaration in 1854 that science was nothing but *"trained and organised common sense,"* suggested that science was an exact body of knowledge which had been forged through the power of human reason (3:45). Science conferred upon human kind the power to construct a whole from a part, just as Zadig, reasoning from evidence to origins, described physical phenomena which he had never witnessed. Like his famous detective ancestor, Cuvier began with a fragment—a mere bone, perhaps—and through a careful process of induction and deduction synthesized a whole (4:18). The implication behind Huxley's Zadig essay was that scientific thought was essentially a refinement of common sense, and that scientific theory aimed at defining reality rather than at the accumulation of a distinct, independent, and self-consistent body of thought. An important question was whether the primary allegiance of a theory was to its own internal consistency or to an external reality. Few modern theorists would unreservedly support Huxley's position that the theoretical whole was an accurate representation of external reality or that scientific thought was common-sensical.[9]

On the other hand, Huxley's "The Progress of Science: 1837–1887" (1887), a key late Victorian essay, revealed that his theory of the relationship between scientific construct and external reality was more complex than has often been supposed. He made several important observations on science which anticipated modern attitudes. He rejected the idea that science was a process of discerning truth in which the methodological interventions of man led by rote from fact to discovery:

> It is a favourite popular delusion that the scientific inquirer is under a sort of moral obligation to abstain from going beyond that generalisation of observed facts which is absurdly called "Baconian" induction. But any one who is practically acquainted with scientific work is aware that those who refuse to go beyond fact, rarely get as far as fact; and any one who has studied the history of science knows that almost every great step therein has been made by the "anticipation of Nature," that is, by the invention of hypotheses, which, through verifiable, often had very little foundation to start with. [1:62]

Huxley rejected the idea that scientific activity was a kind of mechanized arranging of factual data to achieve a routine, determined result, emphasizing, rather, the elements of chance and creativity upon which discovery depended. Furthermore, scientific generalizations and hypotheses were neither absolute nor uniform, but were only useful and accurate within defined limits, and therefore could be accepted only under conditions as truth (1:64). Verifiable hypotheses were to be considered "not as ideal truths, the real entities of an intelligible world behind phenomena, but as a symbolical language, by the aid of which Nature can be interpreted in terms apprehensible by our intellects" (1:65). Each of these observations dismissed the idea of an absolute correlation between the scientific description of nature or process and the reality, such as it might be, of physical nature. This insight was important, for, while the popular imagination frequently considered scientific principle as absolute in some rigid and undeniable sense, often by extension thinking of the scientist himself as an absolutist, the reverse was actually the case: the scientist's success depended on his recognition of a given system's limitations. The "scientific 'criticism of life,'" Huxley declared in "Science and Culture," appealed not to authority but to nature: "It admits that all our interpretations of natural fact are more or less imperfect and symbolic, and bids the learner seek for truth not among words but among things. It warns us that the assertion which outstrips evidence is not only a blunder but a crime" (3:150).

ii. naturalism

In his effort to identify the bond between science and culture, Huxley searched for a critical concept which would establish significant common ground occupied by science and society. By 1892, when he wrote his "Prologue" to *Controverted Questions*, he had long dissociated natural and social order and was preparing for his Romanes lecture, "Evolution and Ethics," in which he was to formulate his declaration of ethical independence. While his earlier speculations on natural order had often been geared to the discovery of a principle which would unify natural law with social law, he abandoned the attempt sometime between 1869 and 1871, when he wrote "Scientific Education" and "Administrative Nihilism," respectively. In "Scientific Education," he declared that there was a "struggle for existence, which goes on as fiercely beneath the smooth surface of modern society, as among the wild inhabitants of the woods" (3:114). Scientific knowledge strengthened one's powers of attack. Two years later in "Administrative Nihilism," written in support of Forster's Education Act, he launched a vigorous attack on what he identified as social "laissez-faire," or the unrestricted pursuit of self-interest. He quoted widely from Locke, Hobbes, Humboldt, and Kant, but even so, his laissez-faire sounded most like Arnold's "doing as one likes" in *Culture and Anarchy*.

Arnold's essays appeared as an edition in 1869, and it would be difficult to imagine Huxley, with all his enthusiasm and, indeed, anxiety, over order, not picking up a major new work by Arnold with "anarchy" in its title. He had jokingly referred to the Bishop Wilson of *Culture and Anarchy* in a note to Arnold in July 1869, in which he sought the return of an umbrella he had left at Arnold's house (*LL*, 1:335). Most likely the two had discussed *Culture and Anarchy* at some length during the visit.

Huxley's "Administrative Nihilism" made a dramatic departure from his earlier essays, becoming the first of a series of essays on political and social thought which culminated in his final attack on social laissez-faireism in "Evolution and Ethics." Huxley argued the need to curtail self-interest and pointed out the superior virtues of social cooperation over social competition. The target was Herbert Spencer, who had systematically borrowed constructs from the biological sciences to fashion his models for society. Spencer more than anyone else showed Huxley the overwhelming problems entailed in using scientific systems, a priori, as models for society. This included Darwinian natural selection. By 1871, Huxley had taken up a position in opposition to the new naturalism. Nevertheless, he maintained that the natural order was a vital factor in the state of art and that it must remain the focus of significant human activity.

That Huxley was constantly searching for critical principles which linked natural order with society and culture is suggested by the large number of critical terms he adopted. Of the three main critical principles he followed over a period of fifty years, the earliest was the "thätige Skepsis" which he borrowed from Goethe and which emphasized a kind of Romantic doubt or scepticism, stressing the unceasing effort to overcome, attaining a positive, if conditional, principle of belief. Inside the back cover of his voyage diary, Huxley wrote:

> "Thätige Skepsis." "An *Active Scepticism* is that which unceasingly strives to overcome itself and by well directed research to attain to a kind of conditional certainty."[10]

Well before the mid-fifties, he had seen in scientific research a possible avenue to the conquest of doubt. The term appeared again in his essay, "On Descartes' 'Discourse Touching the Method of Using One's Reason Rightly and of Seeking Scientific Truth'" (1870), an essay Arnold admired and one Huxley regarded as central to his own critical theory. Descartes was the first modern, he declared, to make it a matter of religious duty "to strip off all his beliefs and reduce himself to a state of intellectual nakedness, until such time as he could satisfy himself which were fit to be worn" (1:170). The object of such doubt was not to destroy, but, as Goethe had observed, to arrive at foundations and to conquer itself. Again, in 1892, Huxley used the term in "An Apologetic Irenicon" to counter the charge of Frederic Harrison that, unlike positivism, agnosticism did not attempt to reconstruct what it dismantled. The spirit of the agnostic position, Huxley declared, was contained in Goethe's "thätige Skepsis," which "enjoins the clearing of the ground, not in a spirit of wanton mischief, not for destruction's sake, but with the distinct purpose of fitting the site for those constructive operations which must be the ultimate object of every rational man."[11]

Along with "thätige Skepsis," Huxley's "agnosticism" functioned as a critical principle which urged the use of empirical method to tutor the reason. It was a somewhat more conservative term since it suggested the withholding of assent, the suspension of belief, as well as the innate human limitation for determining truth. Even more significant was the implication that belief or faith should not influence action, since they had no basis in verifiable reality. The sole basis of behavior, Huxley argued, should be consistent with verifiable truth. The central problem raised by the agnostic principle was, predictably, the ethical question. Huxley's early alternative to the connection of faith and ethics was to urge a morality based on reason and natural law. As he came to believe that nature was amoral, he was forced to conclude that ethics was based on paradox, having evolved with human consciousness as an independent force that functioned in opposition to the cosmic processes of nature. Consciousness made will capable of revolting against the tyranny of nature through substitution of ethical law for natural law.

In his reexamination of the concept of agnosticism in the 1889 essays, Huxley again closely associated reason and method. Agnosticism was not a creed but a "method," the essence of which was expressed by Socrates and which could be summed up in "Try all things, hold fast by that which is good" (5:245). Positively expressed, the agnostic principle could be stated as: "In matters of the intellect, follow your reason as far as it will take you, without regard to any other consideration" (5:246). But it was never entirely clear what he meant when he advised one to follow reason "as far as it will take you." He did not explore in any detail the precise relationship between reason and method. Certainly if Socrates is to be seen as an agnostic, then Cartesian rationalism, to say nothing of various nine-teenth-century methodologies, is not essential to the "method" or to the "reason" of agnosticism. Indeed, if the agnostic method may be summed up in "Try all things, hold fast by that which is good," then Huxley was not referring to a specific method such as induction or deduction at all, for the concept of "good" is of a different order. The good is above all an idea of value, which can only be formed by making value judgments. It cannot be formulated by means of a rigorous methodology un-less one defines it in terms of process, equating it, for example, with "consistency." Reason, however, as the faculty of judg-ment, can make evaluatons methodologies are powerless to de-termine. Given an idea of the good which in "Evolution and Ethics" Huxley identified with both human sympathy and aesthetic intuition, reason could examine methodological ef-forts in terms of that idea. This seems to be what Huxley was suggesting when he declared that agnosticism was a method which appealed to the reason. In this sense, agnosticism was the fusion of method and reason.

Huxley's reluctance to clearly define what he meant by reason and method had a complicating effect on his thought in general. It did not strengthen its theoretical base; many critics have en-countered a fundamental vagueness when confronting ideas such as Huxley's agnosticism from a theoretical point of view. As A. W. Benn and D. W. Dockrill have both found, there is a certain amorphousness to the term "agnosticism," an apparent clash and confusion between the metaphysical, methodological, and moral implications it held for Huxley at various times.[12] "Science" is another of Huxley's terms which slips from one's grasp if examined too closely, again because it is difficult to understand precisely what he meant by telling us that we must accept the supremacy of reason in our use of method. If by "reason" we understand him to mean a partially intuitive pro-cess of evaluation, a private response to external facts, systems, and phenomena; and by "scientific method" we take him to mean the formal, specialized, yet creative processes governed by induction and deduction, we come closest to the twin aspects of his science and agnosticism. His real aim appears to have been to accommodate two philosophical traditions—the rationalist tradition which, as A. W. Benn notes, made reason the "supreme regulator" of belief and action, and the empiricist tradition which held that knowledge was derived from sensory experience alone.[13] Chesterton considered Huxley one of the most devoted and consistent of Victorian rationalists.[14] Wanting very much to link science with reason, Huxley set out, sagelike, to unify them through his own powers of rhetoric in an attempt to establish a vision of order which could assimilate scientific definition without itself being reduced to an arrangement of scientifically defined parts. Unable to achieve a formal philosophical system equal to his vision—a common enough Victorian predicament—Huxley chose what to him was the only worthwhile alternative: the rhetorical affirmation of a complex vision, which he was unable theoretically to define.[15]

Of his rhetorical objectives, the foremost was to communicate the *value* of scientific activity, not merely as a means to material improvement, but as a way of seeing things, of perceiving truth, however limited. He believed that science was a progressive, if necessarily approximate, revelation of reality. When he declared that agnosticism was a method, he was identifying it as a quantifying process involving induction and deduction. But when he observed that it could be expressed in that most ancient principle, "Try all things, hold fast by that which is good," he was aligning it with the qualitative process of evaluation, of judgment. In this way, he could accept Darwinian theory as the great discovery of the century, yet reject it, as he did in "Administrative Nihilism" (1871) and "Evolution and Ethics" (1893), as the dynamic for human society. It was an important function of reason to prevent the methodological extension of empirical results to the region of the absolute:

> Rational doubt—doubt as a means to the attainment of certainty, either of knowledge or of no knowledge—has been the fire of the intellectual world—the great agent not merely of destruction but of construction. For it is out of doubt of the old that the new springs; and it is doubt of the new that keeps innovation within rational bounds.[16]

Huxley considered agnosticism an antidogmatic principle,

177

aimed against the dogmas of materialism and naturalism as well as those of traditional theology. Indeed, agnosticism was attacked as strenuously by the materialists as by the traditional theologians. In his introduction to the English edition of *Socialism: Utopian and Scientific,* Engels in 1892, made a sweeping polemical attack on agnosticism, arguing that it was nothing but " 'shamefaced' materialism."[17] And he went on to claim the mantle of science for historical materialism.

Huxley's critical theory assumed the "scientific naturalism" of his 1892 "Prologue" to *Controverted Questions.* As he had done in coining the term "agnosticism," he conceived his scientific naturalism as an antithesis, this time of "supernaturalism." The qualification "scientific" was necessary to distinguish his conception of naturalism from Spencer's a priori version. Associating scientific naturalism with the ideal of intellectual freedom, he argued that naturalism, with its reference to physical nature and to empirical standards of independence, elevated private judgment to a higher social and cultural truth than public judgment, which he identified with all authoritarian structure. Law, whether scientific or civil, was based on human experience and reason, and was a great cultural inheritance, the only force capable of opposing the dogmas of public judgment and imposed definition, whether formulated by religious or by civil authority.

Scientific naturalism, Huxley argued, was the intellectual descendant of "private judgment" or reason; these had become historical forces through the evolving human consciousness which created opposition to dogmas imposed by authorities of given historical periods (5:38). Scientific naturalism was in this sense a historical term, the logical outcome of a cultural evolution which found its most immediate origin in the Renaissance with the rejection of the old medieval standard of Church authority. The historical progress of private judgment was an intellectual evolution which Huxley believed advanced in an almost deterministic pattern, comparable to the historical dialectic of Marx. The intellectual tyranny of dogma was for Huxley an antiprogressive historical force equivalent to Marx's concept of economic tyranny. But Huxley's criticism applied to proletarian as well as to religious dogma; Marxist societies forged through the regimented imposition of definition would ultimately generate the opposition such historical phenomena had always inspired. The issue of private judgment would inevitably rise anew as a powerful historical force.

"The goal of the humanists," Huxley maintained, "whether they were aware of it or not, was the attainment of the complete intellectual freedom of the antique philosopher" (5:14). By intellectual freedom, he meant the speculative freedom which he associated with Greek philosophy, as opposed to the intellectual serfdom he associated with the "dogmas of mediaeval Supernaturalism" and subsequent Protestant authoritarianism (5:12). Nineteenth-century science had inherited the Renaissance humanistic tradition in the sense that it advocated the use of human reason in the examination of nature as the avenue to truth. The "New Reformation" of modern science was to continue where the old Reformation had failed; it would advance the rule of reason over human affairs. While Erasmus was the "arch-humanist" and the spiritual father of the nineteenth-century spirit of scientific inquiry, Descartes was the first to formulate a clear method for pursuing the essential goals of the humanists:

> It is important to note that the principle of the scientific Naturalism of the latter half of the nineteenth century, in which the intellectual movement of the Renascence has culminated, and which was first clearly formulated by Descartes, leads not to the denial of the existence of any Supernature; but simply to the denial of the validity of the evidence adduced in favour of this, or of that, extant form of Supernaturalism. [5:38–39]

Scientific naturalism provided the basis for human knowledge of nature, revolutionizing traditional fields of knowledge, often times shriveling them to mere bits and fragments of ideas. "Scientific historical criticism" had "reduced the annals of heroic Greece and regal Rome to the level of fables"; "scientific literary criticism" had assailed the "unity of authorship of the *Iliad*," not to mention the Bible; "scientific physical criticism" had reduced the earth to a satellite, and the solar system "to one of millions of groups of like cosmic specks, circling, at unimaginable distances from one another through infinite space"

(5:32–33). Natural explanation was replacing supernatural explanation; but the cost to tradition was monumental.

Having coined "scientific naturalism" as an antithetical term to "supernaturalism," Huxley was caught off guard two years later by A. J. Balfour who, in his *The Foundations of Belief*, attacked the concept of naturalism and classed Mill, Spencer, and Huxley together as its advocates.[18] While all three could be said to hold that phenomena must be traced to natural causes, they differed widely in their general theories. Spencer's naturalism was older and formulated in different philosophical terms than Huxley's scientific naturalism, and while Huxley had borrowed substantially from Mill, he was more a rationalist than a utilitarian.[19] Balfour's attack and Huxley's two replies, the second of which was never published in his lifetime, demonstrated that the concept of naturalism had become complicated and that a struggle had taken shape to forge a controlling theory through which to channel the tremendous social and cultural forces generated by Victorian science and technology.

While Spencerian naturalism had rejected supernaturalism, Spencer's organic theory elevated evolutionary development, including Darwinian natural selection, to the region of the absolute. It was a "universal" and "necessary" principle, the very foundation of reality: "The universal and necessary tendency towards supremacy and multiplication of the best, applying to the organic creation as a whole as well as to each species . . . tends ever to maintain those most superior organisms which, in one way or another, escape the invasions of the inferior."[20] Man was an animal in the natural world and, guided primarily by instinct, a creature with an impotent will, responding to environmental force as formulated along the lines of Darwin's *Origin*. Progress, Spencer declared in *The Principles of Sociology*, was the product of "universal conflict" leading to greater diversity and higher organization.[21] Huxley found methodological fault with the notion that the biological laissez-faire of Darwin could be transposed to history or society. The real difference between the naturalism of Huxley and Spencer is that for Huxley scientific naturalism was a critical principle; for Spencer, naturalism was a theory of reality, an ontology.

While he placed a fundamental value on the importance of

private judgment and intellectual freedom, Huxley was most insistent in his opposition to the concept of natural rights, arguing that rights were the result of laws rather than of abstract systems formulated according to what man was ideally supposed to be. In 1890, he wrote a series of political essays which appeared in four of the early issues of the *Nineteenth Century*. Together, they reflected a somewhat complicated effort to attack Rousseau and Henry George for their a priori defenses of "natural rights," to defend the right of property ownership on the basis of its legal sanctions, to reject the principle of social laissez-faire, and to emphasize the value of the communal effort and the advantages of a strong central government.[22] As a political thinker, Huxley escapes most conventional definitions. He leaned toward the conservative side in his strong emphasis on social order and rationalism; yet his rejection of laissez-faire and his stress on communal effort often seem to place him within the progressive camp. Certainly he was not radical. In his "On the Natural Inequality of Men," he argued that men were born with unequal abilities; although primitive men did not appear to have owned land privately, they were not therefore equal, because they governed by the laws of physical strength. Social organization diminished the sway of the powerful over the weak. Huxley argued that human society was a construct of human consciousness, and that law and ethics had no justification in nature. Like Mill, he rejected Rousseau's concepts of natural and social man as based on a false premise of the benevolence of primitive man. Huxley defended property ownership with the explanation that the right to property was originally established in a condition of social laissez-faire, and that it was the inevitable result of a primitive situation in which men were naturally unequal in their abilities (1:334). Thus while he defended private ownership as a social reality, he did not defend it as an ideal.

Again in his "Capital—the Mother of Labor: An Economical Problem Discussed from a Physiological Point of View," Huxley took what at first seemed a conservative approach to the labor theory of value advocated by the socialists. However, upon close examination of his essay, one finds not an argument that the capitalist system of economics is the sound alternative approach to the distribution of wealth, but a reminder that "vital capital," the essential energy of living organisms, is impossible for the human organism to produce. Green plants alone were "the chief and, for practical purposes, the sole producers of that vital capital which we have seen to be the necessary antecedent of every act of labour" (9:155). The essay is an interesting, if somewhat bizarre, approach to the economics of capital and labor; in it Huxley's primary objective was to establish the likelihood that the classical socialist and capitalist economic duality of capital and labor is itself a fallacy, since the true capital of society is its vital capital, the physiological energy which drives the human organism. Huxley rejects the labor theory of value and denies that financial capital is able to produce "vital capital." He concludes by asserting that both capital and labor in their traditional senses are inconsistent with the more fundamental physiological realities of life.

Huxley's series of political essays suffers from the lack of a thesis. He was not sympathetic to traditional conservative thought and value; and he criticized socialist politics by associating them with regimentation. His desire for social and political order led him to reject the program of revolution advocated by the Marxists, and his high esteem for freedom of speech and individual liberty led him to oppose the tyranny of the majority. On the other hand, his belief that government itself was an instrument which should promote the general well-being of society against the privilege of the few convinced him of the importance of a strong central government which would function as a progressive organ for the improvement of the whole. His ethical vision, in its emphasis on social cooperation, on strengthening the polity through diminishing competition among individuals, had definite socialist overtones. In "Government: Anarchy or Regimentation" (1890), he attacked both laissez-faire individualism, which he equated with anarchy, and " 'regimental' Socialism," which he identified with the Communist International and with the forceful use of the state as an instrument for the organization of men (1:393). This was a force which would ultimately destroy individual liberties and establish an "artificial equality" at the expense of natural inequalities manifested in varieties of human talent and taste.

"But there is no necessary connection between socialism and regimentation," he added, and he accepted in principle the possibility of men voluntarily organizing according to socialist ideals. Ultimately, Huxley emerges as a political critic without a true political conviction or philosophy, a fatal flaw which lessened the impact and influence of his political thought as a whole.

By 1894, Huxley had long thought in terms of two separate worlds, each with its own history. These were the worlds of "civil history" and "natural history" which, in a fragment written after "Evolution and Ethics," he suggested were discrete but interlocking spheres of activity:

> In the Romanes Lecture I use the term "Natural History" as correlate and complement of "Civil History"—which I conceive to be its received & proper sense. Civil history deals with man in the state of art or civilization; natural history with man & the rest of the world in the state of nature. I have said that the ethics of evolution . . . is applied Natural History because it supposes that the struggle for existence on which progress in the "Natural History" world depends goes on & is the condition of progress in civil society.
> The complete logical consequence of that doctrine is the ultra individualism of the philosophical anarchists—the half way to it is the "astynomocracy" of laissez faire philosophy. Practical results of it are seen in the ignoring of the value of the state; the denial of its authority & of the duties of the individual toward it; which seems to me quite as mischievous as the antique errors in the other direction—perhaps more so.[23]

The distinctions he was making had particularly important implications for his critical theory, for if natural history were a "world" distinct from civil history, then values, insights, and laws that described one world would be independent of those that described the other. Progress was not simply the extension into society of the evolutionary principle of natural history. There was in fact, a clash, between social progress and progress in nature. Radical individualism or doing as one likes was consistent with natural law; but civil history began with "self-renunciation" or "abstinence by the individual from executing some of his possibilities of action."[24]

In his two histories theory, Huxley had given up his earlier tendencies to see natural law as a great existential unity.[25] The investigation of nature through the activity of research had not produced the values that Huxley in his youth had looked forward to so confidently. He did not reject the validity of his earlier determinism or abandon the idea of the great, universal order of nature. Indeed, as cited earlier, he had argued in the last days of his life to Balfour that rather than denying the existence of reason in the universe, natural science had to regard it as "reason *in excelsis*," far superior to that incarnate in man.[26] But whatever it was that bound the ethical process to its antagonistic parent, the cosmic process, remained to be disclosed. Years later Whitehead would reassert the primary ethical value of human cooperation in the creation of a state of art:

> The other side of the evolutionary machine, the neglected side, is expressed by the word *creativeness*. The organisms can create their own environment. For this purpose, the single organism is almost helpless. The adequate forces require societies of coöperating organisms. But with such coöperation and in proportion to the effort put forward, the environment has a plasticity which alters the whole ethical aspect of evolution.[27]

The communal effort to create, numerous organisms working together to establish the State of Art, these also were Huxley's final great objects. Humanity must forge its own ethical environment; it must create value.

iii. science and humanism

Three interrelated aspects of Huxley's thought aligned him with the humanistic tradition: his steady focus on man as the reference for significant knowledge, his emphasis on the reasoning faculty as the ultimate basis for knowledge of the external world, and his insistence on the dignity and uniqueness of man as a civilized and ethical being. He was not oriented within the classical humanist tradition of England, however: his notions of curriculum were decidedly at variance with that tradition, whose outstanding Victorian representative was Matthew Arnold. Huxley's debate with Arnold over the relative merits of scientific and classical humanistic studies was significant, for both men were professionally concerned with English education and understood the historical origins of their debate.

Like Arnold, Huxley had read widely in classical literature, seeking a more penetrating insight into the present by studying the history of Western thought and culture. Fascinated with Greek Stoical thought, he had long-lived ambitions to establish a modern philosophical system which would synthesize the bold Stoical monism, with its epistemological triad of physics, logic, and ethics, with the ethical system of Spinoza and the methods of Victorian science and technology. Huxley looked to Greek rationalism for a new morality and world view; he found a direct connection between the Stoical Logos and Spinoza's deity. This in turn inspired the great kaleidoscope that Huxley, in "Scientific and Pseudo-Scientific Realism," imagined as the true macrocosmic symmetry. His notebooks were filled with elaborate notes from Anaximander, Diogenes, and other speculative thinkers who had struggled to penetrate the mystery of the material universe. In private a passionate metaphysical speculator, Huxley found a powerful stimulus for his imagination in the enthusiasm of classical thought for its science, its impassioned yet methodical study of physical nature, its unflinching certainty that to grapple with the problems of material nature was to begin the gaining of wisdom and knowledge. This had been the path of such learned men as Empedocles, Heraclitus, Zeno, Socrates, and Aristotle, all of whom had been sophisticated and shrewd observers of material phenomena.

Huxley, however, was unable to accept the theodicy which enjoined men to see the ultimate good in social laissez-faire, and he was unable to confirm an alternative, ideal entity or structure in which to posit ultimate truth. He was left with the final philosophical impasse, from which he was unable to discover a systematic exit, of a macrocosm which was "reason *in excelsis*" and a cosmic process bearing grimly down, as in "Evolution and Ethics," in opposition to all that was essential to human civilization. In his own philosophical terms, to combat the cosmos was to struggle against reason itself.

From his studies in Greek thought, however, Huxley discovered the historical dimension of scientific speculation and discovered as well that natural philosophy frequently provided the foundation upon which other cultural efforts were based. Cultures grew from shared assumptions on the character of man's intersection with nature, an intersection which was thought of as reality; and the most basic constructs of a given culture could be said to begin with the physical speculation of those who belonged to its scientific tradition. While Huxley had found that natural order itself had no moral content, he was still able to assert without contradiction that scientific naturalism was an effective critical method, based on the axiom that "nature is the expression of a definite order with which nothing interferes, and that the chief business of mankind is to learn that order and govern themselves accordingly" (3:150). This assertion, which was the central argument of his "Science and Culture," raised the formal issue with Arnold over education and curriculum—the classical humanistic concerns. More fundamentally, it raised the question of what knowledge would enable the individual to enter into a valid criticism of modern life.

Arnold himself had great reservations about the possibilities of finding an ethical value in nature, and, like Huxley, was inclined to locate the moral center in human reason. The same alien cosmos loomed before his Empedocles, whose deep insight into the order of physical nature could not stir the hope which ultimately justified his continuing existence. An interesting equivalent to Huxley's ideal of the man of science, Empedocles was Arnold's dramatization of the purely rational vision; stoical intellect and moral insight were unable to compensate for the increased agony of a consciousness unable to escape itself. Arnold overlooked, however, the spontaneity and creative impulse that accompanied the scientific quest, the escape from self that scientific critics like Huxley and, more recently, George Sarton, identified with the scientific vision:

> When this scientific objectivity is carried high enough it leads to a particular kind of disinterestedness which is more fundamental than the disinterestedness of the most generous man. It is not so much a matter of generosity as of forgetfulness and abandonment of self. Every scientist (as every artist or saint) who is sufficiently absorbed in his task reaches sooner or later that stage of ecstasy (unfortunately impermanent), when the thought of self is entirely vanished, and he can think of naught else but the work at hand, his

own vision of beauty and truth, and the ideal world which he is creating. In comparison with such heavenly ecstasy, all other rewards—such as money and honors—become strangely futile and incongruous.[28]

Empedocles, unable to escape from self into the imagination, struggled, via the consciousness, to contend with conditions that were beyond the influence of human will:

> In vain our pent wills fret,
> And would the world subdue.
> Limits we did not set
> Condition all we do;
> Born into life we are, and life must be our mould.[29]

Having lost the vision of beauty in the macrocosm, he was left only with a rational consciousness, "a naked, eternally restless mind," which now, for lack of an object, preyed inward upon him.

Certainly, as Arnold had admitted, Empedocles presented few solutions to the dilemma of existence. But Arnold also understood the necessity of learning the physical conditions which defined the human "mould." To Huxley's query in "Science and Culture" of how one was to formulate an adequate criticism of life without consulting the ideas of men of science, Arnold did not hesitate to respond that he had, indeed, included the great scientific trends of thought in his cultural program of sweetness and light. In *Culture and Anarchy*, he had identified the "genuine scientific passion" with a curiosity he described as "a desire after the things of the mind simply for their own sakes and for the pleasure of seeing them as they are."[30] This impulse was part of the human passion for culture, the desire to augment the excellence of one's own nature which was, in effect, the source of Empedocles' drive toward perfection. However, there was another source of culture, Arnold argued, more properly described as a *"study of perfection,"* and which had predominantly "social" motives.[31] This realm of culture extended beyond that of Empedocles, the isolated intellect, and was preferred by Arnold to other concepts of culture as the "more interesting and far-reaching." Social perfection was the fundamental idea of culture, social perfection which went beyond mere individual accomplishment to the notion of cultural accomplishment; this was to be sought in "the idea of perfection as an inward condition of the mind and spirit."[32]

In "Science and Culture," Huxley acknowledged Arnold's breadth of cultural appreciation, but he was convinced that Arnold's intention in *Culture and Anarchy* was to establish the classical subject matter of conventional British education as the exclusive educational curriculum. In an argument that he recognized was opposed to the traditional humanist ideal, he declared that modern social conditions made it desirable to abandon the study of Greek and Latin texts; furthermore, "for the purpose of attaining real culture, an exclusively scientific education is at least as effectual as an exclusively literary education" (3:141).

The distinctive character of Victorian times, Huxley held, "lies in the vast and constantly increasing part which is played by natural knowledge" (3:149). There were two propositions in Arnold's critical theory: "The first, that a criticism of life is the essence of culture; the second, that literature contains the materials which suffice for the construction of such a criticism" (3:143). Huxley agreed to the first proposition: "Culture certainly means something quite different from learning or technical skill. It implies the possession of an ideal, and the habit of critically estimating the value of things by comparison with a theoretic standard. Perfect culture should supply a complete theory of life, based upon a clear knowledge alike of its possibilities and of its limitations" (3:143). Huxley went on to trace the development of humanism in the Renaissance, arguing that it presented to the European mind, just emerging from the Middle Ages, a new art and a new science, imported through studies of classical thought. Humanism provided an example of "perfect intellectual freedom—of unhesitating acceptance of reason as the sole guide to truth and the supreme arbiter of conduct" (3:148). This, he agreed, had a profound effect on Renaissance education, and became the guiding spirit of humanist culture. The new humanists failed to understand, however, that the knowledge furnished by the study of classical texts had long since ceased to be the broadening and liberating force it had once been to a culture just emerging from the medieval period. The languages of Greek and Latin, which were formerly the sole avenues to the liberation of the intellect had become highly specialized studies in a modern age which possessed the widest range of knowledge ever before available to mankind.

Huxley's final argument against classical humanism would be voiced in his "Prologue" to *Controverted Questions* (1892), where he maintained that "the goal of the humanists, whether they were aware of it or not, was the attainment of the complete intellectual freedom of the antique philosopher" (5:14). Humanism sought above all to liberate through knowledge, to provide the rational insight which would set the intellect free. In "Science and Culture," he had declared that the great advantage of the "scientific 'criticism of life' " was that it appealed "not to authority, nor to what anybody may have thought or said, but to nature" (3:150). In essence, scientific criticism supplied a reference independent of human authority and human subjectivity.

By contrast, Arnold believed freedom was implicitly conferred on the intellect which had grasped the vision of wholeness that had inspired the Greek mind. In his Rede lecture, which was printed in the *Nineteenth Century* in August 1882, Arnold challenged Huxley's "Science and Culture" and addressed the issue of classical humanism. Certainly not a less brilliant controversialist than Huxley, Arnold, disarming his readers with modest references to the "poor humanist," turned defense to offense by observing that Huxley had confused literature with *"belles lettres."* He agreed with Wolf, the critic of Homer, who held that "all learning is scientific which is systematically laid out and followed up to its original sources, and that a genuine humanism is scientific."[33] The scientific study of cultures demanded that one attend to them in their original languages. Arnold thus laid claim to a scientific basis for humanistic education.

He went on to argue that the force of the humanistic approach could be traced to the ancient argument of Socrates, contained in the Diotimian monologue of the *Symposium*, that man felt as his fundamental desire the need for the good. Arnold converted this argument into a naturalistic thesis by equating the notion of fundamental desire to the biological concept of "instinct.' According to Arnoldian naturalism:

> Following our *instinct* for intellect and knowledge, we acquire pieces of knowledge; and presently, in the generality of men, there arises the desire to relate these pieces of knowledge to our sense for conduct, to our sense for beauty,—and there is weariness and dissatisfaction if the desire is baulked. Now in this desire lies, I think, the strength of that hold which letters have upon us.[34]

In this move, Arnold sought to link the human quest for perfection with human instinct for the good, suggesting that civilization had an organic, biological basis. He identified the instinct for the good with the fundamental biological instinct of self preservation:

> As before, it is not on any weak pleadings of my own that I rely for convincing the gainsayers; it is on the constitution of human nature itself, and on the *instinct* of *self-preservation* in humanity. The *instinct* for beauty is set in human nature, as surely as the *instinct* for knowledge is set there, or the *instinct* for conduct.[35]

Scientific knowledge, Arnold held, as Wordsworth had in his preface to the *Lyrical Ballads*, would ultimately be humanized for all through the force of literature; but for the uninitiated it remained raw, inorganic knowledge, removed from the great human instincts. It was analytical and fundamental, but as yet unassimilated, valued by virtue of the intellect, but not by virtue of the emotion. "Humane letters," by contrast, engaged the instincts because they appealed to emotion, to beauty, and to conduct. This, Arnold declared, was the great source of appeal of medieval knowledge; it answered to the instinctual need for the good that was itself part of the human identity. Man was not man without these things; and "Man's happiness consists in his being able to preserve his own essence," as Spinoza had once declared.[36] Thus the notion of self-preservation was to be taken in the sense of preserving one's essence as well as existence. Scientific knowledge was fundamental to physical self-preservation; for some, it was a great emotional and imaginative realm as well. But humane letters, history, literature, philosophy had the explicit responsibility of spiritual self-

190

preservation, the preservation of human nature and identity. In the end, this must be accounted the more fundamental need.

The humanistic pursuit of Greek letters carried the instinct for beauty and knowledge and conduct to its epitome, since it alone presented the vision of harmony that answered to the deepest needs of men, the desire for wholeness. Leonardo himself, artist and arch-scientist of the Renaissance, by his own admission, Arnold pointed out, lacked the "antique symmetry," and felt this his one great fault. The ultimate end of the study of classical civilization, Arnold held, was to deliver to the modern mind a vision of symmetry in beauty, knowledge, and conduct which it then would apply to its own conditions and surroundings.

Arnold and Huxley remained at odds on the issue of humanistic education in England. The correspondence between the two men, however, was intimate and good humored, and while they recognized their fundamental differences, they also recognized the profound similarities in their general values. Neither sought, although Huxley has often been accused of seeking, the kind of disciplinary exclusivity that would become more common in the following century.[37] Although Josiah Mason had excluded "mere literary instruction and education," Huxley pointed out, the new school was to provide instruction in English, French, and German; these would open the way to the "three greatest literatures of the modern world" (3:140, 150). It is worth remembering that Huxley had had only a year of general instruction at Ealing School where Latin and Greek grammar were central to the curriculum. This was the school he had once characterized as having been run by "baby-farmers" (1:5). In spite of this, he had learned, through private effort, Greek and Latin, Italian, French, and German, and had read widely in the literature and philosophy of both modern and ancient civilizations. He questioned the value of the classical humanistic education, not only because he had never experienced its possibilities, but because he had acquired his own knowledge through independent study and research. Arnold, the product of private tutors, Winchester College, Rugby, and Oxford, a living representative of English humanism, saw differently, for his family had long been intimately associated with classical education in England. Huxley placed little value on tradition; his success and rise to influence had come through the new knowledge of Victorian science, and he sought to justify its independent value as a social and cultural activity.

With some concern over the possible misunderstanding of his "Science and Culture," Huxley wrote a second essay, "On Science and Art in Relation to Education," which was delivered at the Liverpool Institute in early 1883 after Arnold had presented his "Literature and Science" as the Rede lecture at Cambridge.[38] While neither an exclusively literary nor scientific education was the ideal, the sciences, if one were to insist on disciplinary exclusivity as so many traditionalists had indeed been doing, were as useful and enlightening a basis in the preparation of one for a criticism of life as the literary arts could be. He agreed with Arnold, however, that it was not a question of whether men of science or of art should dominate; they should, above all, understand one another (3:179). The proper philological study of ancient Greek civilization, he admitted, "affords a splendid and noble education," but it still was incomplete and beyond the practical means of most (3:182). Modern education was obliged to give due attention to the realities of the present which it should strive to alter, as far as possible, for the better. The Greek genius had been one of symmetry, it was true, but a symmetry conceived in the context of its own present, an integration of its science, philosophy and letters. The classical humanistic ideal of Victorian England, Huxley argued, provided an education which lacked the very spirit of symmetry it sought in Greek civilization, for it had abandoned the present for a harmonious vision of the past.

Literature and art, Huxley concluded, were justly esteemed as great emotional and imaginative realms of humanity; the best literature, such as that of Shakespeare, "satisfies the artistic instinct of the youngest and harmonises with the ripest and richest experience of the oldest" (3:179). Huxley had always been sensitive to artistic beauty; in his "Universities: Actual and Ideal" (1874), he had observed, perhaps even thinking of Arnold's *Culture and Anarchy*:

> But the man who is all morality and intellect, although he may be good and even great, is, after all, only half a man. There is beauty in

192

the moral world and in the intellectual world; but there is also a beauty which is neither moral nor intellectual—the beauty of the world of Art. There are men who are devoid of the power of seeing it, as there are men who are born deaf and blind, and the loss of those, as of these, is simply infinite. There are others in whom it is an overpowering passion; happy men, born with the productive, or at lowest, the appreciative, genius of the Artist. [3:205]

He took pains that his advocacy of scientific education not be interpreted to mean that he believed literary education should be weakened. He believed that both curricula were capable of being taught without sacrificing one to the other. Furthermore, science and art were not discrete intellectual and aesthetic entities, as they were commonly regarded. In a fragment manuscript, he had written:

> In the great majority of our thoughts, however, the scientific and the aesthetic elements are inseparably commingled. . . . There is hardly a work of art which does not contain a scientific element— hardly a great artist who is not in the broad sense of the word a man of science—while the greatest works of art might be characterized as science . . . moulded by feeling. . . . If culture is the even and balanced development of all our faculties and if education is the means of obtaining culture then it is absurd to imagine that there can be any antagonisms between science and art or between science and literature as art.[39]

Huxley's thought consistently returned to his focus in *Man's Place in Nature:* "The question of questions for mankind—the problem which underlies all others, and is more deeply interesting than any other—is the ascertainment of the place which Man occupies in nature and of his relations to the universe of things" (7:77). He insisted that the answer had to be sought in physical nature itself. This was the central idea behind his critical terms, *thätige Skepsis,* agnosticism, and scientific naturalism. And it was an important source for his grandson's "scientific humanism":

> Scientific Humanism is a protest against supernaturalism: the human spirit, now in its individual, now in its corporate aspects, is the source of all values and the highest reality we know. . . . It insists on human values as the norms for our aims, but insists equally that they cannot adjust themselves in right perspective and

193

emphasis except as part of the picture of the world provided by science.[40]

For Julian Huxley, as for his grandfather, the sciences were to provide insights into the structure of external reality, which were then to be modified according to values, presumably rationalist, derived from the human spirit. This looked back to Huxley's fusion of method and reason. Scientific thought was not, according to Julian Huxley, to set itself up "as an external code or framework as did revealed religion in the past."[41] The same distinction moved Thomas Huxley to seek a critical function for the scientific vision: to join reason with method was to protect humanity from absolutist systems, whether scientifically or religiously inspired.

While Huxley and Arnold were close and kindred spirits, drawn together by their shared sense of value in their broad humanist outlooks, deep divisions between them remained. Striving for a concept of critical reason that would reflect their personal visions, both sought to throw new light on the changes that appeared to be transforming their society into something entirely new. For Huxley imagination fulfilled a role subordinate to reason, however, while for Arnold it was reason's equal. In "Scientific and Pseudo-Scientific Realism" (1887), Huxley had declared that "if imagination is used within the limits laid down by science, disorder is unimaginable" (5:73). This also meant the end of the miraculous. One remembers how Browning's Arab physician, Karshish, "the not-incurious in God's handiwork," good-natured scholar that he was, could not escape the rational prejudice of his method.[42] For him, the structure of the perception had become the essence of its reality: face to face with divinity, he saw only irregularity. The goodness and beauty of the idea, the simple yet wonderful harmony implicit in the miraculous possibility of Lazarus' cure, was not enough to override the earnest physician's reason, though it nearly succeeded—"The very God! think, Abib."

Arnold associated reason closely with imagination, conceiving of them, although not very coherently, as a single, continuous faculty. This established a dual guardianship over the mind, where neither the purely imaginative nor the purely rational construct was to be accepted. "The main element of the modern spirit's life," he declared, "is neither the sense and understanding, nor the heart and imagination; it is the imaginative reason."[43] Fruitful, harmonious thought, Arnold believed, was achieved through a combination of reason and emotion, sense and imagination; it was the humanization and personalization of knowledge. Searching for a way to avoid what he believed was the dilemma of Empedoclean speculation divorced from emotion, he urged the establishment of an alternative cultural ideal modeled on that of Hellenic harmony and spontaneity. Huxley, in his different way, sought unity as well. His impassioned dream of "reason *in excelsis*" was not in the end so different from Arnold's imaginative reason.

Accepting the new relationship between man and nature constituted the most difficult of Victorian adjustments, since it considerably altered the most fundamental of cultural ideas—the human self-image. Huxley and Arnold both experienced the widening of the chasm between natural process and traditional ideas of self with a growing sense of alienation, a fact which moved them to the search for sources of human value and dignity consonant with the new realities of the coming era. It is in this light that Huxley's call for revolution against nature needs to be understood, for he was revolting against a lifeless paradigm he had constructed himself—that of the cosmic kaleidoscope and of biological man—in the interests of humanly-centered ideas of reason, ethics and community. If to moderns his call for revolution against nature sounds ominous, it is partly because we no longer share in his conception of cosmic organization; more deeply, it is because we fear a Pyrrhic victory over nature. Whether, as Freud asserted, we are still and necessarily in open revolt remains a question, and one which, given our growing technological potency, we can ignore only at our profound peril.

The observations and insights of Huxley and Arnold are of prime significance to the modern age, for both men, in a striking anticipation of modern sensibility, sought ways of locating centers of value and independence in an age that seemed to be losing, amid the confusion of social transition, its sense of restraint and liberty. The independent locus of human dignity, standards of value to modify raw social, political, and economical forces, were found by both men in the humanist values of the past, Huxley locating them in the speculative tradition of science, and Arnold locating them in the syncretic traditions of classical literature. In the Renaissance, the dignity of human knowledge found eloquent spokesmen like Galileo and Bacon, just as in Greek civilization it was expressed in the speculative rapture of the rationalist inquiry into nature. In modern thought, we refer to Einstein and Eliot, to Sakharov and Solzhenitsyn, in our search for the loci of free, spiritual thought amid absolutism. Science and art have always provided humanity with twin refuges—centers of value which are free, when genuine, from dogma and public authority. Both flourish in spite of doctrine, for both celebrate the freedoms of imagination, speculation, and emotion. In science and the rigor of its independent appeal to nature, Huxley found a witness to the mystery and enactment of human intellectual freedom; and this became the frame and measure for his own human identity.

Notes

notes for introduction

1. Alfred North Whitehead, *Science and the Modern World*, p. 141.
2. Walter Houghton, *The Victorian Frame of Mind, 1830–1870*, p. 22.
3. M. H. Abrams, *Natural Supernaturalism*, pp. 66–69.
4. See, for example, Charles S. Blinderman, "T. H. Huxley's Theory of Aesthetics," p. 51.
5. Quoted in William Irvine, *Apes, Angels, and Victorians*, p. 30.
6. Lionel Trilling, "Science, Literature and Culture," p. 475.
7. Oliver Elton, *A Survey of English Literature, 1780–1880*, 3:77.

notes for chapter I

1. William Whewell, *The Philosophy of the Inductive Sciences*, 1:cxiii.
2. David Scott, "On Leonardo Da Vinci and Correggio," *Blackwood's Magazine* 48 (August 1840): 273.
3. Alfred North Whitehead, *Science and the Modern World*, p. 142.
4. *T. H. Huxley's Diary of the Voyage of H. M. S. Rattlesnake*, p. 99.
5. 2 July 1849, T. H. Huxley, Correspondence with Henrietta Heathorn: 1847–1854, fol. 70, Imperial College of Science and Technology, London. Material from this collection is quoted with permission from the Governors, Imperial College of Science and Technology. In quoting from Huxley's manuscripts, I have made minor alterations in the punctuation.
6. *T. H. Huxley's Diary*, p. 26.
7. Beatrice Webb, *My Apprenticeship*, p. 28.
8. 2 July 1849, Huxley-Heathorn Correspondence, fol. 70.
9. See Thomas Carlyle, *The Works of Thomas Carlyle*, ed. Henry Duff Traill, vol. 27, *Critical and Miscellaneous Essays* (1904), pp. 112–13.
10. Ibid., vol. 26, *Critical and Miscellaneous Essays* (1904), pp. 17–18.
11. See also Cyril Bibby, *T. H. Huxley*, pp. 12–13.
12. George Gordon Byron, *Cain, A Mystery*, in *The Complete Poetical Works of Byron*, ed. Paul E. More, p. 648. See also *T. H. Huxley's Diary*, p. 26.
13. For a catalogue of the Huxley-Heathorn correspondence for this period, see Jeanne Pingree, *Thomas Henry Huxley: List of His Correspondence with Miss Henrietta Heathorn, 1847–1854*.

14. 31 December 1848, Huxley-Heathorn Correspondence, fol. 40.
15. 18 August 1851, Huxley-Heathorn Correspondence, fol. 162.
16. Quoted in Bibby, *T. H. Huxley*, p. 5.
17. Cf. Houston Peterson, *Huxley, Prophet of Science*, pp. 14–15.
18. See also William Irvine, "Carlyle and T. H. Huxley," pp. 198–99.
19. 12 May 1849, Huxley-Heathorn Correspondence, fol. 57.
20. 7 May 1851, Huxley-Heathorn Correspondence, fol. 147.
21. 2 September 1848, Huxley-Heathorn Correspondence, fol. 37.
22. 23 September 1851, Huxley-Heathorn Correspondence, fol. 166.
23. Thomas Carlyle, *Sartor Resartus*, ed. Charles F. Harrold, pp. 191–92.
24. John Ruskin, *The Works of John Ruskin*, ed. E. T. Cook and Alexander Wedderburn, vol. 22, *The Eagle's Nest: Ten Lectures on the Relation of Natural Science to Art* (1906), p. 138.
25. Ibid. See also Walter F. Cannon, "The Normative Role of Science in Early Victorian Thought," p. 500.
26. The Huxley Papers, Imperial College of Science and Technology, London, 45:86. Material from this collection is quoted with permission from the Governors, Imperial College of Science and Technology.
27. Charles Dickens, *The New Oxford Illustrated Dickens*, vol. 3, *Bleak House* (1948), pp. 845–47.
28. Karl Marx and Friedrich Engels, *The Communist Manifesto*, in *The Essential Works of Marxism*, ed. Arthur P. Mendel, p. 18.
29. John Henry Cardinal Newman, *The Idea of a University, Defined and Illustrated*, pp. 106–7.
30. Ruskin, *Eagle's Nest*, p. 135.
31. Phyllis Rose, "Huxley, Holmes, and the Scientist as Aesthete," p. 22.
32. Mary Shelley, *Frankenstein or the Modern Prometheus*, ed. James Rieger, p. 47.
33. Quoted in Bibby, *T. H. Huxley*, p. 98; see also pp. 96–101.
34. The term "Huxley theater" is not used in comparative reference to the critical study by Robert Garis, *The Dickens Theatre* (Oxford: Clarendon Press, 1965).

notes for chapter II

1. Thomas Carlyle, "Characteristics," in *Works*, vol. 27, *Critical and Miscellaneous Essays*, p. 8.
2. *T. H. Huxley's Diary*, p. 70. See also Huxley's "Professor Tyndall," p. 3.
3. See also William Irvine, "Carlyle and T. H. Huxley," p. 197.

4. Carlyle, "Characteristics," pp. 4, 13.

5. Irvine, "Carlyle and T. H. Huxley," p. 205.

6. 28 June 1851, T. H. Huxley, Correspondence with Henrietta Heathorn: 1847–1854, fol. 155.

7. Gertrude Himmelfarb, *Darwin and the Darwinian Revolution*, p. 387.

8. 17 July 1850, Huxley-Heathorn Correspondence, fol. 112.

9. Herbert Spencer, *Education: Intellectual, Moral, and Physical*, p. 91. See also Cyril Bibby, *T. H. Huxley*, pp. 57–58.

10. Spencer, *Education*, p. 90.

11. John Tyndall, *Fragments of Science*, 2:335.

12. T. H. Huxley, "Professor Tyndall," p. 3.

13. Carlyle, *Sartor Resartus*, p. 15.

14. Charles Darwin, *The Autobiography of Charles Darwin, and Selected Letters*, ed. Francis Darwin, pp. 38–39. Cf. Charles Kingsley, *Scientific Lectures and Essays*, pp. 249, 333. In marked contrast, Kingsley, in his lecture entitled "Science," proclaimed Carlyle's writings to be "instinct with the very spirit of science." And he urged young men of science to read Carlyle: "It is a small matter to me—and I doubt not to him—whether you will agree with his special conclusions: but his premises and his method are irrefragable; for they stand on the 'Voluntatem Dei in rebus revelatam'—on fact and common sense." In his essay "The Natural Theology of the Future," Kingsley suggested that Carlyle's attack on mechanism was aimed at the eighteenth century deists.

15. Carlyle, *Sartor Resartus*, pp. 317–18. See also Frank M. Turner, "Victorian Scientific Naturalism and Thomas Carlyle," p. 336.

16. Carlyle, *Sartor Resartus*, p. 191.

17. Ibid., p. 246.

18. John Tyndall, "Personal Recollections of Thomas Carlyle," in *New Fragments*, p. 385.

19. Carlyle, *Sartor Resartus*, p. 216.

20. Ibid., p. 313.

21. See also Turner, "Victorian Scientific Naturalism," p. 333.

22. Carlyle, *Sartor Resartus*, p. 317.

23. Turner, "Victorian Scientific Naturalism," p. 336.

24. Carlyle, *Sartor Resartus*, p. 315.

25. Ibid., p. 308. In "Christianity and Physical Science," Newman observed that an "inductive theology," taking as its subject matter "Scripture, Antiquity, Nature," was certain to yield conflicting results. Without a unifying dogma, he argued, the physical theologian was limited to arriving at the attributes of power, wisdom, and goodness

for his god: "and of these, most of power, and least of goodness." See John Henry Cardinal Newman, *The Idea of a University*, pp. 446–47, 453.

26. Caryle, *Sartor Resartus*, p. 256.

27. Ibid., p. 257.

28. See Charles C. Gillispie, *Genesis and Geology*, p. 40.

29. Darwin, *Autobiography*, p. 39.

30. Abrams, *Natural Supernaturalism*, p. 68.

31. Irvine, "Carlyle and T. H. Huxley," p. 200.

32. Oma Stanley, "Thomas Henry Huxley's Treatment of Nature," p. 120. Questions raised by Irvine and Stanley touch on the important issue of technical language. Darwin's language in *On the Origin of Species* was sometimes self-contradictory when he referred to nature as an active agent, and he was forced to appeal to convention in order to answer arguments that his concept of natural selection was essentially teleological. For example, his observation that "man selects only for his own good: Nature only for that of the being which she tends" suggested that nature was a unified, purposeful entity. In answer to charges that he was personifying nature, Darwin observed: "It is difficult to avoid personifying the word Nature; but I mean by Nature, only the aggregate action and product of many natural laws, and by laws the sequence of events as ascertained by us. With a little familiarity such superficial objections will be forgotten." See *On the Origin of Species*, 6th ed., pp. 63, 65. Walter F. Cannon concludes that Darwin drew on traditional British naturalist vocabulary for his personification of nature. See Cannon's "Darwin's Vision in *On the Origin of Species*," p. 158. Huxley and Tyndall were more influenced by the Romantic tradition in their use of language than was Darwin.

33. See Irvine, "Carlyle and T. H. Huxley," p. 200.

34. Carlyle, *Works*, vol. 10, *Past and Present* (1903), p. 7.

35. Ibid., vol. 5, *On Heroes, Hero-Worship and the Heroic in History* (1903), p. 8.

36. T. H. Huxley, *Lay Sermons, Addresses, and Reviews*, pp. 117–18. David Roos establishes the date of this essay in his bibliographical essay, "Neglected Bibliographic Aspects of the Works of Thomas Henry Huxley."

37. Carlyle, *Sartor Resartus*, p. 36.

38. Ibid., p. 52.

39. Ibid., p. 222.

40. See also Huxley's letter of 31 October to the *Pall Mall* in *LL*, 1:301–2.

41. Huxley's stand on emancipation was nevertheless quite strong;

he called for complete equality in educational opportunities. See T. H. Huxley, *Collected Essays*, 3:68.

42. In a letter to John E. Cairnes in May 1865, Mill commented favorably on Huxley's "Emancipation—Black and White" which had just appeared in the *Reader*, "notwithstanding," Mill added, "what I venture to think heretical physiology, which, however, he clearly sees, and as clearly shows, not to affect in the smallest degree the moral, political or educational questions, either as regards Negroes or women." See *Collected Works of John Stuart Mill*, vol. 16, *The Later Letters of John Stuart Mill*, ed. Francis E. Mineka and Dwight N. Lindley (1972), p. 1058.

43. Carlyle, *On Heroes*, p. 155. See also pp. 106-8.

44. Ibid., p. 61.

45. Ibid., pp. 8–9.

46. Ibid., p. 108.

47. Ibid., p. 8.

48. John Tyndall observed in his "Personal Recollections of Thomas Carlyle," *New Fragments*, p. 384, that "Carlyle would have found 'The Hero as Man of Science' a . . . fitting theme. He had mastered the 'Principia,' and was well aware of the vast revolutionary change wrought, not by Science only, but in the whole world of thought by the theory of gravitation."

49. Carlyle, *On Heroes*, p. 55.

50. Carlyle, *Sartor Resartus*, pp. 167–68.

51. Carlyle, *Past and Present*, p. 182.

notes for chapter III

1. The Huxley Papers, Imperial College of Science and Technology, London, 38:53–54.

2. Ibid.

3. Ibid.

4. Ibid., p. 27.

5. For a consideration of the aesthetic aspects of Huxley's drive toward unity, see Charles S. Blinderman, "T. H. Huxley's Theory of Aesthetics," pp. 49–55.

6. See also Walter Houghton, "The Rhetoric of T. H. Huxley," pp. 164–65.

7. John Stuart Mill, *Autobiography*, ed. Jack Stillinger, p. 81.

8. See Gordon S. Haight, *George Eliot: A Biography*, pp. 137–38. See also D. Noble, "George Henry Lewes, George Eliot and the Physiological Society," pp. 45p–54p.

9. For a detailed account of Huxley's controversies with the English positivists, see Sidney Eisen, "Huxley and the Positivists," pp. 337–58.

10. T. H. Huxley, *Lay Sermons, Addresses, and Reviews,* pp. 148–49.

11. Ibid. See also Walter Houghton, *The Victorian Frame of Mind,* pp. 322–23.

12. T. H. Huxley, *Lay Sermons, Addresses, and Reviews,* pp. 159–60.

13. Ibid., p. 162.

14. Ibid., p. 164.

15. See Eisen, "Huxley and the Positivists," p. 358.

16. Huxley's attack on the "'Darkest England' Scheme" was made in a series of letters to the *Times* in December 1890, and January 1891, which were collected, along with a preface and introductory essay, in a pamphlet titled "Social Diseases and Worse Remedies" and published later in 1891. The complete work is included in *Evolution and Ethics,* vol. 9 of Huxley's *Collected Essays,* pp. 188–334.

17. Basil Willey, *Nineteenth Century Studies: Coleridge to Matthew Arnold,* pp. 202–3.

18. William Wordsworth, *The Poetical Works of William Wordsworth,* ed. Ernest de Selincourt and Helen Darbishire, 2:395.

19. "On the Morphology of the Cephalous Mollusca, as Illustrated by the Anatomy of Certain Heteropoda and Pteropoda Collected During the Voyage of H. M. S. *Rattlesnake* in 1846–50," pp. 62–63. See also Blinderman, "T. H. Huxley's Theory of Aesthetics," pp. 49–50.

20. *T. H. Huxley's Diary,* pp. 47–48.

21. William Irvine, *Apes, Angels, and Victorians,* p. 249.

22. In his controversy with W. S. Lilly, Huxley identified the concept of determinism both with the philosophical notion of "the universality of causation" and the theological concept of predestination, citing precedents both in Augustine and Calvin. See *Collected Essays,* 9:139.

23. R. G. Collingwood, *The Idea of Nature,* pp. 104–5, 134–35.

24. Blinderman, "T. H. Huxley: A Re-evaluation of his Philosophy," pp. 58–60. "We approach much closer to Huxley's meaning," Blinderman suggests, "not through considering the rival claims of materialism and idealism as 'true' depicters of the universe, but by remembering what he said of causality: that it is a verbal symbol." See also P. Chalmers Mitchell, *Thomas Henry Huxley,* pp. 224–226.

25. Huxley credited Hume as one source of his suggestion that consciousness is related to molecular change—see *Collected Essays,* 6:94–99. Huxley's prediction that various mechanical equivalents to express consciousness would eventually be found has been realized in a range of modern instrumentation—see *Collected Essays,* 2:163–64. But

see also "Science and Morals," *Collected Essays,* 9:130, where he declared the existence of "a third thing in the universe, to wit, consciousness, which . . . I cannot see to be matter or force, or any conceivable modification of either, however intimately the manifestation of the phenomena of consciousness may be connected with the phenomena known as matter and force."

26. William Hamilton, *Discussions on Philosophy and Literature, Education and University Reform,* p. 21.

27. Hamilton's essay also stood opposed to Spencer's idea of the Unknowable, a fact of which Huxley had long been aware, as Edward Clodd has pointed out. See Huxley's 1889 letter to F. C. Gould in Clodd's *Thomas Henry Huxley,* pp. 246–47.

28. The Huxley Papers, 38:119.

29. Ibid., 132–33. Cf. Huxley's "Scientific and Pseudo-Scientific Realism," *Collected Essays,* 5:62.

30. Ibid., 47:148.

31. See Huxley's *Collected Essays,* 2:112; 4:96–97.

32. T. H. Huxley, "Mr. Balfour's Attack on Agnosticism: II," pp. 316–17.

33. See Alan Willard Brown, *The Metaphysical Society,* p. 62.

34. For a discussion of Huxley's controversies over agnosticism, see D. W. Dockrill, "T. H. Huxley and the Meaning of 'Agnosticism.'"

35. See *Collected Essays,* 5:245. See also D. W. Dockrill, "The Origin and Development of Nineteenth Century English Agnosticism."

36. T. H. Huxley, "Mr. Balfour's Attack on Agnosticism: II," pp. 315–27.

37. Dockrill, "T. H. Huxley and the Meaning of 'Agnosticism,'" pp. 464–65.

38. Henry Mansel, *The Limits of Religious Thought,* p. 119.

39. Ibid., p. 120.

40. Ibid., p. 124.

41. Hannah Arendt, *The Human Condition,* pp. 277–78.

42. See also Arendt, *The Human Condition,* pp. 278–79.

43. 8 April 1889, The Huxley Papers, 27:57.

44. In an unpublished fragment on Newman's writings, Huxley copied among other statements, the following observation from number eighty-five of *Tracts for the Times:* "'What doctrines or rites would be left to us, if we demanded the clearest and fullest evidence before we believed anything? What would the Gospel consist of? Would there be any revelation at all left?' It is not quite clear that Dr. Newman thinks there would," Huxley responded, "and it is certain that in his opinion the resulting creed would be a very short one. If it

had not hit his own teaching as hardly as it does Protestantism, so acute a dialectician might easily have demonstrated that the primitive Christian creed was indeed a very short one consisting of the explicit belief in God & in Jesus as the Messiah and the implicit belief in the Satans & devils." Quoted from The Huxley Papers, 47:196.

notes for chapter IV

1. Joseph Warren Beach, *The Concept of Nature in Nineteenth-Century English Poetry*, p. 16.

2. Alfred Lord Tennyson, *The Poems of Tennyson*, ed. Christopher Ricks, p. 912.

3. Matthew Arnold, *The Poems of Matthew Arnold*, ed. Kenneth Allot, p. 56. For the alternative ending of 1869, see p. 56n.

4. William Irvine, *Apes, Angels, and Victorians*, p. 142. For a general account of the publication of *Man's Place in Nature*, see Irvine, pp. 135–50.

5. Houston Peterson, *Huxley: Prophet of Science*, p. 145. For a recent brief assessment of Huxley's main thesis, see William Strauss, Jr., "Huxley's *Evidence as to Man's Place in Nature*—a Century Later," pp. 160–67.

6. A. O. Lovejoy, *The Great Chain of Being*, pp. 233–36.

7. A detailed consideration of Huxley's controversy with Owen is given in Charles S. Blinderman's "The Great Bone Case," pp. 370–93. See also Irvine, *Apes, Angels, and Victorians*, pp. 38–41; and P. Chalmers Mitchell, *Thomas Henry Huxley*, pp. 130–35.

8. T. H. Huxley, "Researches into the Structure of the Ascidians," in *Scientific Memoirs*, Supplement, p. 194.

9. T. H. Huxley, review of *Vestiges of the Natural History of Creation*, [by Richard Chambers], 10th ed., in *Scientific Memoirs*, supplement, pp. 2–3.

10. T. H. Huxley, "The Cell Theory," in *Scientific Memoirs* 1:277–78. For an account of Huxley's role in the vitalist-mechanist issue as it turned on the protoplasmic theory of life, see Gerald Geison's essay, "The Protoplasmic Theory of Life and the Vitalist-Mechanist Debate," pp. 273–92.

11. T. H. Huxley, "On the Present State of Knowledge as to the Structure and Functions of Nerve," in *Scientific Memoirs* 1:319.

12. T. H. Huxley, "The Cell Theory," in *Scientific Memoirs* 1:249–50.

13. Cf. Michael Bartholomew, "Huxley's Defence of Darwin," p. 526. Bartholomew argues that Huxley's "anti-Darwinian" commitments concerning the history of life are revealed in his refusal to make

the detailed technical defense of descent with modification that others might have made. Huxley's defense, however, was largely concerned with what he spoke of as the "philosophical questions which underlie all physical science" (2:121). These were not questions of the "style" of Darwin's science, but rather questions of the philosophical assumptions upon which Darwin had constructed his primary ideas. Huxley's commitment to—and willingness to explore—scientific naturalism made him an ideal public defender of the *Origin*.

14. Huxley dropped his "A Succinct History of the Controversy Respecting the Cerebral Structure of Man and Apes" from *Man's Place in Nature* in the *Collected Essays*, vol. 7. Owen, basing his argument on the supposed absence in lower primates of "the third lobe, the posterior horn of the lateral ventricle, and the hippocampus minor," apparently deliberately distorted published findings to the contrary; he went so far as to create a special subclass—"Archencephala"—apart from and superior to the rest of the mammals in which to preserve the uniqueness of man. For Huxley's summary of the argument, see *Man's Place in Nature*, ed. Ashley Montague, pp. 133–38. See also Irvine, *Apes, Angels and Victorians*, pp. 39–41, and Blinderman, *"The Great Bone Case,"* pp. 370–75.

15. Ernest Jones, *The Life and Work of Sigmund Freud*, vol. 1 (1957), pp. 54, 245. See also vol. 3 (1953), p. 155.

16. Masao Miyoshi, *The Divided Self*, pp. 86, x–xii.

17. Thomas Carlyle, *Works*, vol. 10, *Past and Present* (1903), p. 7.

18. The English title was "On the Crania of the Most Ancient Races of Man." See Huxley, *Collected Essays*, 7:168n.

19. In addition to discoveries of human fossils on the Continent, a less radical but highly suggestive fossil skull called the "Riverbed Skull" was discovered along the River Trent in Nottinghamshire. Huxley studied and described the skull in 1861—see John Cameron, *The Skull of British Neolithic Man*, pp. 35–36. According to Cameron, numerous Neolithic skeletons were discovered in England in the 1880s. However, the great discovery was made by the Dutch physician, Eugene Dubois, who found *Pithecanthropos erectus* in Java in 1891. Some four months before his death, in a letter to J. D. Hooker, Huxley noted the discovery and enclosed a sketch of what Dubois's "missing link" should look like—see *LL*, 2:417.

20. Cf. Blinderman, "The Great Bone Case," p. 392. See also Stanley Renner, "The Garden of Civilization," p. 110.

21. See A. Conan Doyle, *The Hound of the Baskervilles*, in *The Annotated Sherlock Holmes*, ed. William S. Baring-Gould, 2:48, 52, 66, for prehistoric themes.

22. The most obvious literary parallel is Stevenson's Dr. Jekyll and Mr. Hyde (1886), with the important difference that the two aspects, Jekyll and Hyde, are conscious of each other. See Robert Louis Stevenson, "Strange Case of Dr. Jekyll and Mr. Hyde," in *The Complete Short Stories of Robert Louis Stevenson*, ed. Charles Neider, pp. 519–21.

23. Irvine, *Apes, Angels, and Victorians*, p. 130.

24. John Stuart Mill, "Nature," in *Collected Works*, ed. F. E. L. Priestley, Francis E. Mineka, et al., 10:401–2.

25. Ibid., p. 381.

26. Ibid., p. 385.

27. Ibid., p. 394.

28. Ibid., pp. 377–78.

29. Ibid., p. 385.

30. Ibid., p. 395.

31. Ibid., p. 396.

32. Ibid., pp. 379–80.

33. Ibid., p. 373.

34. Irvine, pp. 346–47. See also Gertrude Himmelfarb, *Darwin and the Darwinian Revolution*, p. 383.

35. Peterson, *Huxley: Prophet of Science*, p. 283; Irvine, *Apes, Angels, and Victorians*, p. 348.

36. See also Richard W. Noland, "T. H. Huxley on Culture," pp. 95, 100, 105. Noland points out similarities between the cultural visions of Huxley and Freud. He finds that Huxley made no original contributions to cultural anthropology or social philosophy, but that he performed the service of transmitting ideas current in the last two decades of the century.

37. See Mill, "Nature," pp. 375, 379. Huxley observed in a manuscript fragment: "The term, 'Nature,' strictly covers the whole phenomenal world: and therefore includes those operations of man and their results which we call art and the artificer. Nevertheless, common usage draws a very proper distinction between natural on the one hand and the artificial on the other. The Venus of Milo and the Forth Bridge are no doubt works of nature in the sense that they are works of man and man is part of nature;—yet to call them works of nature would be a piece of misleading pedantry." Quoted from the Huxley Papers, Imperial College, London, 45:123.

38. Charles Darwin, *The Descent of Man*, 2d ed., rev., pp. 632–33. Darwin noted how man's scrupulous care in breeding pedigrees is not matched in his own breeding habits. He advocated a limited control over human selection, once the laws of inheritance are thoroughly known.

39. Thomas Hardy, *The Collected Poems of Thomas Hardy* (1960), pp. 101–3.

40. Sigmund Freud, *The Future of an Illusion,* trans. W. D. Robson-Scott, p. 20.

41. Darwin, *The Descent of Man,* pp. 624–25.

42. Ibid., p. 625. See also Himmelfarb, *Darwin and the Darwinian Revolution,* p. 352.

43. See, for example, Petr Kropotkin, "Mutual Aid among Animals," Part 1, pp. 337–38. In his extended study of ethics—*Ethics: Origin and Development,* pp. 14–16—Kropotkin spoke of "realistic ethics" as part of his thesis that cooperation was the "predominant fact of nature." He reasoned, in this manner, that morality had an instinctual basis and that nature itself furnished an ethical model for human society.

44. Mill, "Utilitarianism," in *Collected Works,* 10:231.

45. See, for example, *Civilization and Its Discontents,* trans. James Strachey, pp. 42–43.

46. Ibid., p. 59.

47. Irvine, *Apes, Angels, and Victorians,* p. 348.

48. Arnold, "In Harmony with Nature," *Poems,* p. 54.

49. Freud, *Civilization and Its Discontents,* p. 22.

50. Ibid., p. 24.

notes for chapter V

1. Matthew Arnold, "The Function of Criticism at the Present Time," in *Complete Prose Works,* vol. 3, *Lectures and Essays in Criticism,* p. 261.

2. Ibid.

3. Several studies have been made of Huxley's style and rhetoric, including Walter Houghton's "The Rhetoric of T. H. Huxley," pp. 159–75, and Aldous Huxley's "T. H. Huxley as a Literary Man," *The Olive Tree,* pp. 47–83. Aldous Huxley examines a number of his grandfather's rhetorical techniques, rejecting, however, Chesterton's claim that Huxley was more a literary than a scientific man. See G. K. Chesterton, *The Victorian Age in Literature,* p. 26. Charles S. Blinderman argues in "T. H. Huxley's Theory of Aesthetics," pp. 54–55, that it was Huxley's "genius as a creator of order which contributed to his fame." Blinderman also cites H. L. Mencken's claim that Huxley was "one of the few great stylists that England has produced since the time of Anne." Joseph Gardner, in "A Huxley Essay as 'Poem,'" argues that Huxley's "On the Physical Basis of Life," which is often cited as a

classic of Victorian materialism, has a complex metaphorical structure which repudiates materialism.

4. Walter Houghton, *The Victorian Frame of Mind*, pp. 94–95.

5. The Huxley Papers, Imperial College, London, 47:122–23. See also Huxley's "Mr. Balfour's Attack on Agnosticism: II," p. 317.

6. Arnold, "Heinrich Heine," in *Complete Prose Works*, 3:113.

7. See, for example, Arnold, *Culture and Anarchy*, in *Complete Prose Works*, 5:94. "But, finally," Arnold observes, "perfection—as culture from a thorough disinterested study of human nature and human experience learns to conceive it,—is a harmonious expansion of *all* the powers which make the beauty and worth of human nature, and is not consistent with the over-development of any one power at the expense of the rest."

8. Arnold, "The Function of Criticism at the Present Time," p. 264.

9. See, for example, Thomas S. Kuhn, *The Structure of Scientific Revolutions*, 2nd ed., pp. 206–7. Werner Heisenberg, in his *Physics and Philosophy*; p. 200, points out that scientific concepts are "idealizations" and that "through this process of idealization and precise definition the immediate connection with reality is lost." In a different but relevant context, A. N. Whitehead in his *Science and the Modern World*, pp. 23–24, declares that "Science has never shaken off the impress of its origin in the historical revolt of the later Renaissance. It has remained predominantly an anti-rationalistic movement, based upon a naïve faith. What reasoning it has wanted, has been borrowed from mathematics which is a surviving relic of Greek rationalism, following the deductive method. Science repudiates philosophy. In other words, it has never cared to justify its faith or to explain its meanings; and has remained blandly indifferent to its refutation by Hume."

10. *T. H. Huxley's Diary*, p. 278.

11. T. H. Huxley, "An Apologetic Irenicon," p. 565.

12. A. W. Benn, *The History of English Rationalism in the Nineteenth Century*, 2:453. See also D. W. Dockrill, "T. H. Huxley and the Meaning of Agnosticism," p. 465.

13. Benn, *History of English Rationalism*, 1:1. See note 19 below.

14. G. K. Chesterton, *The Victorian Age in Literature*, p. 127.

15. See John Holloway, *The Victorian Sage*, pp. 10–12.

16. The Huxley Papers, 45:10.

17. Friedrich Engels, "Introduction [to the English edition of 1892]," *Socialism: Utopian and Scientific*, trans. Edward Aveling, p. 18.

18. Arthur J. Balfour, *The Foundations of Belief*, pp. 124–25.

19. Huxley's rationalism adheres to values generally expressed by A. W. Benn in chapter 1 of his *History of English Rationalism in the Nineteenth Century*, pp. 1–15: "Rationalism might be defined as the

method and doctrine of those who strive to make reason the supreme regulator of their beliefs and of their actions; who try to think and speak in terms to which fixed and intelligible senses are attached" (p. 1). Benn considered agnosticism an intimate philosophical relative to rationalism, observing that Huxley's definition of agnosticism "covers rationalism in the wide sense," but that it admits to an ignorance that the rationalist is unaware of. For both rationalist and agnostic, however, "the appeal is to reason, and to reason alone. But reason in the hands of the agnostic is applied to the destruction of non-religious metaphysics rather than to the destruction of religious belief" (p. 14). Yet, "of those who in England accept the extreme results of rationalism, the immense majority call themselves, and are called by others, agnostics."

20. Herbert Spencer, *The Principles of Biology*, 1:355.

21. Herbert Spencer, *The Principles of Sociology*, 2:240.

22. The essays were: "The Natural Inequality of Men"; "Natural Rights and Political Rights"; "Capital, the Mother of Labor"; and "Government: Anarchy or Regimentation," in order of appearance. For a discussion of conservative trends in Huxley's political thought see William Irvine, *Apes, Angels, and Victorians*, pp. 334–36. See also Cyril Bibby, *T. H. Huxley: Scientist, Humanist and Educator*, pp. 51–63.

23. The Huxley Papers, 45:42–43.

24. Ibid., 45.

25. For an important critical essay on Huxley's final philosophical position, see John Dewey, "Evolution and Ethics." Dewey, who knew Huxley's Romanes lecture intimately, recalls that "many felt as if they had received a blow knocking the breath out of their bodies. To some it appeared that Mr. Huxley had executed a sudden *volte-face* and had given up his belief in the unity of the evolutionary process." Dewey argues that aggressive forms of "self-assertion" are transformed in society into positive factors in the ethical process (p. 330). He rejects the notion that there can be any opposition between natural and moral processes (pp. 334–36).

26. T. H. Huxley, "Mr. Balfour's Attack on Agnosticism: II," p. 317.

27. A. N. Whitehead, *Science and the Modern World*, pp. 164–65.

28. George Sarton, *The History of Science and the Problems of To-day*, pp. 27–28. Arnold's expertise in science was slight, as Fred A. Dudley has argued in "Matthew Arnold and Science." His concept of science was framed more in classical natural speculation, just as his critical theory looked to classical notions of symmetry and harmony. Huxley was deeply versed in the classical idea of science as well, which gave his debate with Arnold a distinct historical context.

29. Arnold, "Empedocles on Etna," in *Poems*, p. 164.

30. Arnold, *Culture and Anarchy*, p. 91.

31. Ibid.

32. Ibid., p. 95.

33. Arnold, "Literature and Science," in *Complete Prose Works*, 10:57.

34. Ibid., p. 62. (Italics are mine.)

35. Ibid., pp. 70–71. (Italics are mine.)

36. Ibid., p. 67.

37. See also Cyril Bibby, "Thomas Henry Huxley and University Development," p. 107.

38. For an examination and dating of the public platform behind the Huxley-Arnold debate, see David A. Roos, "Matthew Arnold and Thomas Henry Huxley: Two Speeches at the Royal Academy, 1881 and 1883," pp. 316–24.

39. The Huxley Papers, 42: 147–48.

40. Julian Huxley, *What Dare I Think?*, pp. 180–81.

41. Ibid., p. 182.

42. Robert Browning, "An Epistle, Containing the Strange Medical Experience of Karshish . . . ," *The Complete Poetical Works of Browning*, ed. Horace E. Scudder, pp. 338–41.

43. Arnold, "Pagan and Mediaeval Religious Sentiment," in *Complete Prose Works*, 3:230.

Selected Bibliography

Abrams, M. H. *Natural Supernaturalism: Tradition and Revolution in Romantic Literature*. New York: Norton, 1973.

Arendt, Hannah. *The Human Condition*. Chicago: University of Chicago Press, 1958.

Arnold, Matthew. *The Complete Prose Works of Matthew Arnold*. Edited by R. H. Super. 11 vols. Ann Arbor: University of Michigan Press, 1960–77.

_____. *The Poems of Matthew Arnold*. Edited by Kenneth Allott. London: Longmans, 1965.

Ashforth, Albert. *Thomas Henry Huxley*. Twayne's English Authors Series, no. 84. New York: Twayne, 1969.

Balfour, Arthur J. *The Foundations of Belief*. New York: Longmans, Green, 1895.

Bartholomew, Michael. "Huxley's Defence of Darwin." *Annals of Science* 32 (1975): 525–35.

Beach, Joseph W. *The Concept of Nature in Nineteenth-Century English Poetry*. New York: Pageant, 1956.

Benn, A. W. *The History of English Rationalism in the Nineteenth Century*. 2 vols. New York: Longmans, Green, 1906.

Bibby, Cyril. *T. H. Huxley: Scientist, Humanist and Educator*. New York: Horizon, 1960.

_____. "Thomas Henry Huxley and University Development." *Victorian Studies* 2 (1958): 97–116.

Blinderman, Charles S. "The Great Bone Case." *Perspectives in Biology and Medicine* 14 (1971): 370–93.

_____. "T. H. Huxley: A Re-evaluation of his Philosophy." *Rationalist Annual*, 1966, pp. 50–62.

_____. "T. H. Huxley's Theory of Aesthetics: Unity in Diversity." *Journal of Aesthetics and Art Criticism* 21 (1962): 49–56.

Brown, Alan Willard. *The Metaphysical Society: Victorian Minds in Crisis, 1869–1880*. New York: Columbia University Press, 1947.

Browning, Robert. *The Complete Poetical Works of Browning*. Edited by Horace E. Scudder. Cambridge Edition. Boston: Houghton Mifflin, 1895.

Byron, George Gordon. *The Complete Poetical Works of Byron*. Edited by Paul E. More. Cambridge, Mass.: Houghton Mifflin, 1933.

211

Cameron, John. *The Skull of British Neolithic Man*. London: Williams and Norgate, 1934.

Cannon, Walter F. "Darwin's Vision in *On the Origin of Species*." In *The Art of Victorian Prose*, edited by George Levine and William Madden, pp. 154–76. New York: Oxford University Press, 1968.

———. "The Normative Role of Science in Early Victorian Thought." *Journal of the History of Ideas* 25 (1964): 487–502.

Carlyle, Thomas. *Sartor Resartus: The Life and Opinions of Herr Teufelsdröckh*. Edited by Charles F. Harrold. New York: Odyssey Press, 1937.

———. *The Works of Thomas Carlyle*. Edited by Henry Duff Traill. Edinburgh Edition. 30 vols. New York: Scribner's, 1903–4.

Chesterton, G. K. *The Victorian Age in Literature*. 1913. Reprint. London: Oxford University Press, 1946.

Collingwood, R. G. *The Idea of Nature*. 1945. Reprint. New York: Oxford University Press, 1972.

Clodd, Edward. *Thomas Henry Huxley*. New York: Dodd, Mead, 1902.

Darwin, Charles. *The Autobiography of Charles Darwin, and Selected Letters*. Edited by Francis Darwin. 1892. Reprint. New York: Dover, 1958.

———. *The Descent of Man*. 2d ed., rev. New York: D. Appleton, 1909.

———. *On the Origin of Species*. 6th ed. New York: D. Appleton, 1882.

Dawson, Warren R. *The Huxley Papers: A Descriptive Catalogue of the Correspondence, Manuscripts and Miscellaneous Papers of the Rt. Hon. Thomas Henry Huxley*. London: Macmillan, 1946.

Dewey, John. "Evolution and Ethics." *Monist* (Chicago), 8 (1898): 321–41.

Dickens, Charles. *The New Oxford Illustrated Dickens*. 21 vols. London: Oxford University Press, 1948–58.

Dockrill, D. W. "The Origin and Development of Nineteenth Century English Agnosticism." *Historical Journal* (University of Newcastle, New South Wales), 1, no. 4 (1971): 3–31.

———. "T. H. Huxley and the Meaning of 'Agnosticism.'" *Theology* (London), 74 (October 1971): 461–77.

Doyle, A. Conan. *The Annotated Sherlock Holmes*. Edited by William S. Baring-Gould. 2 vols. New York: Clarkson N. Potter, 1967.

Dudley, Fred A. "Matthew Arnold and Science." *PMLA*, 57 (March 1942), 275–94.

Eisen, Sidney. "Huxley and the Positivists." *Victorian Studies*, 7 (1964): 337–58.

Elton, Oliver. *A Survey of English Literature, 1780–1880*. 4 vols. New York: Macmillan, 1920.

Engels, Friedrich "Introduction [to the English Edition of 1882]." *Socialism: Utopian and Scientific.* Translated by Edward Aveling. Chicago: Charles H. Kerr, 1908.

Freud, Sigmund. *Civilization and Its Discontents.* Translated by James Strachey. New York: Norton, 1962.

——. *The Future of an Illusion.* Translated by W. D. Robson-Scott. New York: Doubleday, 1964.

Gardner, Joseph H. "A Huxley Essay as 'Poem.'" *Victorian Studies,* 14 (1970): 177–91.

Geison, Gerald L. "The Protoplasmic Theory of Life and the Vitalist-Mechanist Debate." *Isis* 60 (1969): 273–92.

Gillispie, Charles Coulston. *Genesis and Geology: A Study in the Relations of Scientific Thought, Natural Theology, and Social Opinion in Great Britain, 1790–1850.* 1951. Reprint. New York: Harper, 1959.

Haight, Gordon S. *George Eliot: A Biography.* New York: Oxford University Press, 1968.

Hamilton, William. *Discussions on Philosophy and Literature, Education and University Reform.* New York: Harper, 1860.

Hardy, Thomas. *The Collected Poems of Thomas Hardy.* London: Macmillan, 1960.

Heisenberg, Werner. *Physics and Philosophy: The Revolution in Modern Science.* 1958. Reprint. New York: Harper and Row, 1962.

Himmelfarb, Gertrude. *Darwin and the Darwinian Revolution.* New York: Doubleday, 1959.

Holloway, John. *The Victorian Sage: Studies in Argument.* 1953. Reprint. New York: Norton, 1965.

Houghton, Walter. "The Rhetoric of T. H. Huxley." *University of Toronto Quarterly* 18 (1949): 159–75.

——. *The Victorian Frame of Mind: 1830–1870.* New Haven: Yale University Press, 1957.

Huxley, Aldous. *The Olive Tree.* New York: Harper and Brothers, 1937.

Huxley, Julian. *What Dare I Think?* New York: Harper, 1931.

Huxley, Julian, and Huxley, Thomas Henry. *Touchstone for Ethics: 1893–1943.* New York: Harper, 1947.

Huxley, Leonard. *Life and Letters of Thomas Henry Huxley.* 2 vols. New York: D. Appleton, 1900.

Huxley, Thomas Henry. "An Apologetic Irenicon." *Fortnightly Review* 58 (1892): 557–71.

——. *Collected Essays.* 9 vols. London: Macmillan, 1893–94.

——. *Critiques and Addresses.* London: Macmillan, 1873.

——. *Lay Sermons, Addresses, and Reviews.* New York: D. Appleton, 1871.

_____. *Man's Place in Nature*. Edited by Ashley Montague. Ann Arbor: University of Michigan Press, 1959.

_____. Mr. Balfour's Attack on Agnosticism. *Nineteenth Century* 37 (1895): 527–40.

_____. "Mr. Balfour's Attack on Agnosticism: II." In *Huxley: Prophet of Science*, by Houston Peterson, pp. 315–27. New York: Longmans, Green, 1932.

_____. "On the Morphology of the Cephalous Mollusca, as Illustrated by the Anatomy of Certain Heteropoda and Pteropoda Collected during the Voyage of H. M. S. *Rattlesnake* in 1846–50." *Philosophical Transactions of the Royal Society of London* 143 pt. 1 (1853): 29–65.

_____. "Professor Tyndall." *Nineteenth Century* 35 (1894): 1–11.

_____. *The Scientific Memoirs of Thomas Henry Huxley*. Edited by Michael Foster and E. Ray Lankester. 4 vols. and Supplement. London: Macmillan 1898–1903.

_____. *T. H. Huxley's Diary of the Voyage of H. M. S.* Rattlesnake. Edited by Julian Huxley. Garden City, N.Y.: Doubleday, Doran, 1936.

Irvine, William. *Apes, Angels, and Victorians: The Story of Darwin, Huxley and Evolution*. New York: McGraw-Hill, 1955.

_____. "Carlyle and T. H. Huxley." In *Victorian Literature: Modern Essays in Criticism*. Edited by Austin Wright, pp. 193–207. New York: Oxford University Press, 1961.

Jones, Ernest. *The Life and Work of Sigmund Freud*. 3 vols. New York: Basic Books, 1953–57.

Kingsley, Charles. *Scientific Lectures and Essays*. London: Macmillan, 1899.

Kropotkin, Prince [Petr]. *Ethics: Origin and Development*. Translated by Louis S. Friedland and Joseph R. Piroshnikoff. New York: Benjamin Blom, 1968.

_____. "Mutual Aid among Animals," Part 1. *Nineteenth Century* 28 (1890): 337–54.

Kuhn, Thomas. *The Structure of Scientific Revolutions*. 2d ed. Chicago: University of Chicago Press, 1973.

Lovejoy, A. O. *The Great Chain of Being: A Study in the History of an Idea*. Cambridge, Mass.: Harvard University Press, 1936.

Lyell, Charles. *The Principles of Geology, Being an Attempt to Explain the Former Changes of the Earth's Surface, by Reference to Causes Now in Operation*. 3 vols. London: John Murray, 1830–33.

Mansel, Henry Longueville. *The Limits of Religious Thought, Examined in Eight Lectures*. 4th Edition. London: John Murray, 1859.

Marx, Karl, and Engels, Friedrich. *The Essential Works of Marxism*. Edited by Arthur P. Mendel. New York: Bantam, 1971.

214

Mill, John Stuart. *Autobiography*. Edited by Jack Stillinger. Boston: Houghton Mifflin, 1969.

———. *Collected Works of John Stuart Mill*. Edited by F. E. L. Priestley, Francis E. Mineka, et al. 17 vols. Toronto: University of Toronto Press, 1963–72.

Mitchell, P. Chalmers. *Thomas Henry Huxley: a Sketch of His Life and Work*. New York: Putnam's, 1900.

Miyoshi, Masao. *The Divided Self: A Perspective on the Literature of the Victorians*. New York: New York University Press, 1969.

Newman, John Henry Cardinal. *The Idea of a University, Defined and Illustrated*. New York: Longmans, Green, 1931.

Noble, D. "George Henry Lewes, George Eliot, and the Physiological Society." *The Journal of Physiology* 263 (1976): 45p–54p.

Noland, Richard W. "T. H. Huxley on Culture." *Personalist* 45 (1964): 94–111.

Peterson, Houston. *Huxley: Prophet of Science*. New York: Longmans, 1932.

Pingree, Jeanne. *Thomas Henry Huxley: List of His Correspondence with Miss Henrietta Heathorn, 1847–1854*. London: Imperial College of Science and Technology, 1969.

Renner, Stanley. "The Garden of Civilization: Conrad, Huxley, and the Ethics of Evolution." *Conradiana* 7 (1975): 109–20.

Roos, David. "Matthew Arnold and Thomas Henry Huxley: Two Speeches at the Royal Academy, 1881 and 1883." *Journal of Modern Philology* 74 (1977): 316–24.

———. "Neglected Bibliographic Aspects of the Works of Thomas Henry Huxley." *Journal of the Society for the Bibliography of Natural History*. Forthcoming, 1978.

Rose, Phyllis. "Huxley, Holmes, and the Scientist as Aesthete." *Victorian Newsletter* 38 (Fall 1970): 22–24.

Ruskin, John. *The Works of John Ruskin*. Edited by E. T. Cook and Alexander Wedderburn. 39 vols. London: George Allen, 1903–12.

Sarton, George. *The History of Science and the Problems of To-day*. Washington, D.C.: W. F. Roberts, 1935.

Scott, David. "On Leonardo Da Vinci and Correggio." *Blackwood's Magazine* 48 (1840): 270–80.

Shelley, Mary. *Frankenstein or the Modern Prometheus*. Edited by James Rieger. New York: Bobbs-Merrill, 1974.

Spencer, Herbert. *Education: Intellectual, Moral, and Physical*. New York: D. Appleton, 1886.

———. *The Principles of Biology*. 2 vols. New York: D. Appleton, 1871.

———. *The Principles of Sociology*. 3 vols. New York: D. Appleton, 1900–1901.

Stanley, Oma. "T. H. Huxley's Treatment of Nature." *Journal of the History of Ideas* 18 (1957): 120–27.

Stevenson, Robert Louis. *The Complete Short Stories of Robert Louis Stevenson.* Edited by Charles Neider. New York: Doubleday, 1969.

Strauss, William, Jr. "Huxley's *Evidence as to Man's Place in Nature*—a Century Later." *Medicine, Science, and Culture: Historical Essays in Honor of Owsei Temkin.* Edited by Lloyd G. Stevenson and Robert P. Multhauf. Baltimore: Johns Hopkins Press, 1968, pp. 160–67.

Tennyson, Alfred Lord. *The Poems of Tennyson.* Edited by Christopher Ricks. London: Longmans, 1969.

Trilling, Lionel. "Science, Literature and Culture: A Comment on the Snow-Leavis Controversy." *Commentary* 33 (June 1962): 461–77.

Turner, Frank M. "Victorian Scientific Naturalism and Thomas Carlyle." *Victorian Studies* 17 (1975): 325–43.

Tyndall, John. *Fragments of Science: A Series of Detached Essays, Addresses, and Reviews.* 2 vols. New York: D. Appleton, 1896.

———. *New Fragments.* London: Longmans, Green, 1892.

Webb, Beatrice. *My Apprenticeship.* New York: Longmans, Green, 1926.

Whewell, William. *The Philosophy of the Inductive Sciences, Founded upon Their History.* 2 vols. London: John Parker, 1840.

Whitehead, Alfred North. *Science and the Modern World.* New York: Macmillan, 1925.

Willey, Basil. *Nineteenth Century Studies: Coleridge to Matthew Arnold.* New York: Columbia University Press, 1949.

Wordsworth, William. *The Poetical Works of William Wordsworth.* Edited by Ernest de Selincourt and Helen Darbishire. 5 vols. Oxford: Clarendon Press, 1952–59.

Index